Ella El

INDIAN
LEGENDS
OF
CANADA

McCLELLAND AND STEWART

DESIGN: *Frank Newfeld*

CANADIAN CATALOGUING IN PUBLICATION DATA

Clark, Ella Elizabeth, 1896 –
    Indian legends of Canada

Bibliography: p.

ISBN 0-7710-2121-6bd. ISBN 0-7710-2139-9

1. Indians of North America – Canada – Legends.
I. Title

E78.C2C56   398.2'0971   C61-1360

The Canadian Publishers

McClelland and Stewart Limited
25 Hollinger Road, Toronto

MANUFACTURED IN CANADA BY WEBCOM LTD.

✳

Acknowledgements

Like other anthologies, this one is the product of many minds and many hands. To my helpers who are living, I express my appreciation here :

To the following Indians of Alberta, for information and for stories related to me directly : Enoch Baptiste (interpreted by Horace Holloway), Mrs. Eliza Hunter, and Chief Walking Buffalo, of the Stoney or Assiniboine tribe; Albert Lightning, Cree; One Gun, Blackfeet; Pat Grasshopper (interpreted by Jim Simeon) and Mrs. Daisy Otter, Sarcee.

To Norman Luxton of the Banff Trading Post, Banff, Alberta, and Mr. and Mrs. Philip Godsell of Calgary for their personal introductions to the Indians listed above.

To Mrs. Marie Brent, Republic, Washington, for "Coyote and Shuswap Falls" and for her great-grandfather's speech in "The First White Men and the Revenge of Chief Nicola."

To Dr. M. W. Stirling, Director, Bureau of American Ethnology, Smithsonian Institution, Washington, D.C., for permission to use from the manuscript collection "How the Animals Climbed into the Sky" and "The Origin of the Mackenzie River."

To Mrs. Edith Gostick, Provincial Librarian, Provincial Library, Edmonton, Alberta, for permission to use "Legend of the White Horses on Chief Mountain" in the manuscript collection.

To B. A. McKelvie, Cobble Hill, British Columbia, for permission to use, from his private collection, "A Legend of Siwash Rock, Vancouver" and "Simon Fraser, Chief of the Sky People."

For assistance in locating materials, I am indebted to Miss Audrey Dawe, National Museum of Canada, Ottawa; Miss Inez Mitchell, Provincial Library, Victoria, B.C.; Miss Edith Hilton, Provincial Library, Edmonton; Mrs. Margaret Blaker, Bureau of American Ethnology, Smithsonian Institution, Washington, D.C.; Mrs. Eugenia Langford, Library of the Department of the Interior, Washington, D.C.; the librarians at the American Museum of Natural History, New York City; the librarians and the pages in the American History Room of the New York City Public Library, and also the people responsible for the remarkable cataloguing in that great library; and several librarians in my home library at Washington State University, Pullman, Washington.

To my colleague Florence Diesman I am grateful for her critical reading of the entire manuscript.

Language Families Represented in this Volume

ALGONQUIAN
Abnaki:
Blackfeet: 68, 73, 101
Chippewa or Ojibwa: 5, 8, 50, 53, 74, 80, 86, 87, 88, 91, 122, 129, 133, 137, 138, 161, 162
Cree: 8, 10, 96, 98
Malecite: 144
Micmac: 37, 81, 124, 127, 164, 165
Ottawa: 97, 172
Passamaquoddy: 156

ATHAPASCAN
Chipewyan: 84
Dogrib: 19, 107, 109
Sarcee: 46, 66, 99
Slavey: 19, 112

IROQUOIAN
Huron-Wyandot: 1, 59, 62, 79
Iroquois: 1, 57, 59, 77, 83, 131
Cayuga:
Mohawk:
Oneida:
Onondaga: 148, 153
Seneca: 40, 44, 55, 93, 94, 126, 147, 158
Tuscarora: 3

KITUAHAN
Kootenay: 35

SALISHAN
Cowichan: 21, 25, 121, 167, 175
Lillooet: 114
Okanagan: 64, 106, 177
Shuswap: 106, 177
Squamish: 32, 116
Thompson: 27, 30

SIOUAN
Assiniboine (Stoney): 103, 104, 105, 142, 181

SKITTAGETAN
Haida: 15, 63, 119

WAKASHAN
Nootka: 23, 170

ESKIMO: 113

Contents

✳

NATURE MYTHS AND BEAST FABLES

✳

MYTHS AND LEGENDS OF LANDSCAPE FEATURES

✳

A MEDLEY OF STORIES

✳

PERSONAL NARRATIVES
AND HISTORICAL TRADITIONS

Indian stories and storytelling

This anthology offers the general reader selections from the oral literature of the Indians of Canada. Designed for readers of all ages, it includes myths, legends, personal narratives, and historical traditions from tribes in all the culture areas or physiographic regions of the country.

Some of these areas naturally extended into the present United States, for of course the Indians knew no international boundary. Consequently, most of the stories gathered here, and the customs and beliefs to which they refer, are part of the culture of the Indians of the northern United States and Canada. Tribes represented in this volume from both sides of the present border include the Seneca, Onondaga, and other Iroquois tribes, the Abnaki, Malecite, and Passamaquoddy, all in the eastern part of the continent; the Ottawa, Huron-Wyandot, and Chippewa, of the Great Lakes area; the Assiniboine, Blackfeet, Cree, Kootenay, and Okanagan, of the western plains and plateau.

Knowing that the general reader likes variety of theme, I have selected relatively few tales from the creator-culture-hero-trickster cycles, which predominate in most of the collections published for anthropologists and folklorists. Those tales are strikingly similar, from the valley of the St. Lawrence to the Queen Charlotte Islands in the Pacific. Instead, I have searched for the most interesting examples of each type of narrative mentioned by writers who were entertained by Indian storytellers in the mid-nineteenth century.

Secondly, aware of the need expressed by teachers and others for a book of myths and legends that will provide a background for a study of the American Indians, I have included a large proportion of narratives that reveal the every-day life, the beliefs, and the ceremonies of the early Americans. The staple foods in different areas, the ritualistic uses of wampum and of tobacco, the guardian spirit quest, the sweat lodge, the Sun Dance and other aspects of native religion, the efforts of some tribes to bring about a lasting peace with traditional enemies—many facets of aboriginal life in northern North America are revealed, not only in Section II, but in other stories throughout this book.

And, thirdly, desirous of a book of Indian stories that can be read in families and in schools, I have excluded tales with brutal and erotic themes. This procedure of course, is not new; for generations, the myths and legends of the ancient Greeks, Romans, and Norsemen have been similarly screened for similar purposes.

In this connection, it is interesting to note that the late J. N. B. Hewitt, who was with the Bureau of American Ethnology of the

Smithsonian Institution from 1886 until 1937, denied that obscenity was a "dominant characteristic of American Indian myths and legendary lore." Many collectors, he added, have not taken time to discover "the philosophic and the poetic legends and myths so sacred to these thoughtful people. The inevitable result of this method of research is the wholly erroneous view of the ethical character of the myths and legends and stories of the American Indian." Hewitt's concentrated study was of the tribes speaking the Iroquoian languages, but he collected materials also in Chippewa, Ottawa, Delaware, and some other languages.

In similar vein, the pioneer ethnographer Horatio Hale had written of the Hurons in 1874: "What chiefly struck me, in listening to the narratives of the old chief, was the strong moral element apparent in them. That this element was not given to them by the narrator, but was inherent in the tales themselves, was evident from the fact that it appeared in the same stories when related by others, in widely different versions." Some students of other tribes probably would not agree with Hewitt's and Hale's idea of the motive in Indian tales.

Some facts about Indian storytelling when it was still one of "the lively arts" were recorded by nineteenth-century travellers and missionaries. Anna Jameson, an English writer, spent several months among the Chippewas in the 1830's and went "among them quite familiarly." Of them she wrote: "Like the Arabians, they have among them story-tellers by profession, persons who go about from lodge to lodge amusing the inmates with traditional tales, histories of the wars and exploits of their ancestors, or inventions of their own, which are sometimes in the form of allegories or parables, and are either intended to teach some moral lesson or are extravagant inventions, having no other purpose but to excite wonder or amazement.

"The story-tellers are estimated according to their eloquence and powers of invention, and are always welcome—sure of the best place in the wigwam and the choicest mess of food wherever they go. Some individuals, not story-tellers by profession, possess and exercise these gifts of memory and invention."

Mrs. John H. Kinzie, who lived among the Chippewas from 1830 to 1833, also wrote about the professional storytellers who had attentive audiences for their historical, biographical, and fictitious narratives, "however oft-told and familiar the matter they recite. It is in this way that their traditions are preserved and handed down unimpaired from generation to generation."

"Excellence in this art [of storytelling]," wrote John Gilman in 1835, "is a highly valued accomplishment, whether the excellence be in tragedy or comedy. . . . The Northern Indian is a peculiarly imaginative being, easily . . . moved by the creations of fancy, the legendary lore or traditions told by some father of the tribe around the lodge fire or at their casual resting places during a hunt or a war party." J. G. Kohl, a German travelling around Lake Superior in 1855, was "no little surprised at finding how greatly this [narrative] talent was spread." Everyone seemed to possess it, both men and women.

Some narrators used their own imagination to change and to expand the stories that were related for amusement only. But certain kinds of stories—creation myths, myths explaining the origin of sacred ceremonies—these, to use the words of Horatio Hale, "were, in a certain sense, articles of religion and were handed down with scrupulous exactness."

The histrionic ability of a skilful Indian storyteller was well described by two travellers who, during many evenings in 1862–65, heard a Cree in the north country relate long hunting stories: "The appropriate gestures and expressive pantomime with which an Indian illustrates his speech render it easy to understand. . . . The scene described was partly acted; the motions of the game, the stealthy approach of the hunter, the taking aim, the shot, the cry of the animal, or the noise of its dashing away, and the pursuit, were all given as the tale went on."

To entertain listeners of all ages, to instruct the young, to preserve history and rituals and beliefs were the chief purposes of storytelling among the American Indians, as among other early peoples. An additional motive or value has been stated by a well-educated Indian of the early twentieth century: In the winter months, "when everyone clings to the hearth fire . . . the minds of the people crave stimulation. They demand that their imagination be kindled and that from sordid life they be lifted to the fairylands of pure imagination. The storyteller who can lift the individual out of self and transport him to the land of magic, where he may picture himself a superman performing mighty feats, is in great demand."

Myths of creation and of the origin of tribal customs, historical narratives, tales of ancestral heroes, of hunting and of war, allegories and parables—these types of stories were referred to by the nineteenth-century writers just quoted. Others mentioned stories about dwarfs, giants, witches, monsters, serpents, stars ("the most beautiful legends of the Micmacs are about the heavens"), love, landscape features, humanized animals, and of course the endless cycles of tales about a superhuman being who was sometimes the great benefactor of the tribe and sometimes buffoon or trickster.

The storytelling, with rare exceptions, was restricted to the long winter evenings. In fact, many tribes had a belief similar to this of the Crees: "During the summer, no stories founded on fiction were ever told; the Indians believing that if any 'fairy' tales were told during that season when they were supposed to use all their time to the best advantage, the narrator would have his life destroyed by the lizard, which would suck his blood."

Toads or snakes, other Indians said, would creep into their beds if stories were related before the first snow fell. This belief, thought Hewitt, was probably the survival of some religious taboo that forbade the telling of sacred myths except during certain seasons of the year.

An old woman of the far north would not tell stories in the summer, for then the spirits were abroad. "They can hear us, and they don't like being talked about. But in the cold winter they are far away and cannot hear, so they are not likely to be offended." It was a widespread belief that spirits were in a torpid state during the winter. An old Huron-Wyandot would not entertain in the summer because "too many animals could hear these stories, which might hurt their feelings."

But certain kinds of tales might be related on special occasions. In the old days, before a war expedition, the head chief might ask a storyteller for some "rousing war adventure of their ancestors." And at the Sun Dance festival of the Blackfeet of the western plains, warriors told of their earlier deeds and the old men related some of the important traditions of the tribe.

It is indeed fortunate for our knowledge of the oral literature of the North American Indians that several men and women in the early nineteenth century had sufficient interest to record a few of the stories that pleased them. By the time of professional collectors of folklore on this continent, much had been lost. The folklorist Jeremiah Curtin wrote of the Senecas in 1883: "It was only the old who possessed any knowledge of Seneca mythology—the middle-aged and young men had 'thrown it away.' If the myths in this book had not been collected at that time, they would have been lost." And in 1888 the ethnographer A. F. Chamberlain wrote similarly of the Indians on Scugog Island, Ontario: "These stories are only known to the older generation . . . and will soon be lost to oblivion if not taken down at once."

Among the Western tribes, especially in the isolated regions, storytelling customs were retained into the twentieth century. Reverend John McLean, however, wrote of the Blackfeet of Alberta about 1890: "I have listened to some of these legends as told, over and over again, for the past nine years, and I find that the young men are not able to relate them as accurately as the aged; besides, as the country is becoming settled with white people, they are less disposed to tell to others their native religious ideas, lest they be laughed at, because of not believing the same things as their superior brethren of the white race. As the children grow up, they are forgetting these things, and the years are not far distant when the folklore of the Blackfeet will be greatly changed and many of their traditions forgotten."

An educated Indian chief, Elias Johnson, in a book about Iroquois legends and traditions published in 1881, explained some of the difficulties inherent in gathering and in understanding the folktales of the Indians: "It is very difficult for a stranger to rightly understand the morals of their stories, though it is said by those who know them best that the story was always an illustration of some moral principle.

"To strangers they offer all the rites of hospitality, but do not open their hearts. If you ask them, they will tell you a story, but it will not be such a story as they tell when alone. They will fear your ridicule and suppress their humor and pathos; so thoroughly have they learned to distrust pale faces that when they know that he who is present is a friend, they will still shrink from admitting him within the secret portals of their heart.

"And when you have learned all that language can convey, there are still a thousand images, suggestions and associations recurring to the Indian, which can strike no chord in your heart. The myriad voices of nature are dumb to you, but to them they are full of life and power."

Some of these difficulties are inherent in transferring thoughts and images from writers of any culture to readers of another, even from one individual to another. Nevertheless, there is no better way of understanding the life and personality of the American Indians of the past than through their folktales. Whether written or oral, literature reveals and interprets life. Readers of today, like the audiences of the storytellers in former years, can be instructed while being entertained by these myths, legends, and historical traditions of thirty North American Indian tribes.

TALES OF LONG AGO

WHEN THE WORLD WAS YOUNG

 HURON AND IROQUOIS

The creation myth of the Hurons and the Iroquois

This creation myth was related in 1874, north of Lake Erie, by a Huron sub-chief who was then about seventy-five years of age. It is probably the oldest detailed recording of the origin myth that was once related, with some variations in minor details, by the Hurons and by the Six Nations of the Iroquois. As the old storyteller "had heard the myth in his youth from the elders of his people, their joint recollections would carry it back to the middle of the [eighteenth] century, when the customs and traditions of the Wendat were retained in their full vigour."

The tribe that called themselves "Wendat" were nicknamed "Hurons" by the French; their name was corrupted to "Wyandot" by the British.

Among the Hurons, the twin brothers in the story were called Tijuskeha, meaning "Good Man," and Tawiskrong, meaning "like flint." Among the Iroquois nations, the evil brother was named Tawiskarow; the good brother, Teharonhiawagon, meaning "the Master of Life." In Sketches of Ancient History of the Six Nations written by a Tuscarora (David Cusick) the two brothers are called the "Good Mind" and the "Bad Mind."

In the beginning, there was nothing but water—nothing but a wide, wide sea. The only people in the world were the animals that live in and on water.

Then down from the sky world a woman fell, a divine person. Two loons flying over the water happened to look up and see her falling. Quickly they placed themselves beneath her and joined their bodies to make a cushion for her to rest upon. Thus they saved her from drowning.

While they held her, they cried with a loud voice to the other animals, asking their help. Now the cry of the loon can be heard at a great distance over water, and so the other creatures gathered quickly.

As soon as Great Turtle learned the reason for the call, he stepped forth from the council.

"Give her to me," he said to the loons. "Put her on my back. My back is broad."

And so the loons were relieved of their burden. Then the council, discussing what they should do to save the life of the woman, decided that she must have earth to live on. So Great Turtle sent the creatures, one by one, to dive to the bottom of the sea and bring up some earth. Beaver, Muskrat, Diver, and others made the attempt. Some remained below so long that when they rose they were dead. Great Turtle looked at the mouth of each one, but could find no trace of earth. At last Toad dived. After a long time he arose, almost dead from weariness. Searching Toad's mouth, Great Turtle found some earth. This he gave to the woman.

She took the earth and placed it carefully around the edge of Great Turtle's shell. There it became the beginning of dry land. On all sides, the land grew larger and larger, until at last it formed a great country, one where trees and other plants could live and grow. All this country was borne on the back of Great Turtle, and it is yet today. Great Turtle still bears the earth on his back.

After a while, the woman gave birth to twins, who had very different dispositions. Even before they were born, they struggled and disputed. The mother heard one of them say that he was willing to be born in the usual manner; the other angrily refused to be born in that way. So he broke through his mother's side and killed her.

She was buried in the earth, and from her body grew the plants that the new earth needed for the people who were to be created. From her head grew the pumpkin vine, from her breasts the corn, and from her limbs the bean.

The twins were not men, but supernatural beings; they were to prepare the new earth to be the home of man. As they grew up, they showed their different dispositions in everything they did. Finding that they could not live together, each went his own way and took his portion of the earth. Their first act was to create animals of different kinds.

Evil Brother, whose name means "flint-like," created fierce and monstrous animals, to terrify and destroy mankind. He created serpents, panthers, wolves, bears—all of enormous size—and huge mosquitoes that were as large as turkeys. And he made an immense toad that drank up all the fresh water that was on the earth.

Good Brother, at the same time, was creating the harmless and useful animals—the dog, the deer, the elk, the buffalo, and many birds. Among them was the partridge. To the surprise of Good Brother, Partridge rose in the air and flew toward the country of Evil Brother.

"Where are you going?" asked Good Brother.

"I am going to look for water," answered Partridge. "There is none here, and I have heard that there is some in the land of Flint."

Good Brother followed Partridge, and soon he reached the land of Evil Brother. There he was met by the giant snakes, the fierce beasts, and the enormous insects his brother had created. Good Brother overcame them. He could not destroy them, but he made them smaller and less fierce, so that human beings would be able to master them.

Then Good Brother came to the giant toad. He cut open the toad and let the water flow forth into the land. Thus rivers were formed. Good Brother wanted each stream to have a two-fold current, so that one side of the river would flow in one direction and the other side in the opposite direction.

"In this way, people can always float downstream," he explained.

"That would not be good for the people," said Evil Brother. "They should have to work one way."

So he made the rivers flow downstream only. And to make paddling a canoe harder and more dangerous, he created rapids and waterfalls and whirlpools in the rivers.

In a dream, Good Brother was warned by the spirit of his mother to be careful, lest Evil Brother destroy him by treachery. When the twin brothers saw that they would always disagree, they decided to have a duel. The one who was victorious would be the master of the world. They decided also that each of them should tell the other what weapon could destroy him.

"I can be destroyed," said Good Brother, "only if I am beaten to death by a bag full of corn or beans."

"I can be destroyed," said Evil Brother, "only if I am beaten to death with the antler of a deer or the horn of some other animal."

They set off a fighting ground, and Evil Brother started the combat. He struck his brother with a bag of corn or beans, chased him over the fighting ground, and pounded him until he was nearly lifeless. His mother's spirit revived him and he recovered his strength.

Then Good Brother seized a deer's antler, pursued his brother, and beat him until he killed the evil one.

After his death, Evil Brother appeared to his brother and said, "I am going to the far west. Hereafter, all men will go to the west after death."

And so until the Christian missionaries came to our land, the spirits of dead Indians went to the far west and lived there.

The Tuscaroras, one of the six tribes in "The Iroquois League of Nations" (see p. 142), had an interesting addition to this creation myth of the Iroquois-speaking people. The Tuscaroras were living along the Roanoke River in North Carolina, in southeastern United

States, when the first white colonists came to that region. After the American Revolution, the members of the tribe and of the other Iroquoian tribes that had sided with Great Britain against the colonies were given a reserve along the Grand River, in Ontario. In another of the traditions of the Tuscaroras, their ancestors had lived, centuries earlier, along the St. Lawrence River, which they called Kanawage.

Ages after the creation of the world, the plants, and the animals, Sky Holder decided to create people to live on the earth and enjoy the things he had created. The people would be stronger, braver, and more beautiful than anything he had created earlier. So from the heart of the Great Island, where they had been subsisting on moles, Sky Holder brought out six pairs. They were to become the ancestors of the greatest of all people.

The first pair were left beside a large river; their children and grandchildren became known as the Mohawk people. The second pair were told to make their home beside a large stone; their descendants became the Oneidas. The word *Oneida* means "upright stone." The third pair were left to make their home on a high hill or mountain called *Onondaga*; their descendants are known as the Onondagas.

The fourth pair were told to make their home near a long lake that has a mountain rising from the water. Their family's Indian name means "a great pipe." They have long been known as the Cayugas. The fifth pair were directed to live near a knoll south of another lake. Their Indian name means "possessing a door." They have long been known as the Senecas.

The sixth pair, the ones who became the ancestors of the Tuscaroras, were led by Sky Holder to a land farther south, toward the noon-day sun, until they reached the bank of the great water and the mouth of a river. That river is now called the Roanoke. They were directed to make their home along its banks. Sky Holder stayed with them a while and taught them to make and to use the bow and arrow. He taught them other useful crafts and arts. That is why the Tuscaroras know that they are the people preferred by Sky Holder.

The Onondagas, however, believe that they are the chosen people because they have been honoured by possessing the council fire. Each of the other four nations—the Mohawk, the Oneida, the Cayuga, and the Seneca—has some reason for believing it to be the nation preferred by Sky Holder.

When the six pairs were living in the heart of the Great Island, all spoke the same language. After they were separated and made their homes in different places, each nation altered the Iroquois language somewhat. But the changes were not great enough to make any of them lose the understanding of what the others said.

Years later, when the descendants of the six pairs became scattered, some families lived in areas where the bear was the principal game; so they were called the Bear clan. Others lived where beavers were trapped; so they were called the Beaver clan. The Deer, Wolf, Tortoise, and Eel clans received their names for similar reasons. The Turtle clan had a more complex history: during a very hot summer the pool in which the mud turtles lived became dry. So they started out to look for a new house. One of them, a particularly fat one, suffered a good deal from the exercise he was not used to. Finally, for comfort in walking he threw off his shell. He continued to change his appearance until, in a short time, this fat and lazy turtle became a man, the ancestor of the Turtle clan.

 CHIPPEWA

Nanabozho of the Chippewas

Nanabozho, born on an island at the outlet of Lake Superior, was the first son of a spirit from on high and a woman on the earth. Quickly he grew to manhood. By that time his footsteps were so long that he could easily cross the widest river or lake in one stride. He could seize the lightning in his hands, and his voice was like the roar of a great lake in a storm. If cataracts in the rivers were in his way, he tore them out.

Nanabozho could transform himself into any animal or object of nature, and he conversed with all living creatures. After the great flood that once covered the earth, he restored the land and all that lives upon it. Then he created the first Chippewas. Later he took from the animals the gift of speech because they conspired against the human race.

As the mighty ruler of all the earth, Nanabozho controlled the weather and the seasons. He covered the earth with snow in winter and chained all the streams with ice. At his command the terrible storms broke loose from their caves and lashed the waters of the lakes into white foam. At his command also, the gentle winds blew, the mountains became covered with green, and the flowers of spring bloomed everywhere.

Nanabozho did many things for the people he had created. He killed fierce monsters that endangered them, on land and in the water. The fossil bones of extinct animals, which white men have discovered, are the remains of those monsters of long, long ago.

He brought his people the first fire, and taught them how to make arrowpoints, lances, and hatchets. He taught them how to hunt, how to build canoes, how to cultivate corn and beans and squash for their food. After watching a spider trapping flies, Nanabozho showed men how to make nets for catching fish. After finding that the sap of the maple tree is sweet, he made sugar of it and showed people how to make it. He invented the picture-writing on rocks, and also learned the art of painting the face before going to war. He showed his people what herbs to use for medicine. And so the Chippewas, when gathering roots and herbs, leave a small offering to Nanabozho beside the spot where they found the plants.

Nanabozho changed the appearance of the Chippewa country. By damming up the rivers in order to catch beaver, he formed Lake Superior. The dirt he threw out became the Apostle Islands. As he travelled through the world, he marked each day's journey with piles of stones. They are our mountains, and the valleys below them are the prints of his feet. All along Lake Superior, every strangely-formed rock, every cape and island, all the rapids and cataracts in the rivers that flow into the lake—each of these has some connection with the wonderful deeds of Nanabozho.

Along the Ottawa River are the prints of his footsteps and a round hole that is the kettle which he dropped when pursuing a stone giant; into this hole each passing Indian places bits of tobacco for Nanabozho, with a request for a safe journey. Beside Lake Superior is a stone where he rested and smoked his pipe after jumping across the lake; there every Chippewa who passes leaves a little tobacco, so that Nanabozho may continue to smoke in his lodge in the west.

He taught the Chippewas all the rites and mysteries of their religion. From the spirits he received four gifts that he was to hand on to his successors: the sacred drum, which he and others would use at the side of sick people; the sacred rattle, with which he could extend the life of a patient; tobacco, to be an emblem of peace; and a dog, to be his companion and the companion of others.

All the knowledge which the shamans have concerning the rules and ceremonies of religion, Nanabozho received from the spirits. He built a lodge, as they directed him; and as late as 1887, he was said to be present at the Sacred Medicine Lodge when the Grand Medicine rite was performed.

He lived for a thousand years, some people say. According to some storytellers, he was killed in a fierce battle with the Evil One and was buried on the north shore of Lake Superior, east of Thunder Bay. According to others, he was buried on Michipicoten Island. Indians never pass by these places without offering him the smoke of their tobacco or dropping tobacco on the water.

Other people believe that he is still alive; when they hear noises inside the mountains, they know that Nanabozho is continuing his creative work. Some believe that he lives in a northern sea, where he reposes on a great island of floating ice, guarded by the northern lights. People with this belief fear that white men may find his retreat. If they do, and if Nanabozho should step again on the earth, "it will burst into flames and all living creatures will be destroyed."

This summary of the deeds of Nanabozho is made up of details recorded chiefly by travellers and students between 1721 and 1850. They heard the fireside tales before the Chippewas or Ojibways were greatly influenced by white man's culture. "The northern division of Ojibway," wrote W. J. Hoffman in 1887, "were slow to adopt the teachings of the missionaries." The name of this mythical personage and great benefactor is spelled in various ways, including *Manibozho, Nanibojou, Nannebush, Michabou, Winabojo.* He was sometimes referred to as "the Great Light," "the Spirit of Light," "the Great White One." The ethnologist J. N. B. Hewitt, writing in 1912, considered him "the impersonation of life, the active, quickening power of life."

To the Indians of the past, Nanabozho myths had religious significance. But in most of the Chippewa tales recorded in this century, Nanabozho is not the benefactor of mankind, the culture-hero, and does not have a spiritual meaning. Instead, by some incongruity which Chippewas of today cannot explain, he is often identified with a trickster and with the Great Hare. In the fire myth, for instance, he took the form of a hare and was burned; consequently, all rabbits since that time have had brown spots on their fur. In many tales, Nanabozho, or the Great Hare, is a mischief-maker, a trickster who is often the victim of his own stupid attempts to deceive others.

Some of the stories related about him are identical with the episodes in "Some Adventures of Wisakedjak," in this volume. Nanabozho and Wisakedjak are occasionally spoken of as cousins. Tales about them furnish much of the comedy in Algonquian oral literature; in the storytelling days, they were accompanied by the chuckles of the narrator and the laughter of his audience.

The beginning of the Cree world

Several forms of this myth of creation and of the great flood have been recorded from different Algonquian tribes. The Crees were western members of the Algonquian family, which is the largest of the language groups of the North American Indians.

This particular version has been selected because it was recorded by the great explorer-geographer, David Thompson, before missionaries had been among the people who related it.

Wisakedjak is the principal character in many Cree tales. His name means "the Flatterer." It is spelled also Weesack-kachack.

After the Creator had made all the animals and had made the first people, he said to Wisakedjak, "Take good care of my people, and teach them how to live. Show them all the bad roots, all the roots that will hurt them and kill them. Do not let the people or the animals quarrel with each other."

But Wisakedjak did not obey the Creator. He let the creatures do whatever they wished to do. Soon they were quarrelling and fighting and shedding much blood.

The Creator, greatly displeased, warned Wisakedjak. "If you do not keep the ground clean, I will take everything away from you, and you will be miserable."

But Wisakedjak did not believe the Creator and did not obey. Becoming more and more careless and disobedient, he tricked the animals and the people and made them angry with each other. They quarrelled and fought so much that the earth became red with blood.

This time the Creator became very angry. "I will take everything away from you and wash the ground clean," he said.

Still Wisakedjak did not believe the Creator. He did not believe until the rains came and the streams began to swell. Day after day, and night after night, the rains continued. The water in the rivers and the lakes rose higher and higher. At last they overflowed their banks and washed the ground clean. The sea came up on the land, and everything was drowned except one Otter, one Beaver, and one Muskrat.

Wisakedjak tried to stop the sea, but it was too strong for him. He sat down on the water and wept. Otter, Beaver, and Muskrat sat beside him and rested their heads on one of his thighs.

In time the rain stopped and the sea left the land. Wisakedjak took courage, but he did not dare to speak to the Creator. After long and sad thoughts about his misery, he said to himself, "If I could get a bit of the old earth beneath the water, I could make a little island for us to live on."

He did not have the power to create anything, but he did have the power to expand what had already been created. As he could not dive and did not know how far it was to the old earth, he did not know what to do. Taking pity on him, the Creator said, "I will give you the power to re-make everything if you will use the old materials buried under the water."

Still floating on the flood, Wisakedjak said to the three animals beside him, "We shall starve unless one of you can bring me a bit of the old ground beneath the water. If you will get it for me, I will make an island for us."

Then he turned to the Otter. "You are brave and strong and active. If you will dive into the water and bring me a bit of earth, I will see that you have plenty of fish to eat."

So the Otter dived, but he came up again without having reached the ground. A second time and a third time Wisakedjak praised Otter and persuaded him to go down once more. When he returned the third time, he was so weary that he could not dive again.

"You are a coward!" exclaimed Wisakedjak. "I am surprised by your weak heart. Beaver, I know, can dive to the bottom of the flood. He will put you to shame."

Then he turned to Beaver. "You are brave and strong and wise. If you will dive into the water and bring me a bit of the old earth, I will make a good house for you on the new island I shall make. There you will be warm in the winter. Dive straight down, as a brave Beaver does."

Twice Beaver dived, and twice he came back without any earth. The second time he was so tired that Wisakedjak had to let him rest for a long time.

"Dive once more," begged Wisakedjak when Beaver had recovered. "If you will bring me a bit of earth, I will make a wife for you."

To obtain a wife, Beaver went down a third time. He stayed so long that he came back almost lifeless, still with no earth in his paws.

Wisakedjak was now very sad. If Otter and Beaver could not reach the bottom of the water, surely Muskrat also would fail. But he must try. He was their only chance.

"You are brave and strong and quick, Muskrat, even if you are small. If you will dive into the water and bring me a bit of the old earth at the bottom, I will make plenty of roots for you to eat. I will create rushes, so that you can make a nice house with rushes and dirt.

"Otter and Beaver are fools," continued Wisakedjak. "They got lost. You will find the ground if you will dive straight down."

So Muskrat jumped head first into the water. Down and down he went, but he brought back nothing. A second time he dived and stayed a long time. When he returned, Wisakedjak looked at his forepaws and sniffed.

"I smell the smell of earth," he said. "Go again. If you bring me even a small piece, I will make a wife for you, Muskrat. She will bear you a great many children. Have a strong heart now. Go straight down, as far as you can go."

This time Muskrat stayed so long that Wisakedjak feared he had drowned. At last they saw some bubbles coming up through the water. Wisakedjak reached down his long arm, seized Muskrat, and pulled him up beside them. The little creature was almost dead, but against his breast held a piece of the old earth.

Joyously, Wisakedjak seized it, and in a short time he had expanded the bit of earth into an island. There he, Muskrat, Otter, and Beaver rested and rejoiced that they had not drowned in the flood.

Some people say that Wisakedjak obtained a bit of wood, from which he made the trees; that he obtained some bones, from which he made the second race of animals.

Others say that the Creator made all things again. He commanded the rivers to take the salt water back to the sea. Then he created mankind, the animals of today, and the trees. He took from Wisakedjak all power over people and animals and left him only the power to flatter and to deceive.

After that, Wisakedjak played tricks upon the animals and led them into much mischief. That is why the Indians tell many stories about him, to amuse themselves during the long winter evenings.

 CREE

Some adventures of Wisakedjak

> There is an old saying among the Cree Indians that if anyone were to tell all the stories about Wisakedjak, he would have to live to be very, very old. The tales never failed to amuse an audience, whether made up of children or of their parents and grandparents.
> The following account of Wisakedjak's adventures was related in 1954 by Albert Lightning. "The story really goes on and on," he said, as he finished speaking. Episodes in this tale are found in stories about Wisakedjak told by the Beaver and the Chipewyan tribes; parallels appear in Nez Perce tales about Coyote.

All our stories are about a being who was a spirit in the form of a human being. He was the first being when the world was made. So he was older than all the animals and all the plants in the world; everything was his younger brother. He could talk to animals and birds, fishes and insects, water and wind, trees, rocks—everything. We call him Wisakedjak.

One day as Wisakedjak was walking along a little stream, he saw a family of prairie chickens, very young ones.

"Little Brothers," he called to them, "what's your name?"

"Prairie chickens," they answered.

"But everything has two names," said Wisakedjak. "What's your other name?"

"Our other name is We-scare-people-unexpectedly," the prairie chickens answered.

"Hoh! You can't scare anyone!" he told them. "You are too little to scare anyone."

After teasing them until they were angry, Wisakedjak went on down the creek. When their mother came home, the children told her what Wisakedjak had done and what he had said to them—that they were too little to scare anyone.

"We will see," said the mother bird.

Then she went around and gathered together all the prairie chickens she could find. Her children told them what Wisakedjak had done and had said.

"Wisakedjak is going down to that cutbank along the creek," the mother hen told the group. "There he will try to jump across the water. Four times he will get ready to jump. On the fourth try he will jump. Then each of you will fly out from your hiding place."

The prairie chickens moved quietly away and hid themselves near the cutbank. Soon Wisakedjak came along.

"If a pretty girl were over there," the birds heard him say to himself, "I would have to jump across the creek."

Three times he looked at the wide creek, and three times he got ready to jump but was afraid to move. A fourth time he got ready, and this time he jumped. As soon as his feet left the ground, all the prairie chickens suddenly fluttered out from their hiding places, flapping their wings and crying. They frightened Wisakedjak so much that he fell into the water.

"Can't scare anyone! Can't scare anyone! Can't scare anyone!" the prairie chickens called to him as they flew away.

Wisakedjak dried himself and walked along until he came to a big lake. There he saw a great flock of birds, birds that lived on both land and water.

"I want you to dance for me," he said to them.

At one end of the lake he made a dance tepee of brush and trees, and in it left a very small door. He invited the birds to enter and then he began to drum and to chant in the middle of the tepee. They danced in a circle around him.

After a few rounds he said to them, "For the next dance, I want all of you to shut your eyes."

So they danced around him with closed eyes. Whenever a fat duck came along, Wisakedjak grabbed it, wrung its neck, and put it behind him. In that way he got a pile of nice, fat ducks.

"After a while I will have a good dinner," he said to himself.

But one bird, the hell-diver, decided to open one eye and see what was going on. He screamed to the others, "Our Elder Brother is killing us. Open your eyes!"

All opened their eyes and rushed out the door.

Then Wisakedjak made a big fire, so that he could roast the birds in the hot coals. When he put them in, he left just their feet sticking out. Nothing but their feet could be seen.

"Now I'll take a nap while they roast," he said to himself. "When I wake up, I will have a big feast."

So he lay down and went to sleep. After a while he woke up, and when he opened his eyes, he saw an animal standing near him. At the time the animals had not been given names.

"Younger Brother," said Wisakedjak, "I am going to have roasted ducks for supper. These birds I am cooking are about done. If you want to eat some of my good supper, you will have to run a race with me.

"We will run around the lake. One of us will run in one direction, the other in the opposite direction. If you get back to the fire first, you will join me in eating. If I get back to the fire first, you will have to sit and watch me eat."

"All right," agreed the animal.

The race started, each going a different direction. Knowing where some shrubs grew along the lake, the animal ran only a little way and then hid in the bushes. After a while he turned back and went to the fire. Pulling out one of the birds, and seeing that it was well done, he ate it. He pulled out another bird and ate it. He ate as fast as possible, going all around the fire and eating everything—everything but the feet and legs. These he pushed back under the ashes. Then he went to the bushes and hid again.

In the meantime, Wisakedjak was running as fast as he could. Because he kept on the outside of the bushes, he did not see the animal. He ran faster and faster, because he wanted to get back to the fire before the other did.

When Wisakedjak got back to the starting point, he saw the feet of the birds sticking out from the fire. Everything seemed to be just as he had left it.

"I guess my Younger Brother is not here," he said. "I will start eating right away."

So he took hold of a pair of feet and pulled. But only feet and legs came out of the ashes.

"I've burned that bird," he said. "I slept too long."

He pulled out another pair of feet. And another. And another. All around the fire he went, pulling out nothing but feet and legs. Only the last two had some meat left on them. Then Wisakedjak knew that the animal had been cheating.

"Come on out of the bushes," he called.

Then Wisakedjak said to him, "In the future when my brothers, human beings, come to the earth, you will be known as fox. People will call you 'the sly fox.'"

He had been tricked by Silver Fox.

That was the beginning of the names of things. Wisakedjak gave names to all the animals and birds, to all the fishes and insects—to everything. As he named them, he told them the way they should live and gave them protection against their enemies.

When he gave names to the fish, he told them they were to live in the water; they could swim away from their enemies. He told the ducks they could live on both land and water.

"You can't swim fast or run fast," he told them, "but you can fly up into the air in a hurry. Fox will not be able to catch you."

He gave Deer a white tail and told him that he would always be able to run fast. Bear can climb a tree or hide himself in his den. Squirrel can run up a tree trunk and hide in the upper branches. Rabbit can sit as if frozen, so that he is almost invisible. Mountain Goat was given a coat as white as the snow around him. Thus Wisakedjak made all the first creatures safe from attack.

"Soon there will be many creatures like me," he told the animals. "They will be known as people. They will have to get their living from you, Younger Brothers. I give you now the chance to decide what you will be to people and where they can find you."

The creatures thought a while and talked a while, deciding where they would live.

"These new people will always be near shelter," continued Wisakedjak. "They will live near the woods, around mountains, but always in reach of water. That means they will always be in reach of you, my brothers.

"About this time of year, in midsummer, they will have the feeling that they must wander into the prairies. They will want to go there to get soft meat that nature provides. Later, birds will be hard to catch. By that time, berries and fruits will be ripe. People will pick them and dry them for use in the winter. Then they will drift back into the woods again.

"The coming of these people cannot be stopped by you," continued Elder Brother. "You will be their firewood, their meat, or their other food. You will furnish them clothing and shelter too. Now you tell me what use you will be to the new people, and where they will be able to find you. I must report to them when they come."

"I will always live near them," said Rabbit. "I will live under the bushes. I will give them meat—sweet and tender meat for their children."

"I will give them warm and comfortable clothing," promised Bear.

"I too will give them clothing and meat and also a house to live in," said Buffalo. "They can use my skin for a house. They can use my bones and horns for many things."

Then Horse joined the council. "The people can use me to carry their things from camp to camp. And they can ride me. I am willing to be their slave."

When Horse had finished speaking, Wisakedjak asked the creatures, "My Younger Brothers, what will you do to protect yourselves from the new people?"

"I don't want to be hit on my body," said Rabbit. "When people want to kill me, they should take a stick and hit me over the head. If they don't kill me in that way, I will scratch them and hurt them with one of my sharp bones."

Then all the other creatures told their Elder Brother how they wanted people to handle them. Later, when the human beings came, Wisakedjak taught them how to kill the first creatures and what use to make of them.

"Now take them and use them as nature planned," Wisakedjak told the new people. "There is to be no cruelty toward them—ever. You must teach your children and your children's children how to catch them and how to use them. They must be treated kindly."

Our Elder Brother also taught the human people what roots to use for food and what herbs to use for sickness. "These were made to be good and to be truly useful. Do not waste them. Always leave some of the roots for next year's crop. Never dig all of the roots."

Wisakedjak intended that everything should last forever, and yet he predicted the coming of the white men.

"Another race of people will come," he said. "They will kill all the buffaloes. They will destroy the twelve food plants that grow along the edge of the mountains. They will waste the forests."

Everything has come to pass as our Elder Brother predicted.

Wisakedjak is now very, very old. Some people say that when he left the Cree country, he went to live on an island far away toward the rising sun. If you will go to the ocean and look toward the east, you will see an island. If you go there, you will see another island much farther east. On that second island Wisakedjak now lives. But if you should land there, he will go underground. He is so old that he is no longer handsome and he wants no one to see him.

 HAIDA

The beginning of the Haida world

> *Almost every tribe had one or more myths about the creation of the world. Among the Coast tribes of British Columbia, Raven was the central figure in the stories of creation. Some people considered him a symbol of creation; others considered him a symbol of an ancient deity.*
>
> *The following is one of several creation myths once told by the Haida Indians of the Queen Charlotte Islands. In many of their villages, the raven was the most important symbol on the totem poles.*

Long, long ago, before the world was created, Sha-lana ruled in his kingdom up in the grey clouds. All below his kingdom was a vast stretch of water.

Raven was the chief servant of Sha-lana. One day Raven made his master angry and so was cast forth from the land of the grey clouds. Back and forth he flew over the vast sea until he became weary. But there was no place where he could rest, no place where he could light.

Angry at finding none, he beat the water with his wings until it reached the clouds on both sides of him. When the water fell back, it was transformed into rocks. There Raven rested. These rocks grew and spread themselves on each side until they stretched from North Island to Cape St. James. Later, the rocks were changed into sand. After several moons had passed, a few trees sprang up on the sand and grew there. After many moons, the sand and the trees had grown into the beautiful islands known today as the Queen Charlotte Islands.

After Raven had enjoyed his kingdom for a while, he became lonely "I need someone to help me with my work here," he said to him self.

One day he piled up on the beach two large heaps of clam shells and transformed them into two human beings. Both of them were female.

In a short time these two beings became unhappy and complained to their creator, Raven.

"You should not have made both of us women," they said.

At first Raven was angered by their complaint, but after thinking about it, he understood why they were unhappy. So he threw limpet shells at one of them and changed her into a man. Then they were happy. The man and the woman became the ancestors of all the Haida people.

Seeing the two people together made Raven feel very lonely. So he made up his mind to visit his former home in Cloudland and try to obtain a wife among the daughters of the chiefs up there.

One bright sunny morning he started on his long journey. He flew high up above the great sea until the land he had created seemed the size of a small mosquito. At last he came to the wall around Shalana's kingdom. There he hid himself until evening. Then he changed himself into the form of a bear, scratched a hole in the wall, and through it entered Cloudland.

There Raven found that everything had changed greatly. He learned that everyone was now a chief, ruled by the Chief of Light, who still had supreme power. The Chief had divided his kingdom into villages and towns, into lands and seas. He had created a moon and stars, and he had made a great sun to rule over all the other bodies of light. Raven observed everything carefully, so that he could make a similar kingdom down on his earth.

At last, still in the form of a bear, Raven was brought before the ruler. As he seemed to be a handsome and tame bear, the Chief kept him as a playmate for his young son. For three years Raven lived in the beautiful lodge of the ruling family. Many of the things that he saw there he decided to take with him when he returned home.

In Cloudland it was the custom for children to disguise themselves, to change themselves into bears or seals or birds. One evening Raven, in the form of a bear, was strolling on the beach, looking for clams for his supper. He saw three bears approaching him, but he knew that they were the children of a chief.

"Now is the time to return to my own country," Raven said to himself.

He transformed himself into a large eagle, swooped down upon the three children-bears, and gathered up one of them. He seized also the sun, which was just then setting, and the fire-stick that was used in kindling fires. With the child in his claws, the sun under one wing and the fire-stick under the other, he started away from the Land of Light.

When the people in the upper world learned that the sun had been stolen, they were alarmed. Many of them rushed to the Great Chief to report the theft.

"Search everywhere, at once," he ordered. "When you find the thief, we will throw him to the ruler of the lower world, the world below the great sea."

Just before the search started, a messenger arrived, crying out, "I saw a large eagle flying off with the sun under one wing!"

Everyone then gave chase, following Raven, still in the form of an eagle. In his hurried flight, Raven dropped the child. The child fell down through the clouds into the sea that was close to Cloudland. Still carrying the sun and the fire-stick, Raven flew away from his pursuers and reached the earth safely.

The child, when it fell into the sea, cried for help. Hearing him, a great shoal of little fish came to his rescue and carried him on their backs to the shore of Cloudland. Today many of these fish swim around Rose-spit, and their forms have been pressed into the blue clay along the near-by beaches.

The Great Chief in Cloudland, a lover of peace, did not allow his people to follow Raven to the earth. He feared that their pursuit might cause the ruler of the lower world to come to Cloudland and give them trouble. Instead, the Great Chief created another sun to shine over his kingdom.

When Raven reached his kingdom, he showed his people how to make fire with the fire-stick he had watched people use in Cloudland. Ever since, the earth has had light and heat, from the sun and from fire.

Other supernatural beings

Similar to Nanabozho of Chippewa mythology and to Wisakedjak of Cree mythology are Napi or Old Man of the Blackfeet, Coyote of the western plateau tribes (and of other tribes in the United States), and Raven of the tribes along the Pacific coast. Each appears as the main character in innumerable stories, sometimes as a human being, sometimes as an animal, always able to do supernatural deeds. Each personage has the same combination of contradictory qualities: cleverness and stupidity, benevolence and malicious mischief.

Raven and Coyote appear in tales in this volume. Napi made the sun and the world, animals and the first people. He created the first buffaloes and told the Indians to shoot them with the bows and arrows he had made. He gave the Blackfeet the first specimens of every article that they use, and they made the copies. Everywhere in the Rocky Mountains are places where Napi slept or walked or hunted. As a culture hero, he was much like Nanabozho; as a cruel prankster and trickster, he was much like Coyote.

Characters similar to them are found in the mythology of many tribes. Mink is one of these supernatural beings. Old-One of some plateau tribes, the Three Brothers, the Four Brothers, and several supernatural beings whose names mean simply "the Changer" travelled about, transforming the early world and its inhabitants into the forms we see today.

Glooscap, the main character in the stories of the Micmacs and the Malecites of New Brunswick and Nova Scotia, appears only as a benefactor and as a human or superhuman being, never as a trickster or as an animal. "Glooscap was the friend and teacher of the Indians. All they knew of the arts he taught them. He taught them the names of the constellations and the stars. He taught them how to hunt and fish and cure what they took, and how to cultivate the ground."

He travelled up and down the St. John River in his stone canoe, and over the land on his snowshoes, improving the life of his people. His canoe was an island, now called Peree Island. His stone kettle is now known as Spencer Island. His snowshoes are the two islands opposite Mactiquack. His carrying strap was the rainbow; when he was at home, he hung it in the sky, so that his people would know that all was well. Finding that enormous beavers were troublesome, he broke their dam with his big stick and so formed the Reversing Falls in the St. John River.

He killed giants and monsters and all the dangerous animals. Large animals that were not dangerous he changed to their present size. He transformed a moose into the Isle of Holt and his pursuing dogs into rocks; the dogs still sit on their haunches, their tongues hanging from their mouths. On a cliff at the Narrows, he made a picture of himself before he left for a distant land. Indians seeing the face and head of Glooscap on the rock used to throw tobacco into the water as a sacrifice, to insure a calm voyage.

Glooscap, usually accompanied by his brother, had many adventures with Half-Stone, with Thunder, with Turtle, and with others of the ancient people. Some storytellers say that he is still living, in the south end of the world. He does not grow old, and he expects to live as long as the world lasts.

Glooscap, the Four Brothers, Old-One, Coyote, Raven, Wisakedjak, and Nanabozho are important characters in some of the stories that follow.

The big snow in the northland

Long ago, the animals and birds and fishes along the shores of Great Slave Lake lived in peace and friendship. All spoke the same language at that time, when the world was new and people had not come out yet. No animal ate another animal. All lived on plants and leaves and berries.

One night in this long ago time, the darkness was very thick and snow began to fall. All night it fell. The night continued, so that it seemed never to have an end. The snow became deeper and deeper. Plants and bushes were covered, and the animals had difficulty in finding food. Many of them died.

At last their chief called a council of all the living.

"Let us send messengers to the Sky World," the council decided. "They will find out from the Sky People what is causing this long night and the deep snow."

So they sent as messengers one member of every kind of animal, bird, and fish that lived on the shores of Great Slave Lake. Those who could not fly were carried on the backs of those who could fly. So all reached the Sky World and passed through the trapdoor.

Beside the trapdoor stood a great lodge made of deer skins. In the lodge were three little bears. This was the home of Black Bear, an animal not on the earth at that time. Their mother, the cubs said, was in her canoe on the lake near by; she had gone out to spear caribou.

The animal people did not like the idea of Black Bear's spearing caribou, one of their own group. But they said nothing about it. Instead, they looked around the lodge. Hanging from the cross-bows overhead were some curious bags.

"What are in those bags?" they asked the cubs.

At first the cubs would not answer. When asked again, they said slowly, "We can't tell you. Wait until our mother comes back. She asked us to stay here and watch them."

"I wonder if those bags have something to do with us," the earth people wondered to themselves. So they asked the cubs again about the bags.

Pressed by their questions, the cubs finally told them.

"This bag contains the winds. That one contains the rain. This one the cold. That one, the fog. This one——"

But they would not say what was in the last bag.

"We dare not tell you about this one," said the youngest cub. "Our mother told us that it is a big secret. If we tell you what is in it, she will be angry when she returns and will spank us."

The visitors felt sure that the last bag contained the sunshine, and sunshine was what they wanted. So they left the lodge and held a council. They saw Black Bear landing her canoe on the far shore of the lake. Quickly they made a plan.

"Mouse, you go to Bear's canoe and gnaw a deep cut in the handle of her paddle close to the blade. When you have finished your work, you signal to Caribou.

"Caribou, as soon as you get the signal, you jump into the lake and begin swimming. Before Black Bear gets close, swim ashore and run into the woods. The rest of us will hide until it is safe to get the bag of sunshine."

Before Fox hid himself, he put his head inside the lodge and said to the cubs, "Keep a lookout for the caribou. It may come near you here."

Mouse ran to the far shore of the lake and gnawed the paddle. As soon as she signalled, Caribou jumped into the water.

The cubs saw him and yelled to their mother. "Mother! Mother! Look at the caribou!"

The earth people, watching from their hiding places, saw Black Bear jump into her canoe, seize the paddle, and begin to stroke as hard as she could. Caribou also watched as he swam. Soon the paddle broke, the canoe turned over, and Black Bear disappeared beneath the waters of the lake.

Caribou swam ashore, Mouse returned to her friends, and all the earth people ran into the lodge. They pulled down the bag they wanted, and in it they found the sun, moon, and stars. These they threw down through the trapdoor. When they opened the door, they saw that snow covered the tops of even the highest pine trees. While they watched, the snow began to melt from the heat of the sun.

Thinking the earth world would soon be safe, the animals started down. But some of them had accidents. Beaver split his tail, and the blood was spilled over Lynx. Moose flattened his nose and Buffalo bruised his back. Ever since then, Beaver's tail has been flat, Lynx has been spotted, Moose has had a flat nose, and Buffalo has had a bump on his back. Since that time also, there have been bears in the earth world, for the three cubs came down with the earth people.

But it was still hard to get food. The snow melted so quickly that the earth was covered with water. The fish, who had been living on the land, found that they could swim and so they carried their friends on their backs. The ducks set to work to pull the land up from beneath the water.

At last the people were so hungry that they sent Raven out to look for dry land. At that time Raven was the most beautiful of all birds.

While looking for land, he found the body of a dead animal. Although he had never before eaten anything except berries and willow leaves, he began to feast on the body of his animal brother. As punishment, he was changed into the bird he is today. All the animals and birds hate him; and even man, who eats everything else, will not taste his flesh.

Then the people sent Ptarmigan out to look for dry land. When Ptarmigan came back, he carried on his back a branch of willow. It was a message of hope. As a reward, ptarmigans turn white when the snow begins to fall in the Barren Land. Thus they warn the animals and the people that winter is near.

But the peaceful and friendly life on Great Slave Lake was no more. When the flood waters had gone, the fish found that they could no longer live on the land; if they did, they would be eaten by the birds and the animals. The birds found that they were safer high in the trees and up in the mountains than anywhere else. Every animal chose the place that suited it best. Soon the birds and fish and beasts could not understand the same language.

Not long afterward, the first human beings came to Great Slave Lake. Since then, there has been no peace.

✳ COWICHAN

The story of the great flood

When the first missionaries came to the Far West, they found that the Indians had traditions of a great flood similar to the flood of Noah's day. The Squamish Indians told about a canoe-load of their ancestors being saved on the top of Mount Baker, a high peak in the Cascade Range.

The Cowichan Indians of Vancouver Island had the following flood tradition.

Long ago the people became so numerous that they spread all over the land. When hunting became scarce, people in the different bands and different villages began to quarrel over their boundaries.

By this time they had become skilled in shaping paddles for their canoes, in weaving baskets, and in dressing skins. From cedar bark they wove material which they made into clothes. From cedar logs they made canoes which they shaped with the help of clam shells.

The canoes were blunt at both ends, just like scows.

Their wise men had the power to foretell the future. One time all the wise men were disturbed by dreams that kept returning to them, for these dreams seemed to predict the destruction of the people. The wise men were greatly troubled and shared their dreams with one another.

"I have dreamed a strange thing," said one of them. "I dreamed that so much rain fell that we were all drowned."

"I dreamed," said another, "that the river rose and flooded the place, and that we were all destroyed."

"So did I," said another wise man.

"And I too."

Unable to understand what these dreams meant, they called a council to decide what the people should do.

"Let us make a raft, a huge raft of many canoes tied together," suggested one of the speakers at the council.

Many people agreed with him. Others laughed at him, believing that the dreams meant nothing.

The people who agreed with the wise speaker set to work to build the raft. After many months they had made sturdy canoes from cedar logs and had tied them together with long ropes of cedar bark. With a huge rope of cedar bark they tied the raft to the top of Mount Cowichan. They passed the long rope through the middle of a large stone on top of the mountain. The stone which was thus used as anchor may still be seen on Mount Cowichan.

All the months the people were building the raft, those who did not believe in dreams laughed at them and scoffed at them. But all marvelled at the huge and beautiful raft when the canoes were finally floated in Cowichan Bay. No one had ever seen such a large raft and such huge cedar-bark ropes.

Not long after the work was done, rain began. The drops were as large as hailstones and so heavy that they killed babies. As the rivers overflowed their banks, all the valleys were covered with water. People climbed up on Mount Cowichan, but that too was soon under water.

When the rain began, the wise men and the people who had believed their warning dreams took their families and food and placed them on the raft. By and by the raft rose with the water. For many days the people lived on the raft, seeing nothing but each other and the great flood. Even the mountains had disappeared. As the rain continued to fall, the people had to bail out the water with their cedar-bark bailers. They were frightened and they prayed for help. But no help came.

At last the rain stopped. Slowly the waters went down, and after a time the raft rested on the top of Mount Cowichan. The cedar rope and the stone anchor had held it. From the top of the mountain the people watched the flood waters disappear until at length they could see their own land.

But what destruction met their eyes! Their homes were gone, and the valleys, once green with forest, were brown with mud and fallen trees. Both sad and glad, they returned to the places where they had lived. There they began to rebuild their village and to take up their old life again.

After many years their numbers had increased so much that their lands were filled with people. Again they quarrelled among themselves, this time so bitterly that they decided to separate. Some of them moved in one direction, some in another. And in this way people spread over the earth.

✳ NOOTKA

How Deer got fire

The origin of fire is a favourite theme of myths in all parts of the world. Fire myths among the North American Indians alone would fill a book.

Long ago, in the early days of the world, Chief Woodpecker was the only one who had fire in his house. Even his own people, the Wolves, had no fire. The Deer people and their wise chief had no fire and did not know how to get any from Woodpecker.

One time the Deer people heard that a winter ceremonial dance was to be held in the dancing house of Woodpecker. They held a secret meeting and there decided to go to Chief Woodpecker's village and get some fire.

"Who will be the one to steal the fire?" they asked.

"I will get fire for you," said Deer.

Then his chief gave him a seaweed bottle containing hair-oil. "Take this with you," he said. "And also this comb and this piece of stone. When you get the fire, you must run. And when the Wolves pursue you, throw the stone between you and them. It will be transformed into a large mountain. When they come near again, throw the comb behind you. It will be transformed into thick bushes. When they come near a third time, throw down the hair-oil. It will be transformed into a large lake.

"Then you must run very fast. You will see Periwinkle Shell on the trail. You will give him the fire, and then you must run to save your life. Now let me put some soft cedar bark on you, so that you can catch the fire with it."

The chief took the soft cedar bark and tied a bunch of it on each of Deer's elbows.

"During one song," continued the chief, "you must dance around the fire. When that song is ended, ask to have the smoke hole opened so that you can have some fresh air. When they have opened the hole, we will sing the second song. In the middle of it, you must touch the fire with your elbows and then jump through the smoke hole."

By the time the council ended, it was dark and time for the dance to begin. Deer and his people started toward the Wolves' dancing house, singing as they went.

When Chief Woodpecker heard them coming, he said to his people, "We will not let the Deer people in, because they might try to steal our fire."

But his daughter begged him to let the people come in, so that she might see Deer dance. "I have been told that he dances very well," she said.

"Open the door, then, and let them in," the chief told his people. "But keep close watch on Deer, and do not let him dance too near the fire. When all are inside, shut the door and put a bar across it, so that he cannot run out."

The Wolves did as their chief ordered. The Deer people began to sing Deer's first dancing song, and he began to dance around the fire.

At the end of the first song, he said to the Wolves, "It is very hot in here. Will you please open the smoke hole, to let in some cool, fresh air?"

"Go and open the smoke hole," said Chief Woodpecker. "It is hot in here, and Deer cannot jump as high as the smoke hole."

When the smoke hole was wide open, the song-leader of the visitors began to sing, and Deer began to dance around the fire again. Whenever Woodpecker saw him go near the fire, he sent one of his men to tell him to keep away. Deer danced faster and faster, whirling and whirling. At last he touched the fire with his elbows, the cedar bark caught fire, and he jumped through the smoke hole.

Off he ran into the woods, the warriors of the Wolf tribe following close behind him. When they came near, he threw the small stone behind him, and it turned into a large mountain. While they were crossing over the mountain, Deer ran a long way. When the Wolves drew near a second time, he threw the comb behind him. It turned into thorny bushes, which caught the Wolves' clothes and slowed them down.

After a while they got through the thorny bushes and almost over-took Deer. But he poured the silver-perch oil on the ground, and suddenly there was a large lake between him and the Wolves. While they were swimming across the lake, Deer saw Periwinkle Shell on the beach.

"Periwinkle," he said, "open your mouth, take this fire into it, and hide it from the Wolves. I have stolen it from Chief Woodpecker's house. Do not tell the Wolves which way I went."

Periwinkle took the fire in his mouth and hid it. Deer ran on ahead.

After a while the Wolves came along and saw Periwinkle sitting beside the trail.

"Which way did Deer go?" they asked.

Periwinkle could not answer, for he could not open his mouth. With his mouth shut, he could only say, "Ho, ho, ho!" And he pointed this way and that way, to confuse them.

So the Wolves lost track of Deer and finally went home without catching him. The fire, which Periwinkle held in his mouth, was shared by everyone, and since then there has been fire in all parts of the world.

✳ COWICHAN

Who was given the fire?

> This fire myth has been selected partly because it contains the moralizing element that early recorders said was frequent in Indian fireside tales.
> It came from the Cowichan Indians of Vancouver Island, and was recorded many years ago by James Deans. He was sent to the Hudson's Bay Company at Fort Victoria in 1853.

Our fathers tell us that very long ago our people did not know the use of fire. They had no need for fire to warm themselves, because they lived in a warm country. They ate their meats raw or dried by the sun. But after a while their climate grew colder. They had to build houses for shelter, and they wished for something to warm their homes.

One time when a number of them were seated around a deer which they had just found in one of their pits, a pretty bird came and fluttered above their heads. It seemed to be either watching them or looking for a share in the meat. Seeing the bird flying about, some people tried to kill it. Others, more kind, said, "Little bird, what do you want?"

"I know your needs," the bird replied, "and I have come to you, bringing the blessings of fire."

"What is fire?" asked all of them.

"Do you see that little flame on my tail?" asked the bird.

"Yes," all answered.

"Well, that is fire. Today each of you must gather a small bunch of pitch wood. With it you can get fire from the flame on my tail. To-morrow morning I will come here early. Every one of you will meet me here, bringing your pitch wood with you."

Early next morning all arrived at the chosen place, where the bird was awaiting their coming.

"Have you brought your pitch wood?" asked the bird.

"Yes," replied all of the people.

"Well, then," said the bird, "I am ready. But before I go, let me tell you the rules. None of you can obtain my fire unless you obey the rules. You must be persevering, and you must do good deeds. You must strive for the fire, in order that you may think more of it. And none need to expect to get it who has not done some good deed.

"Whoever comes up with me," continued the bird, "and puts his pitch wood on my tail, he will have the fire. Are you all ready?"

"Yes," replied everyone.

Away flew the bird, followed by all the people—young and old, men and women and children. Helter-skelter they ran, over rocks and fallen timber, through swamp and stream, over prairies and through forests. Some of them got hurt. Others peeled their shins as they fell off the rocks and stumbled over the logs. Many people splashed through mud and water. Others were badly scratched and had their clothes torn among the bushes. Many turned and went home, saying, "Anything so full of danger is not worth trying for." Other people became so weary they gave up. But the bird kept on.

At last a man came up to it, saying, "Pretty bird, give me your fire. I have kept up with you, and I have never done anything bad."

"That may be true," replied the bird. "But you cannot have my fire because you are too selfish. You care for nobody as long as you yourself are right."

So away flew the bird.

After a while another man came up, saying, "Pretty bird, give me your fire. I have always been good and kind."

"Perhaps you have been," answered the bird. "But you cannot have my fire because you stole your neighbour's wife."

So the bird flew away again. By this time few people followed it, most of them having given up the chase.

At last the bird came to where a woman was taking care of a poor, sick old man. It flew straight to her and said, "Bring your pitch wood here and get the fire."

"Oh, no," said the woman. "I cannot do so because I have done nothing to deserve it. What I am doing is only my duty."

"Take the fire," said the bird. "You are welcome to it. It is yours, for you are always doing good and thinking it only your duty. Take the fire and share it with the other people."

So the woman put her pitch wood on the bird's tail and got the fire. Then she gave some to all the others, and people have never since been without it. Fire has cooked their food and warmed their lodges.

That is how, in the long, long ago, the Cowichans first got fire.

✳ THOMPSON

Coyote and the salmon

Many tribes along the Columbia River and its tributaries related a story similar to this one told by the Thompson River Indians of British Columbia. The Klamath Indians of southern Oregon also had a variant of it concerning the salmon in the Klamath River. The four wooden boxes in the following myth do not appear in other versions. Indian storytellers who speak English pronounce "Coyote" in three syllables and emphasize the second: Kī-ō´-ti.

One time Coyote was crossing a creek which flows into the Thompson River. He fell from the log into the swiftly flowing water and was swept down stream into the river. In danger of being drowned, he turned himself into a small board. As a board, he was carried down the stream to where the Thompson flows into the Fraser River, and from there to the unknown region below.

He floated with the current until he was stopped by a fish-dam, near the mouth of the Fraser. The fish-dam was owned by two old women. When they came to their dam the next morning, they saw the piece of wood.

"That is a nice piece of wood," one of the women said. "It will make a nice dish. I will take it home."

When they had made it into a dish, they placed salmon in it and ate from it. But the fish disappeared so quickly that they could not get enough for a fair meal. One piece of salmon after another they put in the dish, but always it disappeared quickly. At last one of the women became angry and threw the dish into the fire. At once they heard the sound of a baby crying. The sound was coming from the fire.

"Pull it out quickly!" one of the women said. "It is a child! I should like to have a child, to bring up as my own."

So they pulled the child out of the fire, a little boy. He grew up very rapidly. They found him difficult to rear, for he was headstrong and disobedient. Sometimes they took him with them on their wanderings, and sometimes they left him at home.

In their house these women kept four wooden boxes, each of them fitted with a lid.

"Do not take the lids off these boxes," they warned the boy. "Remember that they must never be taken off. Never."

The boy looked as if he understood.

Salmon, the chief food of the women, was a new food to Coyote. There was no salmon in his country, and the Coyote people knew nothing about it. Below the women's dam the river was full of fish, but of course there were none above it. Coyote made up his mind to break the dam and let the salmon go up the rivers to his people.

One day when the women were away, Coyote broke the dam and then went to the house and opened the four wooden boxes.

From one box, smoke came out; from another, wasps; from the third, salmon-flies; from the fourth, beetles.

Then Coyote, running along the bank of the river, was followed by the salmon. The smoke, the wasps, the flies, and the beetles followed the salmon. The people along the upper river saw the great smoke and wondered what it was. Coyote led some of the salmon up the Thompson River to his people, but most of them went on up the Fraser.

That is why smoke-wasps, salmon-flies, blow-flies, and meat-beetles follow the salmon up the streams, even to this day. They become numerous almost as soon as the salmon begin to run. Until Coyote brought the salmon, these insects were not known to the people of the Fraser River country.

After Coyote had taken salmon up these rivers, he went over to the Columbia and led salmon up that river and up the streams that flow into it. After taking the fish to the headwaters of the Okanagan River, he returned and began to lead them up the Similkameen River. Before he had gone far, he saw some girls bathing near the opposite bank.

He called to them, "Do you want any backbone of the humpback salmon?"

"No," they answered. "But we'd like to have part of a mountain sheep."

"I shall not let their people have any salmon," Coyote said to himself.

So he piled up rocks in the river and made a waterfall.

"Now the salmon can never go any farther up this river," Coyote said to himself.

At the same time he caused great numbers of mountain sheep to appear in the Similkameen country. That is why mountain sheep are still plentiful in that country and why the people have to travel to the Thompson, Okanagan, or Columbia rivers to get their supply of salmon.

All along the rivers, Coyote showed the people how to make equipment for catching salmon, and he taught them how to cook it and how to dry it for winter use.

Then he went to another country. There the people did not know how to hunt. They used clubs and stones for killing animals, and because deer run fast and jump far, the hunters had difficulty in killing anything. So Coyote showed the men how to make bows and arrows and how to use them. He taught the women how to cut up meat, how to cure it, how to dress the skins and make them into clothing.

He did many other wonderful things. He changed mosquitoes from large, fierce creatures that killed people into the tiny insects they are today. He turned grass into shells, to be used for ornaments on buckskin clothes. He turned twigs into berry bushes heavy with fruit. He threw fish skins into the river and they became salmon. Because of Coyote, his people had many kinds of food, and life became much easier than it had been when the world was very young.

Some people say that Coyote was the ancestor of all the Indian tribes that lived between the Cascade Mountains and the Rocky Mountains. Others say that he was not their ancestor, but their chief. All these tribes are known as "Coyote people."

Coyote and Old Man

The theme of the power contest, frequent in mythology, appears not only in this myth of the Thompson River Indians but also in similar tales told by their relatives, the Lake, Okanagan, and Colville Indians.

At last Coyote finished his work on earth. He had conquered Ice and Blizzard. He had killed some monsters and had transformed others into harmless creatures of today's world, like marmots and mosquitoes. He had brought salmon up the rivers to be food for his people. He had shown his people how to make and to do many things that made their lives easier and happier.

So the time came when he should meet Old Man.

As Coyote was travelling through the country somewhere southeast of the Columbia River, he met Old Man. But Coyote did not know that this was the "Great Chief," the "Great Mystery," for he looked like any other old man.

Coyote thought to himself, "This old man does not know who I am. He knows nothing about my great powers or about the wonderful things I have done. I will surprise him."

After they had greeted each other, Old Man began to make fun of Coyote as if he were a person of little power. Coyote, annoyed, boasted of the wonders he had performed.

"If you have done all of those wonderful things," said Old Man, "then you must be Coyote. All the people have told me that only Coyote can do such things."

"Yes, I am Coyote. Why do you doubt my powers?"

"If you are Coyote, and if you are as powerful as you say you are," replied Old Man, "change that river and make it run over there."

This Coyote did.

"Now bring it back," ordered Old Man.

This also Coyote did.

"Now place that mountain on the plain," ordered Old Man.

This too Coyote was able to do.

"Put the mountain back where it was," ordered Old Man.

But this Coyote could not do, because Old Man had willed that he should not.

"Why can you not put the mountain back?" asked Old Man.

"I don't know," answered Coyote. "I suppose that you must have greater powers than I have."

Old Man made the mountain go back to the place where it had stood. Then, to test Old Man's power, Coyote said to him, "Move that river."

Old Man did so.

"Move that mountain," ordered Coyote.

Old Man did so. Then he returned the mountain and the river to their original places.

"You must be Old Man, the Great Chief," said Coyote. "I was looking for you."

"Yes, I am the Great Chief," replied Old Man. "You have been on earth for a long time. As you have put it to rights, you have nothing more to do. Soon I am going to leave the earth. You will not return again until I do. Then you will come with me, and we will change things in the world. We will bring the dead back to the land of the living."

Then in a far-away part of the world Old Man made a large house out of ice and put Coyote in it. Inside the house he placed a large log, which should burn forever and forever, and be a fire for Coyote.

In that house of ice Coyote is to stay until Old Man returns to earth. No one knows exactly where the house is, but some people think that it is up in the high mountains where the glaciers are. There Coyote spends most of his time warming himself at his log fire, first on one side, then on the other. When he rolls over, the weather turns cold. No Indian mentions his name during mild weather in the winter time, lest Coyote turn over and the weather change.

Some Indians say that Old Man now lives in the upper world and that he is the maker of rain and snow. Every time he scratches his back, rain or snow falls. Other people say that Old Man lives in the high mountains, where he makes rain and snow and loud noises. That is why Indians do not like to go to the top of a very high mountain.

Some time in the future Coyote and Old Man will return and will again work wonders on the earth. When all is ready, they will bring the dead from the Land of Shades. Then there will be a loud beating of drums, and the dead will appear, borne on the top of red clouds, the northern lights, and tobacco smoke.

Why the salmon come to the Squamish waters

A wooden statue known as the Salmon Chief stands in the museum in Vancouver, British Columbia. Formerly it belonged to the local Indians, the Squamish, who sometime in the past carved it to commemorate the incidents in the following myth.

Long ago when animals and human beings were the same, there were four brothers who went about doing good. They usually travelled on the water, in a canoe. This was not an ordinary canoe; it was really the youngest of the four brothers transformed into that shape.

Coming to the Squamish Indians one time, they were persuaded by the chief to stay a while in his village. Knowing the wonder-working powers of the brothers, the chief said to them, "Won't you bring the salmon people to our shores? We are often short of food. We know that salmon is good, but they never come to our waters."

"We will persuade the salmon people," replied the oldest brother, "if we can find out where they live. We shall have to ask Snookum, the sun."

But it was difficult to get near enough to the sun to ask him anything. He was a wily creature and seldom left the sky. The brothers knew that they would have to use craft to bring him down. After much pondering and discussing, they transformed the youngest brother into a salmon and tied him to the shore with a fishing line. By sporting about in the water, the salmon attracted the attention of Snookum. But before doing anything, the sun also used craft: he caused the three brothers to go into a deep trance. Then in the form of an eagle, Snookum descended from the sky, pounced upon the salmon, and flew away with it, breaking the line as he flew.

When the three brothers awakened from their trance, they used their wonder-working powers again. They transformed the third brother into a whale and tied him to the shore. This time they used a rope, which was stouter than the line they had used for the salmon. Again the sun cast the brothers into a trance and descended from the sky in the form of an eagle. He fixed his claws firmly into the flesh of the floating whale and started aloft with it. This time the rope did not break. Again and again Sun-Eagle tried to break it, but he could not. Neither could he free his claws from the whale's flesh.

While he was still struggling, the two brothers awoke from their trance. They pulled the whale to the shore, dragging the Sun with it. They said to Snookum, "Don't struggle, my friend. You cannot get away without our help, and we will not give it unless you do what we ask you to do."

Knowing that they had outwitted him, Sun-Eagle struggled no more with the whale. "What do you want me to do?" he asked.

"Tell us where the salmon people live," said the oldest brother. "You can see all over the world when you are up in the sky."

"The home of the salmon is a long way off in that direction," replied Sun, pointing toward the west. "If you want to visit them, you must first prepare much medicine and take it with you. Then all will be well."

The brothers released Sun-Eagle, and he flew off into the clouds. After gathering many herbs and making much medicine, they said to the Squamish people, "Get out your canoes and make ready for a long journey. At sunrise tomorrow we will set out for a visit with the salmon people."

Next morning they all started westward. For many days they paddled, and finally they came near an island. But they could not get close to its shores because of a large amount of floating charcoal. One of the Squamish youth tried to walk upon it, but it gave way beneath his feet and he was drowned. Paddling around the charcoal, they went to the other side of the island. There they saw what seemed to be a village. Smoke of all colours rose into the clouds.

"This seems to be the country we are looking for," said the brothers. "Sun told us that this is the home of the salmon people."

So the paddlers took the canoes to the beach, which was very broad and smooth. All the Squamish people went toward the village, the four brothers carrying the medicine with them. They gave some of the medicine to Spring Salmon, the chief of the village. As a result, he was friendly toward the whole party.

In the stream behind the village, Spring Salmon kept a fish-trap. Shortly before the visitors had landed, the chief had directed four of his young people, two boys and two girls, to go into the water and swim up the creek into the salmon-trap. Obeying his orders, they had drawn their blankets up over their heads and walked into the sea. As soon as the water reached their faces, they became salmon. They leaped and played together, just as the salmon do in the running season, and frolicked their way toward the trap in the creek.

So when the time came to welcome the strangers with a feast, Chief Spring Salmon ordered others of his people to go to the salmon-trap, bring back the four fish they would find there, and clean and roast them for the guests. The visitors watched the villagers clean the four salmon, cut them open, and spread them above the flames on a kind of wooden gridiron. When the salmon were cooked, the chief invited his guests to eat.

"Eat all you wish," he said, "but do not throw away any of the bones. Be sure to lay them aside carefully. Do not destroy even a small bone."

The Squamish and the brothers gladly accepted the invitation, partook freely of the roasted salmon, but wondered why they were asked to save the bones.

When all had finished eating, some of the young men of the salmon village carefully picked up the little piles of bones the guests had made, took them to the beach, and threw them into the sea. A few minutes later the four young people who had earlier gone into the water re-appeared and joined the others. For four days the Chief thus entertained his guests with salmon feasts.

The care taken with the bones at each meal excited the curiosity of one of the visitors. On the fourth day he secretly kept back some of the bones and hid them. At the close of the meal, the rest of the salmon bones were collected in the usual manner and cast into the sea. Immediately afterwards, four young people came out of the white water. But one of them, the visitors noticed, was covering his face with his hands.

Approaching Kos, the salmon chief, the youth said, "Not all of the bones were collected. I do not have any for my cheeks and nose."

Turning to his guests, Kos asked, "Did any of you mislay any of your salmon bones? Some are missing." And he pointed to the face of the young man.

Alarmed by the result of his act, the Squamish youth who had hidden the bones brought them out, pretending that he had just found them on the ground. Now all the visitors were certain that their hosts were the salmon people.

Some time later a large number of sea-gulls were seen gathering about an object that floated on the water a little distance from the shore.

"Go out and see what is attracting the gulls," Chief Kos directed one of his young men.

Soon the man returned and reported that it was the body of the Squamish youth who, the visitors had said, had sunk beneath the floating charcoal on the other side of the island. When the body was brought ashore, it was discovered that the eyes were missing. The four brothers had power to restore a corpse to life, but they could not restore lost eyes.

"Can you supply a new pair of eyes?" they asked the salmon chief.

Kos replied that he could and offered first a pair of eyes from Sockeye salmon. They were too small. Then he offered a pair of Cohoe eyes. They also were too small. Then he selected a pair of Dog-salmon eyes. They were exactly the right size. The oldest of the four brothers sprinkled the corpse with some of the medicine they had brought, and the body came to life again. All was well.

"We have come to visit you, Chief Kos, for a special purpose," explained the oldest brother. "We came to ask you to let some of your salmon people visit Squamish waters, come up the streams of the Squamish people. My friends are poor, and they often go hungry We shall be very grateful if your people will sometimes visit them."

"I will do as you request," replied the salmon chief, "on one condition: they must throw all the bones back into the water as you have seen us do. If they will be careful with the bones, my people can return to us again after they visit you."

"We promise," said the four brothers.

"We promise," said all the Squamish people.

Then they made preparations to return to their home across the water, toward the rising sun.

As they were leaving, the salmon chief said, "I will send Spring Salmon to you first in the season. After them I will send the Sockeye, then the Cohoe, then the Dog-salmon, and last of all the Humpback."

Ever since that time, long ago, different kinds of salmon, in that order, have come to the Squamish waters—to the sea, into the straits, and into the streams. And in the days of old, before the coming of white people, the Indians were always very careful to throw the bones of the salmon back into the water.

This is the story carved on the statue of the Salmon Chief of the Squamish.

✳ KOOTENAY

The animals climb into the sky

The theme of a visit to Sky Land by the mythological people of the earth is found in the myths of many tribes in British Columbia and in the State of Washington. The following is from the Kootenays; the Okanagans and the Shuswaps relate almost the same story. About forty versions have been recorded; in them the part played here by the two Hawks is played by Chickadee, Wren, Woodpecker, or Boy Sapsucker.

Long ago, the animal people decided to make a journey to the Sky World. When they wondered how they could get up there, Grizzly Bear, who was their chief, told them he had a plan. He called all the people together and said to them, "Each of you—each animal, bird, and fish—will shoot an arrow upward until a rope of arrows reaches the sky."

All agreed with his plan. Coyote shot the first arrow toward the sky, but it fell down without reaching the spot. Fish, Toad, and Snake tried, but their arrows also fell back. One animal after another tried to hit the sky, but none succeeded. At last two Hawks took their turn. They had already visited the sky and were known to be skilful with the bow and arrow.

For a day and a night their arrows whistled through the air before the animals heard them strike the sky. The two Hawks continued to shoot. Their second arrow hit the notch of the first, the third one hit the notch of the second, and so on. At last they had a rope of arrows that reached almost to the ground. In order to complete the rope, Raven stuck his bill into the notch of the last arrow and braced his feet against the earth. Thus the animals climbed from the earth to the sky.

"Wait a minute," said Glutton, while the first ones were climbing. "I must look after my traps. Then I will be with you."

But when he came back, all the others had gone up the rope, including Raven. Glutton was so angry at being left behind that he pulled down the arrows and scattered them all over the land. This is how the Rocky Mountains came to be.

Before the other animals had reached the sky, Muskrat had climbed up there on his tail. With his spirit-power he had made a number of houses appear on the seashore. There he awaited the other earth people, eager to play a trick on them. The houses were very dirty. When the animal people arrived, Muskrat shot at them from the houses. As soon as he had shot from one place, he ran through a tunnel into the water and then into the next house. From there he shot at them again. In this way he made them believe that many people lived there and were shooting at them.

At last Woodpecker discovered that only the Muskrat lived in those houses. He watched at the hole until Muskrat came out, and then killed him.

When the animal people were ready to return to the earth, they were surprised at not being able to find the rope on which they had climbed up. Their chief thought of a plan and said to them, "Let us make a noose and catch Thunderbird. Then we will put his feathers on ourselves; with their help we will fly down to the earth."

Soon they saw a flash of lightning and heard the Thunderbird coming. Quickly they caught him in a noose and pulled out his feathers. Eagle took the best feathers. The others were divided among many creatures, but there were not enough for all. Those that took feathers flew down and became birds. Others leaped down and became fish or land animals. Coyote used his tail to steer with and so fell gently to the earth. Sucker fell on a rock and broke his bones. He had to borrow new ones, and since then he has been full of bones.

Some people say that the creatures that did not return from the Sky Land were killed by the Sky People and were changed into stars.

Glooscap and his four visitors

The missionary who recorded this story from the Micmacs considered it a parable with several meanings.

Soon after Glooscap had left the Indians, four men agreed to go in search of him. They did not know where he was, but they knew that he could always be found by those who diligently sought him. For many suns and many moons they journeyed. They started in the spring of one year and kept on searching until midsummer of the next year.

Then the men found a small path in the forest that was marked by blazed trees. Following it, they came to a beautiful river, then to a broad and beautiful lake, and soon reached a long spit of land that ran far out into the water. There they climbed a hill and, looking down from the top of it, they saw smoke rising through the trees. In a short time the men came to a large and well-built wigwam.

Entering it, they found two people. On the right sat a middle-aged man, and on the left a very aged woman, doubled over as if she might be more than one hundred years old. Opposite the door a mat was spread out, as if a third person had a seat there.

The man in the wigwam pleasantly welcomed the four visitors and asked them to be seated. But he did not ask the usual questions as to where they were going or where they had come from. After a while, all heard the sound of an approaching canoe and then footsteps. Soon a young man entered the wigwam, well dressed and manly in form and features. His weapons indicated that he had been hunting, and he told the woman that he had brought home some game.

The old woman, weak and tottering, rose with great difficulty, brought in four or five beavers, and started to prepare them for cooking. But so feeble was she that the young man took the knife from her hands and prepared them himself. In a short time, he set before the hungry guests a large portion of the cooked meat.

For seven days the men were hospitably entertained, while they rested from their long journey. The hosts seemed to pay no attention to their worn garments, so full of holes that their skin peeped out in all directions.

One morning the middle-aged man asked the young man to wash their mother's face. As soon as he had done so, her wrinkles vanished and she became young-looking and handsome. Her white hair became black and glossy, and she was dressed in a beautiful robe. Instead of looking old, stooped, and feeble, she now appeared young, straight, and active.

The four visitors looked on in amazement. They knew now that whoever their young host was, he had supernatural powers. Gladly they accepted his invitation to look at the country around his wigwam. Beauty was everywhere. Tall trees with rich foliage and fragrant blossoms stood in rows so straight and far apart that the men could see a long distance in every direction. The air was sweet and balmy. Everything suggested health, repose, and happiness.

After they had enjoyed the scene for a time, their host and guide asked, "Where have you men come from and why are you here?"

"We are in search of Glooscap."

"I am Glooscap," he replied. "What can I do for you?"

"I am a wicked man," said one, "and I have an ugly temper. I wish to be calm, meek, and holy."

"Very well," replied Glooscap. "Your wish will be granted."

"I am poor," said the second man, "and I find it difficult to make a living. I wish to be rich."

"Very well," replied Glooscap. "Your wish shall be granted."

"I am despised by my people," said the third man. "I wish to be loved and respected."

"Your wish shall be granted."

"I wish to live a long time," said the fourth man.

"You have asked a hard thing," said Glooscap, "but I will see what I can do for you."

Next day the three in the wigwam prepared much food, and all four men feasted before starting forth on their return journey. Then Glooscap led them up a hill, very high and difficult to climb. The ground there was rocky, broken, and unfit for cultivation. On the top of the hill, where the sun would shine from morning until night, Glooscap had the men stop. He went to the one who had asked to live a long time, clasped him around the waist, lifted him from the ground, and then set him down again. Glooscap gave him a twist or two as he moved his own hands upward, and then he moved his clasped hands over the man's head. Thus the visitor was transformed into an old, gnarled cedar tree, with limbs growing out, rough and ugly, all the way to the bottom.

"There!" exclaimed Glooscap. "I do not know exactly how many years you will live, but I think you will not be disturbed for a long, long time. No one will have any use for you, and the land around you is of no value. I think you will live to be very, very old."

The three companions were horrified. They not only mourned the loss of their comrade, but they wondered how Glooscap would grant their requests. But he soon calmed their fears. Guiding them back to his lodge, he took three small boxes from his medicine bag and gave one to each of the men. Then he told them to take off their old clothes and put on the new ones which he had ready for them. Each garment was beautifully finished and decorated.

Though now eager to return home, the three men dreaded the long journey that had taken them one whole summer, a winter, and half of a second summer. But Glooscap offered to be their guide. Early next morning, he put on his belt and started off, the three men following. About the middle of the morning they reached the top of a high mountain, from which they could see another high mountain in the blue distance.

"It will take us seven suns to reach that mountain," the men said to each other.

Glooscap made no reply, but pushed on. To the astonishment of the three men, they reached the second mountain in the middle of the afternoon.

"Now look round you," directed Glooscap.

"Why, it is our own country!" they exclaimed in surprise.

All below them was familiar. They saw their own hills and forest, their own lake and river. "There is your village," said Glooscap. And then he left them. Before sunset the three men were at home.

At first no one recognized them because of their new and splendid robes. When they explained who they were, they were surrounded by all the people of the village. Men, women, and children listened in amazement to their adventures.

When they finished their story, the men opened their boxes, which Glooscap had said were not to be opened until the travellers reached home. In each was a powerful ointment, which they immediately rubbed over their bodies.

Immediately their wishes were granted. The man who had been hated by his people was made beautiful in spirit and so fragrant from the perfume of the ointment that his company was sought by all and he became greatly loved. The man who had been very poor became a successful hunter and kept his family supplied with an abundance of game. The one who had confessed to a wicked temper became a righteous man, always calm and meek and devout.

They had found Glooscap, and he had granted them their wishes.

SENECA

The origin of stories

In a Seneca village, long ago, lived a boy whose father and mother died when he was only a few weeks old. The little boy was cared for by a woman who had known his parents. She gave him a name which means Orphan.

The boy grew to be a healthy, active little fellow. When he was old enough, his foster mother gave him a bow and some arrows, and said, "It is time for you to learn to hunt. Tomorrow morning go to the woods and kill all the game birds you can find."

Taking ears of dry corn, the woman shelled off the kernels and parched them in hot ashes. Next morning she gave the boy some of the corn for his breakfast, rolled some in a piece of buckskin, and told him to take it with him.

"You will be gone all day," she said, "and will get hungry."

Orphan Boy started off and soon found plenty of game. When he began to work toward home, he had a good string of birds.

The next morning, while he was eating breakfast, his mother said to him. "You must do your best when hunting, for if you become a good hunter you will always be prosperous."

Each day Orphan Boy started off with his little bundle of parched corn. Each day he brought home more birds than the previous day. On the ninth day he killed so many that he brought them home on his back. His mother tied the birds in little bundles of three or four and distributed them among her neighbours.

The tenth day the boy started off, as usual, and went deeper into the woods than ever. About midday the sinew that held the feathers to his arrow loosened. Looking around for a place where he could sit down while he took the sinew off and wound it on again, he saw a small opening. Near the center of the opening was a high, smooth, flat-topped, round stone. He went to the stone, sprang up on it, and sat down. He unwound the sinew, put it in his mouth to soften, and then arranged the arrow feathers. When he was about to fasten them to the arrow, a voice near him asked, "Shall I tell you stories?"

Orphan Boy looked up expecting to see a man. Not seeing any one, he looked behind the stone and around it, and then began to tie the feathers to his arrow.

"Shall I tell you stories?" asked a voice beside him.

The boy looked in every direction, but saw no one. Then he made up his mind to watch and find out who was trying to fool him. He stopped work and listened, and when the voice again asked, "Shall I tell you stories?" he found that it came from the stone. Then he asked, "What is that? What does it mean to tell stories?"

"It is telling what happened a long time ago. If you will give me your birds, I'll tell you stories."

"You may have the birds."

At once, the stone began telling what happened long ago. When it had finished one story, it began another. The boy sat, with his head down, and listened. Toward night the stone said, "We will rest now. Come again tomorrow. If anyone asks about your birds, say that you have killed so many that they are getting scarce and you have to go a long way to find one."

While going home the boy killed five or six birds. When his mother asked why he had so few, he said that they were scarce, that he had to go far for them.

The next morning Orphan Boy started off with his bow and arrows and little bundle of parched corn, but he forgot to hunt for birds. He was thinking of the stories the stone had told him. When a bird lighted near him he shot it, but he kept straight on toward the opening in the woods. When he got there he put his birds on the stone and called out, "I've come! Here are birds. Now tell me stories."

The stone told story after story. Toward night it said, "Now we must rest till tomorrow."

On the way home the boy looked for birds, but it was late and he found only a few.

That night the mother told her neighbours that when Orphan Boy first began to hunt he had brought home a great many birds. "But now," she continued, "he brings only four or five after being in the woods from morning till night. There is something strange about it. Either he throws the birds away or he gives them to some animal. Or maybe he idles time away, doesn't hunt at all."

She hired a boy to follow Orphan Boy, to keep out of his sight and sometimes shoot a bird. Orphan Boy killed a good many birds; then, about the middle of the forenoon, he suddenly started off toward the east, running as fast as he could. The boy followed till he came to an opening in the woods and saw him climb up and sit down on a large round stone. The hired boy crept nearer and heard talking. When he couldn't see the person Orphan Boy was talking to, he went up and asked, "What are you doing here?"

"Hearing stories."

"What are stories?"

"Telling about things that happened long ago. Put your birds on this stone, and say, 'I've come to hear stories.' "

The boy did as he was told, and straightway the stone began. The boys listened till the sun went down. Then the stone said, "We will rest now. Come again tomorrow."

On the way home Orphan Boy killed three or four birds.

When the woman asked the boy she had sent why her son killed so few birds, he said, "I followed him for a while, then I spoke to him, and after that we hunted together till it was time to come home. We couldn't find many birds."

The next morning the elder boy said, "I'm going with Orphan Boy to hunt. It's good sport." The two started off together. By the middle of the forenoon each boy had a long string of birds. They hurried to the opening, put the birds on the stone, and said, "We have come. Here are the birds! Tell us stories."

They sat on the stone and listened to stories till late in the afternoon. Then the stone said, "We'll rest now till tomorrow."

On the way home the boys shot every bird they could find, but it was late and they did not find many.

Several days went by in this way. Then the foster mother hired two men to follow them.

The next morning, when the boys had a large number of birds, they stopped hunting and hurried to the opening. The men followed and, hiding behind trees, saw them put the birds on a large round stone, then jump up and sit there with their heads down, listening to a man's voice. Every little while the boys said, "Uhn!"

"Let's go there and find out who is talking to those boys," said one man to the other.

They walked quickly to the stone, and asked, "What are you doing, boys?"

The boys were startled, but Orphan Boy said, "You must promise not to tell anyone."

They promised, and then Orphan Boy said, "Jump up and sit on the stone."

When the men had seated themselves on the stone, the boy said, "Go on with the story. We are listening."

The four sat with their heads down, and the stone began to tell stories. When it was almost night the stone said, "Tomorrow all the people in your village must come and listen to my stories. Have each person bring something to eat. You must clean the brush away so that the people can sit on the ground near me."

That night Orphan Boy told the chief about the story-telling stone and gave him the stone's message. The chief sent a runner to give the message to each family in the village.

Early the next morning everyone in the village followed Orphan Boy. When they came to the opening, each person put what he had brought, meat or bread, on the stone. The brush was cleared away, and everyone sat down.

When all was quiet the stone said, "Now I will tell you stories of what happened long ago. There was a world before this. The things that I am going to tell about happened in that world. Some of you will remember every word that I say, some will remember a part of the words, and some will forget them all. But each man must do his best. Hereafter you must tell these stories to one another. Now listen."

Each man bent his head and listened to every word the stone said. Once in a while the boys said "Uhn!" When the sun was almost down, the stone said, "We'll rest now. Come tomorrow and bring meat and bread."

The next morning when the people gathered around the stone, they found that the meat and bread they had left the day before were gone. They put fresh food on the stone, sat in a circle, and waited. When all was quiet, the stone began. Again it told stories till the sun was almost down. Then it said, "Come tomorrow. Tomorrow I will finish the stories of what happened long ago."

Early in the morning the people of the village gathered again and, when all was quiet, the stone began to tell stories. Late in the afternoon, it said, "I have finished! You must keep these stories as long as the world lasts; tell them to your children and your grandchildren, generation after generation. One person will remember them better than another. When you go to a man or a woman to ask for one of these stories, carry something to pay for it, bread or meat, or whatever you have. I know all that happened in the world before this; I have told it to you. When you visit one another, you must tell these things. You must remember them always. I have finished."

And so it has been. From the stone came all the knowledge the Senecas have of the world before this.

A message from the Happy Hunting Grounds

The recorder of the following story considered it "an ancient legend with a modern moral." He and other nineteenth-century students of Iroquois mythology wrote that until the coming of the whites, the Iroquois had no concept of heaven or of a prevailing "Great Spirit." Instead, they believed in many spirits; in their myths, these quickly became attributes of the "Great Spirit."

The Mischief Maker played so many pranks on the early people that all the tribes sent out runners to catch him. Hearing their whoops in every forest, and knowing that he was being hunted, he hurried on and hid in a cave under a rock. The runners did not quite overtake him, but seeing his fresh tracks, they thought they might catch him the next morning.

But next morning, the Mischief Maker was up and far away while his pursuers still slept. That night he hid again, this time in a hollow log. The next afternoon, when he heard whoops very near, he knew that the hunters were gaining on him fast. So he selected a tree with thick branches, broke down the weeds and bushes round it, climbed the tree and hid in its top. His pursuers, losing his tracks in the broken bushes, ran on for a long distance. Then they returned and made camp under the tree.

Smoke from their fire crept up among the branches and rose in a straight column to the sky. The Mischief Maker sailed away on the smoke, going up and up. He passed beautiful lakes and hunting grounds stocked with deer, passed large fields of corn and beans, tobacco and squashes. He saw large groups of handsome Indians, whose wigwams were full of dried venison and bear's meat. And so he went on and on, up and up, until he reached the wigwam of the Great Chief.

Here the Mischief Maker rested and stayed for one hundred moons, observing the customs of the people and learning their language. One morning the Great Chief told him that he must return to his people.

"I don't want to go," replied the Mischief Maker. "I am very happy in this new place."

"These are the Happy Hunting Grounds," said the Chief. "We have admitted you here so that you may know what to teach your people in order that they may get here. Go home, and if you do what I tell you, you may return to remain here forever. You have been allowed here this time, only to observe. When you come again, you may hunt and fish and do whatever you want to do. You must return to earth now and teach what you have learned."

Then a cloud of smoke in the form of an eagle came to the Mischief Maker and, seated on its back, he was carried down to the top of the tree from which he had risen. When he opened his eyes, the sun was shining and he saw that his pursuers had left their camp below. So he descended and travelled on, his mind filled with what he had seen and heard.

"No longer will I play tricks on the people," he said to himself. "Instead, I will tell them what I learned in the Happy Hunting Grounds above."

After a long journey he drew near a village and gave the common signal. Runners came to meet him, and then the head chief and all the people.

"What news do you bring?" he was asked.

"I that was the Mischief Maker am now the Peace Maker," he replied. "The Great Chief took me to the Happy Hunting Grounds, and I am sent back to tell you how to get there."

When he had described all that he had seen, the people built a big fire and danced round it, shouting as they had never shouted before. Then they sat in a circle about the fire, to listen to his message.

"The Great Chief Above, the Great Spirit, is unseen, but he is always about us. He will care for us if we will trust in him. He will never die, and he rules all things for us. He told me that we should return thanks to him, for he changes the seasons and he makes the corn and beans and squashes to grow for us. He is displeased when we kill our brothers.

"He bids us keep away from his wicked brother, the Evil-Minded One. The Evil-Minded One is very bad. He brings pestilence and fevers, lizards and poisonous weeds. He destroys peace and brings war. But if we will obey the words of the Great Spirit, the Evil-Minded One will never harm us.

"The Great Spirit has messengers who aid him in his work. They watch over all the people, take care of mothers and their new-born children, watch over those whom the Evil-Minded One has troubled with disease. The Evil-Minded One also has messengers who do his work. They scatter pestilence and whisper in our ears to tell us to go against the Great Spirit, the Ruler.

"One of the messengers of the Great Spirit is Heno. Heno has a pouch filled with thunderbolts. He gathers clouds and sends rain, and so is a friend of corn and beans and squashes. He also punishes witches and evil persons. Pray to Heno when you plant your seed, and thank him when you gather your crop. Pray also to the Great Spirit, who sends Heno to care for you. Let Heno be called Grandfather.

"There is also the Spirit of the Winds. He moves the winds but is chained to a rock. They trouble him and he tries very hard to get free. When he struggles, the winds are forced away from him, and they blow upon the earth. Sometimes he suffers terrible pain, and then his struggles are violent. The winds are made wild, and they do damage to the earth. When the struggle is over, the Spirit of the Winds goes to sleep, and the winds become quiet also.

"There is a spirit for the corn, another for the beans, another for squashes. They are sisters, living together in the fields, and are very kind to each other. You are to call them 'the Keepers of Our Life.'

"There are spirits in the water, in fire, in all the trees and berries, in herbs and tobacco and grass. They assist the Great Chief, the ruler of all things. Always return thanks to these spirits.

"This is the message that I bring from the Great Spirit. Obey them, and he will give you a place in the Happy Hunting Grounds."

When the Peace Maker had finished his message, he directed the people to throw tobacco on the fire as an offering to the Great Spirit. On the column of its smoke, he was carried away to the Happy Hunting Grounds.

And the people danced and sang around the embers of the council fire.

❋ SARCEE

The guardian spirit quest

> This is not a story, but it will help some readers to understand "A Boy's Vigil and the First Robin," "A Boy's Vision and the First Corn" in this section, the first three narratives in the last section, and minor details in several other stories.
>
> Among many peoples, dreams and visions are considered to be communion with the spirits and therefore are to be heeded, often as predictions of the future. Among the North American Indians, the vision was sought by purification and by fasting in solitude; this guardian spirit quest, in fact, was an important part of native Indian religion, for which a boy was usually instructed by some adult.
>
> The following explanation was given in 1954 by Pat Grasshopper, a very old Sarcee who was interpreted by Jim Simeon. A few details were added by Percy Creighton of the Blood Indians.

My mother told me about the spirits. There are spirits everywhere in nature. I have heard one talking, and it sounded like someone whistling. Spirits make the grass and plants to grow. Spirits cause the winds to blow and the clouds to float across the sky. Every animal and every bird has a spirit.

To get some of the spirit power from nature, and to find a spirit that would be his protector through life, a boy would go out, alone, on his guardian spirit quest. He would first bathe until he was very clean, and then he would live alone for three or four or five days without food. After he had fasted, he would have a vision, and a spirit would speak to him. It would give him a special song and special power. Adults also might go on such a quest, after the death of a child.

A boy who wished bear power, which is very strong spirit power, might lie down beside a bear's den. His vision would be a bear, and he would receive spirit power that would make him able to cure sick people. Strong power would go from him into a sick person, and that person would get well. Another boy might be given the power to become a great hunter or, in the old days, a great warrior. Or he might be given great wisdom and be a wise counsellor of his people.

Only a strong person can stay until the vision comes, for it often comes first in the form of some dangerous animal. The animal tests the person's courage. If he does not run away from it, something talks to him, something that he cannot see. This voice tells him to stay a certain number of nights. At the end of that time, the spirit gives the person power and tells him what his protector will be.

When a person returns from his vigil, he does not reveal what his vision has been. If he should, he would lose some of his spirit power. Later, perhaps years later, during the guardian spirit dances some winter, the name of his protecting spirit will be made known. After that, he will wear some sign of it. If it came from a bear, if his guardian spirit is a bear, he will carry with him a bear's claw. If it is an eagle, he will wear some of the down from beneath an eagle's wing. And he may use his symbol, his token, as a design when he paints his tepee or carves his pipe.

He sings his spirit song when he is trying to heal a sick person or when he is in danger. At any time that he needs the help of his guardian spirit, he sings his power song.

In the old days, a man called upon his spirit power in war. Even a bullet would not go through someone who had strong spirit power. So the guardian spirit quest was very important in the old days.

A boy's vigil and the first robin

When the only son of an old man reached the age for the long fast, his father was eager for him to secure a very strong guardian spirit. He wanted the boy to see, in his vision, a spirit that would make him surpass all other men of his tribe.

So he directed his son to make careful preparation for the vigil, to make himself clean, even to his finger-nails. And he planned that the youth should fast longer than had any of the men in the tribe, men famous for their wisdom or their bravery. Several times the boy bathed in the sweat lodge and plunged into the near-by stream. He scrubbed his body with fir boughs so that he would be clean and pure for the long fast. Meanwhile his father made a little lodge for him, away from the rest of the family and the village, and he put a clean mat on the ground floor of the lodge.

"Now lie quietly on this mat," the father said when the boy had finished his sweating and bathing. "Endure your fast like a man. At the end of twelve days, I will bring you food and give you my blessing."

The boy carefully obeyed all his father's directions. He lay quietly, with his face covered, and waited for the spirit voice to bring him a message. Every morning his father visited him, to encourage him by reminding him of the honour and fame that would come if he would fast for the full twelve days. Seven mornings the boy made no reply to his father's words. He lay motionless, with no sign of discontent.

But on the morning of the ninth day of his fasting, he spoke in a weak voice, "My father, my dreams suggest that evil is to happen to me. May I break my fast now and make a new fast at some later time?"

"My son," his father answered, "you do not know what you are asking. If you get up now, all your glory will depart. Wait patiently a little longer. In only three days you will accomplish your desire. You know that it is for your own good to be patient. I urge you to persevere and to endure a little longer."

The son murmured a reply and covered himself a little closer. The tenth morning he did not stir when his father visited him, but on the eleventh day he repeated his request: "Let me break my fast now." His father replied in almost the same words as before, adding only this promise: "Tomorrow I myself will prepare a meal for you and will bring it to you."

The boy remained silent, lying as motionless as a dead person. No one would have known that he was living but for the gentle movement of his breast.

Next morning the father joyously prepared food for his son and hastened with it to the lodge. He felt sure that his son had been blessed by a vision and by a spirit that would guide him to greatness. As he approached, he was surprised to hear the boy talking. Stooping and looking through a small opening, he was astonished to see that his son was painting himself with red paint. He had already painted his breast and was now finishing his work by painting his shoulders as far back as he could reach.

"My father has destroyed my future as a man," the boy was saying to himself. "He would not listen to my requests. He will be the loser. I shall be happy as a bird, for I have obeyed him. My father only will be the sufferer, for my guardian spirit is just. He has not granted my wish, but he has shown me pity in another way. He has given me another form. Now I must go."

At this moment the father exclaimed in anguish, "My son! My son! Do not leave me, I pray you."

But with the quickness of a bird, the boy had flown to the top of the lodge and perched himself on the highest pole. He had been changed to a robin redbreast. With pity in his eyes, he looked down upon his father and spoke comforting words.

"Do not grieve, my father. Do not regret the change that you see in me. I shall be happier as a bird than I could have been as a man. I shall always be the friend of people, and shall live near their homes. I shall always be happy and contented. Although I shall not be the great warrior you wanted me to be, or be a wise counsellor, I shall be a daily messenger of peace and happiness. I will cheer you by my songs and shall try to inspire in others the light-heartedness and joy I myself feel. This will take the place of the glory you wanted for me, expected of me. I am now free from the cares and pains of human life. My food I shall find in the forests and fields, and my paths and trails will be in the air and the sunshine."

Then stretching himself as if delighted to have wings, the first robin sang one of his sweetest songs and flew away to a neighbouring grove.

A boy's vision and the first corn

Corn, or maize, was so important to the Indians of the eastern and middle sections of the North American continent that they honoured it with many stories, songs, and festivals. This legend and the next have been selected to represent what might be an entire book of tales about maize.

In times past, a poor Indian was living with his wife and children in a beautiful part of the country. He was not skilful in making a living for his family, and his children were too young to help him. But he was a man of kind and contented disposition, always thankful to the Master of Life for every good he received.

The same cheerful disposition was found in his oldest son, Wunzh. He had been obedient from earliest childhood. As he approached adolescence, he was thoughtful, mild, and kind, greatly beloved by his parents and by his younger brothers and sisters.

One day his father said to him, "You are old enough now to undertake the guardian spirit quest. You will try to find out what spirit will be your guide and protector through life."

As soon as the first signs of spring appeared, they built the customary little lodge for the boy, at a solitary spot some distance from their own. There he would not be disturbed during this important and solemn ceremony. There he began his fast, for he must be purified in body before a spirit would speak to him.

The first few days he lived in the lodge, he amused himself in the morning by walking in the woods and over the mountains, examining the early flowers and plants. In this way he prepared himself to enjoy his sleep and, at the same time, stored his mind with pleasant ideas for his dreams. While he rambled through the woods, he felt a strong desire to know how the plants, herbs, and berries grew, without any aid from man. He wondered why some plants were good to eat, others were poisonous, and still others would heal a sick person.

Later when he lay all day in the lodge, too weak from fasting to ramble through the woods, he recalled these questions about the plants. He wished that he would dream of something that would prove a benefit to his father and his family, and to all his people.

"The Great and Good Spirit made all things," the boy said to himself. "To him we owe our lives. But could he not make it easier for us to get our food than by hunting animals and taking fish? I must try to find out in my sleep and my vision."

By the third day he had become so faint and weak that he did not leave his lodge. While lying there, he saw a handsome young man coming down from the sky and advancing toward him. He was richly and gaily dressed. He wore many garments of green and yellow colours, some dark and some light in shade. On his head was a plume of waving feathers. Every movement of his body was graceful.

"I am sent to you, my friend," said the visitor, "by that great and good spirit, the Master of Life, who made all things in the sky and on the earth. He knows your motives in fasting. He sees that you have a kind and unselfish wish to do good to your people, to seek some benefit for them. He knows that you do not ask for strength in war or for the praise of warriors. I am sent to instruct you and to show you how you can do good for your people.

"Arise now, young man, and prepare to wrestle with me. Only in that way can you hope to accomplish what you want to accomplish."

Wunzh knew that he was weak from his fasting, but he felt courage rise in his heart. Immediately he got up, determined to die rather than fail. He began to wrestle and, after long effort, he was almost exhausted. He felt relieved when the beautiful stranger said, "This is enough for the first time, my friend. I will come again to try you."

And smiling on the boy, the visitor ascended in the air in the direction from which he had come.

Next day he returned at the same hour, and the two wrestled again. Wunzh felt that his strength was even less than the day before, but the courage of his mind and heart seemed to increase as his body became weaker. Noticing his faintness, the stranger soon spoke as before. "This is enough. I will come again to test you."

Then he added, "Tomorrow will be your last trial. Be strong, my friend. Only in this way can you overcome me and obtain the favour you wish and seek."

On the third day he again appeared at the same time and renewed the struggle. The poor youth was very faint in body, but he grew stronger in mind at every contest. He was determined to throw his opponent or to die from his effort. After they had wrestled for the same length of time as on the previous mornings, the heavenly stranger stopped.

"I am conquered," he declared. "Let us sit down, and I will instruct you."

So the two sat together in the lodge, and the visitor began to speak.

"You have won what you desire from the Master of Life, my friend. You have wrestled manfully. Tomorrow will be the seventh day of your fasting. Your father will offer you food to strengthen you, but as it is the last day of trial, you will prevail. I know this, and I will tell you what you must do to benefit your family and your tribe.

"Tomorrow I shall meet you and wrestle with you for the last time.

As soon as you have conquered me, you will strip off my garments and throw me down. You will clean the earth of weeds and roots, make it soft, and bury me in the spot. Leave my body in the earth. Do not disturb it, but come occasionally to visit the place, to see whether I have returned to life. Be careful never to let the grass or weeds grow on my grave. Once a month cover me with fresh earth.

"If you follow my directions, you will accomplish your object of doing good to your fellow creatures by teaching them what I have now taught you."

After a few other instructions, the heavenly visitor shook hands with the boy and disappeared.

In the morning the boy's father came to him with a little food.

"My son, you have fasted long enough. If the Good Spirit will favour you, he will do it now. It is seven days since you tasted food. You must not sacrifice your life. The Master of Life does not require that."

"My father," replied Wunzh, "wait till the sun goes down. I have a special reason for fasting until sunset."

"Very well, my son. I shall wait until that hour arrives, and you feel ready to eat."

At the usual hour, the sunset hour, the visitor from the sky returned, and the two wrestled for the last time. In spite of the fact that the boy had refused the food his father had brought, he felt that new strength had been given him and that his courage was greater than ever. He grasped his opponent with supernatural strength, threw him down, took from him his beautiful garments and plume. Finding him dead, the boy buried him on the spot, following all the directions that had been given the day before. He was confident that the stranger would come to life again, as he had promised.

Returning to the family lodge, Wunzh ate a little of the food that had been prepared for him. Life went on as before his vigil and dream, but he never forgot the grave of his friend. Throughout the spring he visited it, pulled out the grass and weeds, and kept the ground soft. Soon he saw the tops of the green plumes coming through the ground. The more carefully he followed the directions to keep the ground soft, the faster the green plumes grew. But he did not tell his father or anyone else about his vigil or about the grave.

Days and weeks passed. One day when the summer was drawing to a close, Wunzh invited his father to follow him. The man had just returned, weary, from a long hunting trip. Together they walked to the quiet, secluded place of the youth's vigil. He had removed the lodge and had kept the weeds from growing on the circle where it had stood. In the center of the spot the father saw, for the first time, a tall and graceful plant with bright-coloured silken hair. It had long green leaves and on every side were golden clusters. Nodding plumes seemed to grow from its top.

"It is my friend, the friend of all people," explained the boy excitedly. "It is the friend who came to me here—*Mondawmin*, the spirit of corn. We need no longer depend upon hunting and fishing only. As long as this gift of the Good Spirit is cherished, as long as it is taken care of, the earth itself will give us a living."

Wunzh then pulled an ear of corn from the stalk.

"See, my father," he said, "this is what I fasted for. The Good Spirit listened to my voice and has sent us something new. Henceforth our people will have maize, as well as fish and game. Life will be easier."

Then the boy repeated to his father the instructions given him by the visitor from the sky.

"These broad husks," he explained, "must be thrown away, just as I pulled off my friend's garments after we wrestled. The ear must be held before the fire till the outer skin becomes brown, not long enough to dry the milk that is within the grain. My friend said that it is good."

Father and son then returned to the family lodge, carrying with them some of the ears from the new plant. There the whole family joined in a feast and gave thanks to the Master of Life, who had sent them the beautiful gift.

Thus corn came into the world. Ever since it has blessed the Chippewas and all their neighbours and friends.

✳ CHIPPEWA

The spirit of the maize

Many years ago, a band of Chippewas had a wonderful yield of maize. So abundant was their crop that they became proud, arrogant, and wasteful. They ate more than they needed, they fed corn to their dogs, and they let corn lie in the fields and rot. Children used cornstalks in their play and then threw them in the mud.

When the people had eaten all they could eat, they buried the remainder of the corn and went off hunting. But though they saw deer and elk, in great herds, they could not catch or kill any. The hunters seemed to be shooting blindly. Every arrow went amiss, and the animals seemed to have twice their usual speed. Without fresh meat, the people soon exhausted the supplies they had brought with them. Hunger was upon them.

Remembering their corn hidden at home, they sent some of their men to get it. But alas! Mice had found it and had eaten the entire store of maize.

Sorrow filled the hearts of all the people when the men returned to the hunting camp, empty-handed. "Why are we being punished?" they asked themselves. They continued to ask the question as they beat their drums and sang their holy songs.

One man among them had taken no part in the waste of the corn. Instead, he had grieved over the way his people had treated the maize, the beautiful gift of the Master of Life. Brooding over the greed and selfishness and wastefulness of his people, he walked alone in the forest. In the distance he heard the sound of beating drums and of singing, as his people tried to appease the spirits they knew they must have angered. He walked on into a wild area of the forest where there were no signs of man.

Suddenly he came to a clearing. In the center of a small meadow was a mound, and on the mound stood a lodge made of birch-bark. As he approached, cries and groans coming from the lodge made him more and more curious. Walking inside, he saw a little man stretched out on dirty, much-worn hides. Pale, sick, miserable-looking, the little man began to speak.

"See what a wretched condition these men have placed me in!" he said to his visitor. "I am their best friend, and yet they have insulted me and dragged me through mud and dirt. They have let dogs tear my garments. In every way possible they have mistreated me. That is why they are now in want. Friends cannot quarrel without inflicting wounds."

The visitor felt troubled, for he knew now whom he was looking upon and listening to. The weak voice continued.

"I am glad that you have come and that you see how wretchedly I live. There is no water in my jug. I have no clothes, not even a leaf to protect me from the cold. Weeds grow in my garden. Beasts of the forest prowl around me. Soon they will devour me. Go back to your people and tell them what you have seen and heard. I am the Spirit of the Maize."

Moved with pity, the good Indian promised and then hurried back to camp. He described the lodge, the sickly appearance, and the wretched living conditions of the good Spirit of the Maize.

"He says that you have brought him to that condition," said the good Indian. "He says also that your wastefulness is the cause of your own misfortune."

Amazed, the people heard the man to the end of his story. Then suddenly they were aware of their wrong-doing. Quickly they broke camp and returned to their village, to their unplanted fields, in which only weeds were growing. There they sacrificed a dog to the Spirit of the Maize and made their fields ready for planting. The little corn that had not been eaten by the mice they carefully placed in the soil, singing the songs that should be sung at planting time.

Somehow they managed to live until harvest time. Then they had a good crop, which they used wisely and carefully Vhen they went hunting the next time, they had good luck, for they were still sorry for their greed and wastefulness.

 ✳ SENECA

The origin of Seneca medicine

> *Three good spirits in the mythology of the Iroquois tribes were the spirits of corn, beans, and squash. They were sisters, fond of each other, growing in the same soil, living together in peace and unity. On still, moonlight nights they could be seen flitting about the fields and be heard rustling among the tall corn.*
>
> *The spirit of corn was dressed in long green leaves and yellow tassels. The spirit of beans wore a wreath of velvety green pods. The spirit of the squashes was clothed in brilliant orange blossoms. The Indians held festivals in their honour and prayed to them as "our life, our supporters."*
>
> *Below is a legend that the Senecas used to relate about two of these favourite plants.*

Long ago, a man went into the woods alone, on a hunting expedition. One night, while camping in a field, he was awakened by the sound of singing and by a noise like the beating of a drum. Unable to sleep, he rose and went in the direction of the sound. To his surprise the place looked as if people lived there. On one side he saw a hill of corn; on the other, a large squash vine with three squashes on it. Apart from all the others three ears of corn were growing.

"There must be some meaning to these things," the man said in his heart.

But he could not think what the meaning was. Curious and uneasy he started off on his day's hunt, determined to come back some evening.

The very next night, as he was sleeping near by, he was again awakened by a noise. When he opened his eyes, he saw a man beside him, looking at him. Coming toward them were a number of people.

"Beware!" said the strange man. "What you saw last night is sacred. You deserve to die."

"No," said the people who had gathered round the hunter. "We will pardon him. Let us share with him our secret. You tell him what the corn and the squash are for."

"Corn and squash are a great medicine for wounds," said the man who had wakened the hunter. "Come with me and I will teach you how to prepare them and how to use them."

The man in the vision led the hunter to a place where he saw a fire and a laurel bush that looked like iron. Around it many people were dancing, singing, and rattling their gourd shells.

"What are your people dancing for?" asked the hunter.

In answer, one of them heated a stick, thrust it through the hunter's right cheek, and then applied some medicine. Quickly the wound healed. Another person heated a stick, thrust it through the hunter's right leg, and then applied some medicine. This wound also healed quickly.

All the time they were showing him the power of their medicine, they were singing a song. They called it the "medicine song," and they taught it to him. Then they showed him how to make the medicine.

When the hunter turned to go home, he saw that the dancers and the others were not human beings, as he had thought. Instead, they were animals—bears, beavers, foxes. As he looked, all of them vanished.

At home again, he followed the directions given him in the vision. He took an ear of corn, dried the cob, and pounded it fine. He took a squash, cut it up, and pounded it. He remembered how much of each he was to mix with water from a running spring. "Always from up the stream, never from down the stream," he remembered.

The medicine he made healed wounds quickly, just as he had been told it would. For many years the man made the medicine, and with it he healed many people. Before he died, he prepared enough to last for over a hundred years.

This was the origin of the great medicine of the Seneca Indians. Every time the deer changed his coat, they made the medicine, singing the song the hunter had heard in his dream vision. While the medicine was being applied to a patient, the people sang the song and rattled a gourd shell as accompaniment.

Also they burned tobacco, for burning tobacco is the same as praying.

The origin of Iroquois medicine

There once was a man who was a great hunter. His generosity was praised throughout the country, for he not only supplied his own family with food, but distributed game among his friends and neighbours. He even called the birds and animals of the forest to share his abundance. For this reason he was known among them as "Protector of Birds and Animals."

He lived the life of a hunter until war broke out between his tribe and a distant tribe. Then he lived the life of a warrior, and showed as much bravery in war as he had shown skill as a hunter. He slew so many of the enemy that all around him lay dead except one, a mighty man of valour. In an unguarded moment, the hunter received a blow on the head from the tomahawk of this enemy. He fell to the earth; the warrior scalped him and fled.

Some of his own party saw him lying there, and supposing him to be dead left him on the battlefield. But a fox who wandered that way recognized the Protector of Birds and Animals. Sad indeed was he to find his friend slain, and he began to consider means of restoring him to life.

"Perhaps some of my friends," said Fox to himself, "may know of a medicine which will heal his wounds."

So saying, Fox ran into the forest and sang a dirge, which was a signal for all the animals to gather. From far and near they came, till hundreds of every kind stood round the body of the dead hunter, asking what had happened.

"I accidentally came this way," replied Fox, "and found our friend stretched lifeless on the earth here."

The animals examined the body closely, to be sure that there was no life in it. Then they held a grand council, with Bear as the leader. When all were ready to listen, Bear asked, "Does anyone know a medicine that will bring the dead man to life?"

Eagerly each animal examined his medicine box, but he found nothing powerful enough to restore life. When they had gone round the circle, they were so sad that they joined in a mournful howl, a dirge for the dead. It was heard by a singing bird, an oriole, and he came quickly to learn its meaning and the meaning of the gathering of all the animals. Bear explained.

"The birds also will be grieved by the death of our friend," said Bear to Oriole. "Will you not invite all of them to come to the council here? Perhaps all of you and all of us together can find a remedy that will restore life."

Soon were gathered together all the birds of the air. Even the great eagle came, though she seldom appeared on the earth. When the birds had examined the body and decided that there was no life in it, the council began again. All decided that their friend's scalp must be obtained from the killer and that any bird or animal who wished to might go in quest of it.

Fox was the first to offer to go. He departed full of hope, but after many days he returned. "I found no trace of man's footsteps anywhere," he reported.

Several others of the creatures were prompted to go on the quest, because of their love for the great hunter. The animals tried first, but were not successful. Then Pigeon Hawk begged to be the first of the birds to search for the man's scalp. "I am swift of wing," he said, "and I can visit the whole world faster than any one else can."

So swiftly did he fly that he returned almost before he was missed by the others. "He went so fast that he could not see anything clearly," they decided.

White Heron was the next to volunteer to go. "I am so slow of wing," he said, "that I will see everything as I pass over the earth."

But on his journey he saw below him a plain filled with bean vines ready to eat. They looked so tempting that he flew down to enjoy a feast. So much did he eat that he could not rise again from the earth. After waiting many days, the council called for some other bird to make the search. This time Crow came forward. "I too am slow of wing, like White Heron," said Crow. "And I so frequently hover over settlements that no one will suspect me if I linger near the one where the scalp is."

When Crow, sailing lazily through the air, spied the smoke of a settlement, he dipped his wings for a closer look. There was the scalp, which he knew must be the one he sought, stretched out to dry. Now the warrior who had taken it had learned that the animals and birds were holding council to plan how to recover it, but when he saw Crow, he was not alarmed. "Crow often hovers near us," he said.

He was not watchful, and so after a few attempts, Crow seized the scalp and flew with it to the council.

But when they tried to fit it to the head of their friend, they found that it was too dry. In vain they searched for something with which to moisten it, until Great Eagle offered her help.

"Listen to my words," she said. "My wings are never furled. Night and day, for many years, the dews of heaven have been collecting on my back, as I sat in my nest above the clouds. Perhaps these waters may have a power no earthly waters can have. We shall see."

Then she plucked a feather from her wing, and it was dipped in the moisture on her back. When the moisture was applied to the shrivelled scalp, it became as fresh and pliable as if just removed. Now it would fit the head, but there must be a healing power to cause the two to unite, some power to awaken life again.

Eager to help, all went forth and brought back rare leaves, flowers, the bark of trees, the flesh of animals and the brains of birds, to make a healing mixture. When it was moistened with dew, the mixture was applied to the scalp. Instantly the scalp became firm, and the hunter sat up. Amazed, he looked around upon his many friends, wondering why they were assembled in such a great number.

"Stand up on your feet," they said to him.

When they found that he could stand and move, they told him the whole story, beginning with Fox's discovery of him on the field of battle. Then they gave him the rest of the medicine that had restored him to life.

"It is the gift of the Good Spirit to man," they explained. "He directed us in the council. He brought Eagle to furnish the heavenly moisture. He gave us wisdom in making the preparation, so that we might give to man a medicine that will heal every wound."

Then the animals left for their homes in the forest, the eagle soared away to the high rocks, the birds of the air flew away to their nests in the tall trees. All were happy because they had given the powerful medicine that had restored to life the Protector of Birds and Animals.

The hunter returned to his home, carrying with him the wonderful medicine. He told all his people about it and about the miracle it had worked. To this day that medicine is used among the Iroquois, by the men and women who are the favourites of the Good Spirit, the Master of Life.

✳   IROQUOIS AND HURON-WYANDOT

The first wampum

Wampum beads, made of certain kinds of shells in some unknown way, were used as money, necklaces, bracelets, ornaments on clothing and on weapons. Strings of wampum and belts of wampum were important in ceremonies, in councils, and as public records. The making of treaties and of alliances was concluded by the presentation of one or more wampum belts, and these were carefully preserved.

By means of designs and colour symbolism, the beads could be

arranged to communicate ideas. White wampum, when used cere-
monially, expressed peace, health, prosperity; purple indicated
hostility, death, sorrow. Wampum belts and wampum strings were
an approach to writing; they preserved the history, the laws, and
the rituals of several tribes.

The Iroquois and the Huron-Wyandots related almost identical
myths about the origin of wampum. The Iroquois said also that
Hiawatha made the first wampum from the plumage of a flock of
ducks that drained a lake he needed to cross.

Long ago, in the days of our first grandfathers, the villages of the
Wyandots stood beside a beautiful lake in the north country. Near
one of the villages was a marsh where cranberries grew.

One day when a girl went out to the marsh to gather cranberries,
she was surprised by a giant bird. It was half a tree tall, and was
frighteningly fierce in appearance. When the girl saw the bird, it was
eating cranberries, and it seemed unable to rise and fly away.

The girl was alarmed. "It is a hook-keh bird!" she said to herself.
Then she ran back to the village and told the chief what she had
seen. Sounding the great shell, he called the council and reported to
them what the girl had seen. All the people were frightened.

The council asked the medicine men to make their medicine and to
find out what the bird was and what it meant. Through their medicine their wise men learned that the bird in the marsh was the
wampum bird, the first wampum bird ever seen in this lower world.

"We must kill the bird and obtain the wampum," the council
decided.

So the chief and all his warriors went to the marsh to slay the
wampum bird. There it was, still eating cranberries. So fierce and
desperate was the bird that the warriors could not get near it with
their clubs.

"We shall have to use our arrows," the chief decided. "The one who
kills the wampum bird with an arrow shall have my daughter for his
wife."

The chief's daughter was a beautiful girl, much desired by the
warriors of the tribe. They shot their arrows at the bird. When the
first arrow struck it, the bird stood up to its full height, half the
height of a tree, and shook off all the wampum with which it was
covered. The precious stuff fell in showers, like rain, all around the
warriors. In an instant the bird was again covered with wampum,
its only plumage. Purple wampum covered its wings; white wampum
covered its body.

Again and again the warriors shot the bird. Each time an arrow
struck it, it stood up to its full height and shook off all the purple
wampum and all the white wampum. While the warriors gathered

the precious stuff, the bird was again covered.

Not a bow-shot could kill it. And still they could not get near enough to strike it with their clubs.

While they were wondering what to do next, a young man came through the woods to the place where they were standing. He was a stranger to them, from another tribe. The warriors wanted to kill him and scalp him, because he was a stranger, but the chief said, "Let him first shoot at the wampum bird."

The youth cut a slender willow from the marsh and with it fashioned a bow. No one saw the arrow leave his bow; no one saw it strike. But all saw the wampum bird drop, and they found an arrow piercing its head. Gathering the wampum that had dropped, the people returned to the village. Not even their largest lodge would hold all the wampum they had found.

The warriors carried with them the youth who had killed the bird. They still wanted to kill him and scalp him, for he had done what they had not been able to do. But again the chief interfered for him.

"My son, tell me where you come from."

"I am a Delaware," the youth replied. "My people live in a village not far away from your village."

The chief and his council sent the young man to bring his people to a great council. At the great council the Wyandots recognized the Delawares as their nephews, and the two peoples made a treaty that has never been broken even unto this day.

The young man was adopted by the Wyandots, and he was given the chief's daughter as a reward for killing the wampum bird.

To confirm the treaty between the two tribes and make it binding, they passed back and forth strings of wampum secured from the bird that the young Delaware had slain. Since that day, the Wyandots have never concluded a treaty without passing the wampum belt.

The Wyandots and their nephews the Delawares lived side by side for a long time. Then the Wyandots came from the north country to live on the banks of the St. Lawrence River.

The first tobacco

Tobacco was regarded as a means of communicating with the spirits. It was offered to appease angry waters, to still tempests, to protect the traveller, to show gratitude to a departed hero or a benevolent spirit. By burning tobacco, a person or a tribe sent a prayer to the spirits. Smoking the ceremonial pipe was the last act of making an agreement or a treaty. Tobacco seeds were planted with ceremony and singing.

The mythical origin of tobacco is given in this Huron-Wyandot story.

Long ago, the Hawk Clan of the Wyandot people lived in a village beside a lake. Clear streams flowed into the lake, coming down from the surrounding hills, where grew tall and beautiful trees. From the village, the hills looked blue.

In the village lived an old man of the Bear Clan and his young wife from the Hawk Clan. Two daughters were born to them, and they were very happy. But when the first daughter was twelve years of age, she died, and her parents suffered much grief. When the second daughter was twelve years of age, she too died. The mother soon died of grief, and the old man was left alone in his lodge. Sad and heavy was his heart, but he went about the village doing good. All the people of the Hawk Clan held him in high esteem.

One day when the old man and some of his neighbours were standing beside the lake, they saw a flock of very large birds come flying over the blue hills. They were giant hawks—half a tree tall they seemed to be.

Astonished, the people watched them circle over the lake and over its shores. Suddenly one of the birds fell to the ground and lay on the shore, its wings thrown above its back like a dove shot with an arrow. For a short time the other hawks soared overhead, dipped and soared again, calling and screaming to each other. Then they flew back over the blue hills from where they had come.

In terror, the people of the village had watched the scene. Up and down the shore of the lake they ran wildly, calling and shouting to each other in their fright. "The great bird is an omen of evil," they said. "What disaster is coming to us?"

Only the old man was not afraid. He tried to quiet the others. "I will go to the bird that fell down," he said.

"Oh, no," said his friends. "Do not go to the hawk."

"I am not afraid," he replied. "I am old, and I am full of sorrow. My life is almost done. The heavens are black, and I am alone. It can matter little if I die, and I am not afraid of death. I will see the stricken hawk."

So the old man started alone toward the fallen bird. The way was longer than he thought, and darkness overtook him. But the hawk remained where it had fallen. As he came toward it, a great flame swept down from the sky and burned the bird to ashes. When the old man came to the spot, ashes lay all about. Within them was a living coal. When he stooped to look at it closely, he saw within the coal of fire the face of his first-born daughter. He picked her up, and she spoke to him.

By this time, people of the village, afraid of what might happen to the old man, had reached the place also. They too heard the voice of the old man's first-born daughter.

"I have returned with a precious gift for my people, the Wyandots. I was sent with it to my own clan, the Hawk people. Here it is."

Then she opened her hands, and the people saw that they were full of very small seeds. These the girl planted in the ashes of the fire from which she had risen. Soon a large field of tobacco grew around the place where the great hawk had lain.

For a time the girl lived with her people. She taught them how to cultivate and cure the tobacco. She taught them to make offerings of it and to smoke it in their pipes.

Thus the Wyandots were more fortunate than any other people They alone had tobacco.

 ✱ HAIDA

The origin of cedar trees

The importance of the cedar tree in the life of the West Coast Indians is suggested in this little story.

After he had made the world, the Great Creator placed the Haida Indians on the Queen Charlotte Islands, these beautiful islands of peace and plenty.

But alas! As soon as the people were settled there, they began to quarrel. And they continued to quarrel. At last the Creator came down from the sky and warned them.

"If you cannot learn to live at peace with each other, you will be destroyed."

Full of shame and grief, they begged him to let them try again, and he granted their request. For a while all were kindly and good and peaceful. But in time, greed and jealousy and other evil traits showed themselves again, and again the people quarrelled.

When the Great Creator came a second time, he said to them, "Now you will receive the punishment you have long deserved."

As soon as he had finished speaking, thick darkness covered the land, and it stayed for many days. When it vanished, all the bad people had been changed into cedar trees.

From the sky came these words from the Creator, the Great Benefactor of Mankind: "When people who can live in peace with each other come to these beautiful islands, they will use the red cedars for many things. With planks of cedar the men will build their lodges. With the trunks of cedar they will make their canoes. From the roots, the women will make their baskets and mats. From the bark, they will take the fibres and weave them into clothing. From the inner bark, they will get food in springtime."

Thus from greed and evil deeds came good. For the cedar trees gave the Haida people most of the things they needed in life.

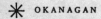 OKANAGAN

The origin of Sweat House

The custom of taking a steam bath in a sweat house or sweat lodge was important in probably every tribe north of Mexico. It was more than a means of cleansing the body; it was also important in medical practice for the cure of diseases, and it was a religious ceremony to insure success in some undertaking of the individual or of the tribe.

The sweat house was built according to tribal traditions, usually facing a lake or stream. After a person had taken a steam bath, he plunged into the water for a swim. This ritual was followed both summer and winter.

Details of the ritual varied somewhat, of course, in different parts of the country. The following story is from the Okanagan of the Western Plateau.

When the world was very young, the Creator, the Great Chief Above, gave names to all the animals. He gave names to Grizzly Bear and Fox, to Eagle and Magpie and Woodpecker, and to all the other creatures. When he named Coyote, the Great Chief Above gave Coyote the power to be chief of all the animal tribes.

When the Creator had named all the animal people, he had one name left. That was Sweat House. He wanted the animal people, and the human beings who would come after them, to know Sweat House. There they could cleanse themselves, both their bodies and their souls. But no animal person was left to take the name. So the Great Chief Above gave the name to his wife. She was glad, for she wanted the people to have a place where they could cleanse themselves and where they would pray for strength, health, and good luck.

Coyote gave the people strict rules about building Sweat House and about using it properly.

"For the framework of the lodge," he said, "use eight or twelve branches of a tree. Use young willow or birch or fir, because those young branches bend easily. Make the frame so low that people will have to stoop when they bathe; then the steam will stay close to their bodies. Cover the frame with bark and grass and earth.

"Heat the stones in a hole beside the entrance to the sweat lodge. Use small, dry-land stones. Do not use river-bed stones, for they will crack. With sticks, roll the hot stones into Sweat House. Close the entrance with a mat or with a branch of fir. Then sprinkle cold water on the stones.

"Remain in the steam as long as you can. Always sing the Sweat-House song, and pray your prayer to the spirit of the Sweat House. Always take a swim after sweating. If you wish very good luck, or if you are preparing for a difficult undertaking, go into the Sweat House several times. Sing the sweat song and the prayer each time.

"When you have finished, pile the stones outside Sweat House. Do not throw them away, and do not step on them. If you do, you will have bad luck. Do not anger the Sweat House. Always treat it well. Treat it as a spirit should be treated."

The frame-poles are the ribs of Sweat House. They represent the wife of the Great Chief Above. She can never be seen, for she is a spirit. But she hears the songs of her people when they are bathing, and she grants their requests. She loves her people, and she has pity for their troubles.

Before a man goes hunting, he dashes water on the hot rocks inside the sweat lodge, and he chants this prayer:

> O! O! Sweat House,
> Take pity on me.
> Let me live to be old.
> Help me.
> Give me power
> So I can kill deer,
> Deer.

If anyone is sick, he asks the spirit of the Sweat House to cure him. And he ends the sweat song with a prayer for health.

A boy once offended Sweat House. When he was about fifteen years old, he became angry because he could not light the sweat-house fire. He kicked the stones out of the fire-pit and scattered them. Almost at once he suffered severe pains, and he was ill for a long time. When his mother learned what he had done, she told the medicine man. The medicine man cured him and warned the boy never to anger Sweat House again. Ever since then, he has remembered that the sweat lodge is a sacred place. Before every sweat, he chants the song as a prayer. When he has finished, he piles the stones outside the Sweat House, and he never touches them with his feet.

 SARCEE

The origin of the beaver bundle

> Medicine bundles were among the most valued possessions of a tribe. A bundle "might be anything from a few feathers wrapped in skin or cloth to a multitude of miscellaneous objects—skins of animals and birds, roots, rocks, stone pipes, etc.—kept inside a large rawhide bag, in which everything had a definite significance and called for a special song whenever its owner exposed it to the light." Possession of a sacred bundle brought the owner good luck and wealth.
>
> Among the Sarcees, one of the two most treasured medicine bundles was the beaver bundle, which was associated with both the Sun Dance and the cultivation of tobacco. The following explanation of its origin was made by a former owner of the beaver bundle.

One time a hunter sighted a buffalo herd not far from a lake. Leaving his horse, he hid himself in a hollow. When the buffaloes drew near, he shot one that was very fat. After rolling the body over on its back, the hunter removed the insides and piled up part of the meat. Then he rolled the body over again, made another pile of the meat, cut off the legs, and knocked off the ribs.

While he was busy cutting up the buffalo, there on the lake shore, a fish came out of the water and circled round him. It was a big fish with a horn on its head.

"Do not be afraid of me, my son," said the fish. "You see that little cloud over there in the sky? Those are the thunderbirds. They are trying to seize me, but as they are afraid of human beings, you will protect me from them."

Then the thunders came down from the sky and said to the hunter, "My son, stand aside. We want to eat that whale. Why did he go to you for protection?"

The hunter answered, "Do not kill him. He came to me for protection."

The thunders spoke again. "My son, he has not as much power as we have."

"That is not true, my son," interrupted the whale. "We who live on the earth have more power than those who live in the sky. The thunders come only once a year. They do not have the power to stay with you. If you give me up to them, you will step over a little water some day. But if you save me, I will give you this bundle."

"My son," said the thunders, "if you give us this big fish, you shall always have whatever you wish for."

The hunter listened to both and pondered upon what both had said. Then he replied, "I pity this whale, but I will also show mercy to you. Spare the whale and take instead this fat buffalo."

The thunders answered, "We are sorry to take your meat, my son, but we will spare the whale."

They moved away a little, then suddenly crashed down and took all the buffalo meat.

After they had gone back to the sky, the whale spoke again to the hunter. "Make a pouch like this one," and he showed the hunter the stomach of a young buffalo. "Fill it as I tell you. I shall help you throughout your life, in gratitude for your saving my life."

Then the hunter led the whale back to the lake. Before it plunged in, the whale said, "Hereafter, always throw something into the lake as an offering to me. Now return home and make the bundle. Place inside the pouch a skin of every living creature. Put some tobacco also in the bundle, and keep some berries in it as food for me. On the inside of the pouch draw my picture; on the outside, draw a picture of the thunders. Do not forget my instructions, and never give your bundle away to any other tribe."

Then before the whale dived into the water, he sang the beaver songs for the hunter.

The man made the beaver bundle according to the instructions of the big fish, and at his death he bequeathed it to another man. So it has been handed down among the Sarcees through all the generations since the time of the hunter.

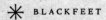 ✳   BLACKFEET

The origin of the Sun Dance

The Sun Dance was the great religious festival of the Plains Indians. The ceremonies of the preparation and of the dance lasted three to ten days, every feature of it being carried out according to ritual.

Among the Blackfeet and Sarcees, it was held only in fulfilment of the vow of a woman whose industriousness and faithfulness to her husband permitted its celebration. In other tribes, a man might make the vow, in gratitude for some favour from the Master of Life.

After being prohibited by both the Canadian and United States governments for a number of years, the Sun Dance was later revived without the feature of self-torture. To the old Indians, the ceremony is filled with symbolism. Each post in the Sun Lodge, all the sacred articles (presented in ceremony to the medicine woman and preserved by her until the next Sun Dance), the whistling, the painted designs on the bodies of the dancers—all these and other details have symbolic meanings.

Some of the symbolism is indicated in "The Vision of Chief Walking Buffalo," p. 132. Other symbolism is suggested in this origin myth from the Blackfeet.

The theme of Star Husband and Star Boy is found in the mythology of many North American tribes, across the continent. Morning Star is said to be Venus; Mistake Morning Star, Jupiter.

The Sun Dance had its origin long ago, when the Blackfeet used dogs instead of horses as beasts of burden and when they used stones instead of wooden pegs to hold down their tepees.

One time, in early summer, our people were camped near the mountains. On a cloudless night, two young girls were sleeping in the long grass outside the family lodge. The older sister, whose name means Feather Woman, awoke before daybreak, just as the Morning Star was rising from the prairie. He was very beautiful, as he shone through the clear air of early morning. The girl lay gazing at the star until he seemed very close to her and she imagined that he was her lover.

At last she awoke her sister, exclaiming, "Look at the Morning Star! He is beautiful, and he must be wise. Many young men have wanted to marry me, but I love only the Morning Star."

A few moons later, when the leaves were turning yellow and the geese were flying southward, Feather Woman went alone to the river for water. As she was returning home, she saw a young man standing before her in the trail. Modestly she turned aside to pass him, but he put out his hand as if to detain her.

Annoyed by his boldness, she exclaimed, "Stand aside! No young man has ever before dared to stop me."

"I am the Morning Star," he replied gently. "One early morning, during the moon of flowers, I saw you sleeping in the grass beside the lodge, and I fell in love with you. Now I come to ask you to return with me to the sky, to the lodge of my father, the Sun. There we will live together in peace and harmony."

Morning Star was tall and straight, and his hair was long and shining. In his hair he wore a yellow plume, and in his hand he carried a juniper branch with a spider web hanging from one end. His beautiful clothes were of soft-tanned skins, and from them came a fragrance of pine and sweet grass.

Feather Woman remembered his beauty in the sky that morning in early summer, and she felt love rise in her heart again. She wanted to go with him, but she said with hesitation, "I must first say farewell to my father and mother."

"No," replied Morning Star. "You must speak to no one. You must tell no one where you are going."

Then he handed her the juniper branch with the spider web, placed the yellow plume in her hair, and gave her directions. "Hold the upper strand of the spider web in your hand, and place your feet on the lower strand. Now close your eyes."

When he told her to open her eyes again, they were in the sky world, standing together before a large lodge.

"This is the home of my parents, the Sun and the Moon," said Morning Star. "Enter and be welcomed by my mother."

It was daytime, and the Sun was away on his long journey. But the Moon was at home. Morning Star addressed his mother. "One night, in the moon of flowers, I saw this girl sleeping on the prairie. I love her and have brought her home as my wife."

The Moon welcomed Feather Woman as her daughter, and when the Sun Chief came home in the evening, he also gladly received her. The Moon dressed her in a soft buckskin dress trimmed with elks' teeth and gave her gifts—wristlets of elks' teeth and an elk-skin robe decorated with sacred paint.

"I give you these gifts," said the Moon, "because you have married our son."

Feather Woman lived happily in the sky with Morning Star, and learned many things. When their child was born, they called him Star Boy.

The Moon then gave Feather Woman a root digger, saying, "This should be used only by pure women. You can dig all kinds of roots with it, but I warn you not to dig up the large turnip growing near the home of Spider Man. You have now a child. To dig up that root would bring unhappiness to all of us."

Everywhere Feather Woman went, she carried the baby and the root digger. She often saw the large turnip but was afraid to touch it. One day, while passing it, she thought of the mysterious warning of the Moon and became curious to see what might be underneath. Laying her baby on the ground, she dug until her root digger stuck fast. She could not move it.

Seeing two large cranes overhead, she called to them to help her. Three times she begged in vain, but on her fourth call they circled and lighted beside her. The chief crane sat on one side of the turnip and his wife on the other. Taking hold of the turnip with his long, sharp bill, he moved it backward and forward, singing the medicine song :

> This root is sacred.
> Wherever I dig,
> My roots are sacred.

Four times he repeated this song—to the north, the south, the east, and the west. After the fourth time, he pulled up the turnip.

Feather Woman, looking down through the hole, saw the earth spread out below. Unknown to her, the turnip had filled the hole through which Morning Star had brought her into the sky. Far below her was the camp of the Blackfeet where she had lived. She could see the young men playing games. She could see the women tanning hides, making lodges, gathering berries on the hills, crossing the meadows to the river for water. For a long while she sat gazing at the familiar scenes. When she turned to go home, she was crying. She felt lonely, and she longed to be back on the green prairies with her own people.

When Feather Woman arrived at the lodge, Morning Star and his mother were waiting.

"You have dug up the sacred root!" said Morning Star, as soon as he saw his wife.

When she did not reply, the Moon said, "I warned you not to dig up the turnip, because I love Star Boy and do not wish to part with him."

Nothing more was said, for it was daytime and the Sun Chief was still away on his long journey. In the evening, almost as soon as he entered the lodge, he asked, "What is the matter, my daughter? You look sad, as if you were in trouble."

"Yes, I am homesick. Today I looked down upon my people."

Then the Sun Chief was angry and said to Morning Star, "If she has disobeyed, you must send her home."

The Moon tried to soften the anger of the Sun, but the chief said again, "She must return to her people. She will no longer be happy with us."

So Morning Star led Feather Woman to the home of the Spider Man, whose web had drawn her up to the sky. He placed on her head the sacred medicine bonnet, which is worn only by pure women. He laid Star Boy on her breast, wrapped them both in the elk-skin robe, and bade her farewell.

Then the Spider Man carefully let them down to the earth, through the hole. It was an evening in midsummer, during the moon when the berries are ripe, that Feather Woman returned to her people. She lived with her parents in their lodge, but she was never happy. Often with Star Boy she went to the summit of a high ridge, and there mourned for her husband. One night she remained alone on the ridge. Before daybreak, when Morning Star rose from the plains, she begged him to take her back. But he refused.

"You disobeyed and therefore cannot return to the sky. Your sin is the cause of your sorrow, and it has brought trouble to you and your people."

Not many moons later, Feather Woman died. Then her father and mother died, and Star Boy was left alone. He was so poor that he had no clothes, not even moccasins. He was so shy that he never played with other children. When the Blackfeet moved camp, he feared to travel with them because the other boys stoned him and abused him. He was sensitive about a mysterious scar on his face, which became more noticeable as he grew older. Ridiculed by everyone, he was often tauntingly called Scarface.

When Star Boy became a young man, he loved a girl of the Blackfeet, the beautiful daughter of an important chief. Scarface, as she called him, sent her a gift, with the message that he wished to marry her. She scornfully told him that she would not accept him until he had removed that scar from his face.

Deeply grieved, the young man consulted with an old medicine woman, his only friend. "The scar was placed on your face by your grandfather, the Sun Chief," the old woman told him. "Only the Sun himself can remove it."

Then Star Boy resolved to go to the sky, to the home of the Sun. The old medicine woman made moccasins for him and gave him a supply of pemmican.

Alone, Star Boy journeyed across the plains and through the mountains, until at last he came to the Big Water toward the setting sun.

For three days and three nights he lay upon the shore, fasting and praying to the Sun Chief. On the evening of the fourth day, he saw a bright trail leading across the water. He travelled along this path until he drew near the home of the Sun. Then he hid and waited. Next morning, the great Sun Chief came from his lodge, ready for his daily journey.

When Star Boy appeared, his grandfather did not recognize him, and was really very angry at the sight of someone from the earth. But the Moon interceded. Morning Star, still young and beautiful, brought dried sweet grass, burned it as incense, and placed the boy in the sacred smoke. When Star Boy had related the story of his long journey because of the rejection of the girl he loved, his father felt sorry for him and understood why his face was sad and worn. "I will help you," promised Morning Star.

Star Boy lived in the lodge of the Sun and Moon with Morning Star. Once when they were hunting together, he saved the life of his father. He killed seven huge and dangerous birds that had threatened the life of Morning Star. All three felt so grateful that the Sun was persuaded to grant the young man's one request: the removal of the scar from his face.

"I will make you my messenger to the Blackfeet," the Sun Chief told Star Boy after he had removed the scar. "Tell them that I will restore their sick people to health if they will give a festival in my honour, once every year."

Then he taught Star Boy all the secrets of the Sun Dance and instructed him in the prayers and the songs to be used. He gave Star Boy two raven feathers to wear as a sign that he came from the Sun, and also a robe of soft-tanned elk-skin.

"This robe must be worn only by a good and virtuous woman," said the Sun. "She can then give the Sun Dance, and the sick will recover."

Morning Star gave his son a magic flute and a wonderful song. "With these," he said, "you will be able to charm the heart of the girl you love."

Star Boy returned to the earth and the Blackfeet camp by the Milky Way, the short path to the earth. He instructed his people concerning the Sun Dance, just as his grandfather had directed. He won the heart of the girl he loved, just as his father, Morning Star, had predicted. Then the Sun Chief took the young couple to the sky, and there he made Star Boy bright and beautiful, just like his father. When both Morning Star and his son appear in the east in the early morning, the Blackfeet often confuse them. So they sometimes call the younger one by a name that means "Mistake Morning Star."

The star that stands still, the north star, is a hole in the sky, the hole through which Feather Woman was drawn up to the Sun lodge and let down again to the earth. Its light is the radiance from the home of the Sun Chief shining through. The half-circle of stars to the east is the Lodge of the Spider Man. Whenever you see the circles of half-buried stones on the plains, stones that were used to hold down the sides of the Blackfeet tepees in the old days, you will know why our fathers called the half-circle of stars the Lodge of the Spider Man.

The gifts that Feather Woman brought from the sky were used in the first Sun Dance and have been used ever since. The sacred medicine bonnet, the dress trimmed with elks' teeth, the turnip digger, the sweet grass for incense, the prongs for lifting hot coals from the fire —these are always used by the woman who makes the vow, and she takes care of them until the next festival. They are the sacred articles of the Sun Dance. They came from the lodge of the Sun, who is honoured by our ceremony.

✳ BLACKFEET

The origin of the Sun Dance songs

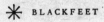

This myth, related in 1954 by a very old Blackfoot called One Gun, has probably been influenced by Christian teachings.

One time, long ago, the Blackfeet were dancing the Sun Dance in full regalia. Dancing with them was the man who had given them the songs they used in the ceremony.

After they had danced a while and had sung all the Sun Dance songs they knew, the man said to them, "Now I will sing a special song. First, I will teach it to the drummers, and then I will dance it. While I am dancing this song, I will not touch the ground. You will see that my feet will stay a short distance above the ground."

When he had taught the drummers his new song, he went to the center of the Sun Dance lodge, almost to the center pole. There he started dancing. Soon he rose above the ground to about the height of a dog. The drummers stopped singing and watched him rise higher than their heads, higher than the Sun Dance lodge, higher than the center pole.

He went higher and higher, higher and higher, until at last he reached the sky. When he was out of sight, his clothes came down. He had disappeared into the sky in human flesh. "Only a good person can go to the sky world," he had told us.

A year after the man disappeared into the sky, we had a Sun Dance down at Medicine Hat. The man, the Great Almighty, came back to us from the sky world and spoke to us.

"My people, I come back to give you good advice. As the sun rises, and as the sun sets, you must say your prayers. The Great Almighty hears well early in the morning and at sunset."

After he had given this advice, he disappeared—just like smoke.

Since that time, we have followed his teaching, for he was a good man. We pass on to every generation his message to pray as the sun rises and as the sun sets. And we still use in the Sun Dance the songs the Great Almighty taught us when he was on the earth.

✳ CHIPPEWA

The spirit of the dead chief

Burial customs of the Indians varied from tribe to tribe. This story reveals some of the customs of the Chippewas of the Great Lakes region.

A Chippewa chief, heading his war party against the Sioux, received an arrow in his breast and fell. No warrior thus slain is ever buried. According to the old custom, he was placed in a sitting posture, his back against a tree, his face toward his fleeing enemies. His head-dress, his ornaments, and all his war-equipment were arranged with care, and thus he was left.

But the chief was not dead. Though he could not move or speak, he saw and heard all that took place near him. When he found that he was left by his friends as if dead, he was seized by rage and anguish. When, lamenting, they took leave of him, he rose up and followed them, but they did not see him. He followed their foot-prints, and wherever they went, he went. When they ran, he ran. When they camped, he slept. But he could not eat with them, and when he spoke, they did not hear him.

"Is it possible, my brothers," he shouted, "that you do not see me, that you do not hear me? Will you let me bleed to death? Will you let me starve in the midst of food? Is there no one will recognize my face or offer me a morsel to eat?"

Thus he lamented and upbraided, but his words did not reach his tribesmen. If they heard his voice at all, they thought it the summer wind rustling through the leaves.

When the war party returned to their village, the women and children came out to welcome them. The chief heard questions about himself; he heard the warriors' answers and the lamentations of his relatives and friends over his death. He tried to make himself heard.

"It is not true!" he shrieked. "I am not dead! I was not left on the battlefield. I am here! I live. I move. See me! Touch me! I shall again raise my spear in battle and sound my drum at the feasts."

But again his people heard no words. They mistook his voice for the wind rustling and whistling among the trees. When he walked to his wigwam, he found his wife tearing her hair and weeping over his death. He tried to comfort her, but she seemed unaware of his presence. He begged her to bind his wounds, but she did not move. He put his mouth close to her ear and shouted, "I am hungry. Give me food!" But his wife thought she heard a mosquito buzzing in her ear.

Angered beyond endurance, and suffering pain, the chief summoned all his strength and struck her on her temple. But she merely raised her hand to her head and said, "I feel a little ache here."

Then the chief began to wonder. Could his body have remained on the field of battle and only his spirit be here among his relatives and friends? He decided to go back and seek his body, a four days' journey from his village. On the fourth day, just as he was approaching the spot where he had been wounded, he saw a flame in the path before him. He tried to step aside and pass it, but he could not. Whichever way he turned, still it was before him.

"Spirit," he exclaimed in anger, "why do you oppose me? Don't you know that I too am a spirit and that I am trying to re-enter my body? Do you think you will make me turn back? Just as I have never been conquered by the enemies of my people, so will I not be conquered by you."

As he finished speaking, he leaped through the flame and found himself seated under a tree on the battlefield. He was dressed in his war array, and his bow and arrows lay beside him.

Looking up, he saw a great war-eagle seated on a bough. In his youth he had dreamed of the war-eagle, and its spirit had become his protecting spirit. For eight days the bird had watched over his body and had prevented the buzzard and the crow from devouring it.

Now the chief was able to bind up his wounds and to return to his people, getting food on the way by using his bow and arrows. When he reached his village, his wife and friends received him with great joy. They listened to his adventures until he had ended.

"It is four days' journey to the land of the spirits," he said as he finished his story. "The spirits need fire every night. So friends and relatives should build the funeral fire on a grave for four nights. If they do not, a man's spirit will have to build and tend the fire for itself. And that task is slavish and irksome."

Ever since then, the Chippewas have lighted the funeral fire on a grave, to light the departed spirit to the land of the dead.

NATURE MYTHS AND BEAST FABLES

 IROQUOIS

"There they dwell in peace"—the Pleiades

"There they dwell in peace" is the meaning of the Iroquois word for the constellation we call the Pleiades. In other Indian traditions they are known as "the Seven Dancers," as "the Seven Perfect Ones," as "They Sit Apart from Others," and as a herd of caribou being chased by three hunters transformed into stars.

There are many Indian myths about the Pleiades—usually thought of as seven stars, occasionally six, occasionally twelve.

The Iroquois explain the origin of the Pleiades in the following myth. The Haidas tell of seven brothers, fishermen, who sailed up to the sky and became the Pleiades. The Blackfeet of the Western Plains tell about a number of little boys who were disappointed because they were not given yellow robes from the skins of buffalo calves; in revenge, they went to the sky and became stars, and every year they stay out of sight during the season when the buffalo calves are yellow.

A long time ago, a party of Indians went through the woods toward a good hunting ground that they knew very well. For several days they were in wild country, travelling leisurely and camping at night. At last they reached a beautiful lake, where grey rocks were crowned with great forest trees. Fish were plentiful in the lake and in the streams that flowed into it. At every jutting point, deer came down the surrounding hills to bathe and to drink in the lake. On the hills and in the valleys grew huge chestnut and beech trees, where squirrels chattered and bears came to take their morning and afternoon meals.

On the shore of the lake the chief halted his party, so that he might give thanks to the Master of Life for their safe arrival at this good hunting ground. The Indian is always thankful.

"Here we will build our lodges for the winter," said the chief. "And may the Great and Good Spirit, who has prospered us on our way, send us plenty of game, good health, and sweet peace."

The pleasant autumn days passed by quickly. Hunting prospered, and all were happy. The children, amusing themselves, decided to dance to their own singing. Every day they met in a quiet spot by the lake to have what they called "a jolly dance." They had danced for some time when, one day, a very old man came to them. He was dressed in white feathers, and his white hair shone like silver. They had seen no one like him before. But stranger than his appearance were his words. In unpleasant voice and with unpleasant words, he warned the children to stop their dancing, but they were so intent on their play that they paid little heed. Again and again the old man came to them and repeated his warning.

But the children continued to hold their jolly dance in a secluded spot beside the lake. One day a little boy who was fond of food suggested, "Let's have a feast tomorrow. If each of us will bring food from home, we can have a big feast here after we have danced."

So when they returned to their lodges, each child asked his parents for food for the feast. All refused them.

"You will waste and spoil it," some said.

"You can eat at home as you should," said others.

So next day they were unable to have the feast they had planned. Their empty stomachs caused them no joy, but they danced as usual. Not long after, as they danced, they found themselves leaving the earth. Their heads felt light with hunger, and they found themselves rising, little by little, into the air. How this happened, they did not know. Could it be caused by the strange old man they had seen?

One child said, "Do not look back. Something strange is taking place."

A woman of their village saw them rising and called to them, but her voice had no effect. The children continued to rise slowly. When the woman reached the camp with the news, all the parents rushed out with food of every kind. They looked up and called piteously to the children, but the little ones would not return. One of them looked back and became a falling star. Another sang as he rose.

Seven of the children reached the sky and were changed into stars. The one who sang as he rose is the faintest of the group. Every falling star recalls the story of the pretty group of dancers we still see in the heavens. White people call them the Pleiades. We call them *Oot-kwa-tah*, which means "There they dwell in peace."

The seven sisters in the sky

Well known is the Greek myth of the seven Pleiades and of the "lost Pleiad," the sister who hid herself for shame because she had married a mortal. Indian tribes as far apart as the Huron-Wyandots of eastern Canada and the Nez Perces of the northwestern United States also related myths about the seven sisters in the sky.

Long ago a young man was having his fasting period near the end of a lake. His fasting lodge stood in a solitary place where no one ever ventured.

One evening when his fast was almost over, he was sitting in the entrance of the lodge. To his surprise he heard the faint sound of singing in the distance. Looking around, he could see nothing that could be making music. Soon the sounds became clearer, and they seemed to be coming from the sky, over the lake.

The young man continued to listen. Soon he thought that the voices were coming from the beach near by. Curious, he slowly and silently crept down toward the lake, through the grasses and reeds that grew between his lodge and the beach. As he crawled along, he noticed that the music was becoming more distinct and seemed to be much closer.

Reaching the shore, he moved the reeds apart with his hands and looked around. On the beach, seven young girls were singing and dancing, hand in hand. All were beautiful, and they were surrounded by the unearthly glow of starlight. One of them was even more beautiful than the others, and the young man fell in love with her at once.

As he tried to get closer to them, a pebble slipped from under his hand and made a noise. The girls started off at once and, climbing into a large basket, vanished into the sky.

In his fasting lodge the young man wondered, the rest of the evening and all the next day, whether the beautiful girls would ever come back. The next evening he listened and watched. After a while he again heard singing in the distance. Happy that the girls were returning, he crept down to the edge of the reeds and the grasses, almost to the beach.

When the girls came down from the sky, the young man was there, looking at them. He saw their big basket land on the beach. He saw them step out of it and begin to sing and dance. So delighted was he with the beautiful sight that he did not move or make a sound, and he kept himself hidden by the reeds.

After dancing as a group for a long time, the girls began to dance singly. Soon the loveliest one of the seven took her turn in a dance by herself. Never had the young man seen anyone so beautiful or any dancing so graceful. Without realizing what he was doing, he rose and expressed his happiness.

Instantly the seven girls climbed into their basket and vanished into the sky, as they had done the first time he saw them.

For several evenings the young man heard them singing and watched the dancing on the shore of the lake. Gradually the desire rose in his heart to capture the girl he had fallen in love with. One evening when they were dancing, he rushed into their midst. As before, the girls ran to the basket, which was swinging near them and hanging from the sky.

The last one to climb into it happened to be the girl whom he loved. So he seized her, just as she laid her hand on the edge of the basket. Clinging fast to her, he too was lifted into the air. But in time, the girl had to quit her hold, and the two of them fell to the ground.

The young man told her about his love for her and asked her to become his wife. The maiden was grieved, but she was not really angry.

"We are seven sisters," she said to him. "And we have always lived together. We are the group of stars that you have often seen in a cluster in the sky. It has long been our custom, this time of year, to come down to the earth to dance and play. I cannot become your wife unless you go up to the sky with us."

So the young man ascended to the sky with the beautiful girl he loved. In the sky land he found everything perfect. Everyone's wishes up there were realized at once, without effort. In the sky land the young man and the maiden lived together as husband and wife.

That is why, on starry nights, we can see among the Pleiades only six of the seven sisters that used to be in the cluster. Sometimes the shadow of the seventh one may be seen, faint and dim.

The great bear and the seven hunters

Early missionaries and travellers in what is now Canada were surprised when they learned that the Indians also knew as "bear stars" the constellation they themselves called the Great Bear or Ursa Major. We call it the Big Dipper also.

The following myth was related by the Algonquian and Iroquois tribes; this is the Micmac version. In their story, the bear is represented only by the four stars in the bowl of the dipper. The three stars that we imagine to be the handle of the dipper or the tail of the bear are, in this myth, the first three of seven hunters pursuing the bear. The hunters are Robin (because the star is reddish in colour), Chickadee (because it is small), Moose Bird, Pigeon, Blue Jay (because that star is blue), and two owls. (The moose bird is the Canada jay.)

The tiny star beside Chickadee is the pot he is carrying; when the bear is killed, he will cook the meat in it. Just above the hunters, a group of smaller stars forms the bear's den.

The myth explains the position of the stars in the constellation in the different seasons. Apparently the constellations Boötes and Corona Borealis are included in the story.

Late in the spring, every year, the bear wakes from her long sleep, leaves her den, and descends to the ground in search of food. Sharp-eyed Chickadee sees her instantly. Being too small to pursue her by himself, he calls the other hunters to assist him. Seven begin the chase, after placing Chickadee and his pot between two of the larger birds so that he will not lose his way. All pursue the bear eagerly, being hungry for meat after the long winter.

Throughout the summer the bear flees across the northern horizon, still pursued by the hunters. In the autumn, those in the rear lose the trail and drop out, one by one. First to disappear from the chase are the two owls, because they are heavier and clumsier than the other birds. But you must not laugh when you learn that the smaller owl, the Acadian owl, has failed to get some of the bear meat. You must not imitate his rasping cry. If you do, he will descend from the sky when you are asleep; with his birch-bark torch, he will set fire to whatever clothing you are wearing.

After the owls, Blue Jay and Pigeon lose their way and drop out of the chase. Only Robin, Chickadee, and Moose Bird are left. They continue their pursuit and at last, about the middle of autumn, they overtake the bear.

Brought to bay, the bear rears up on her hind feet and prepares to defend herself. But Robin pierces her with his arrow, and she falls over on her back. Being very thin in the autumn, Robin is eager to eat some of the bear's fat as soon as possible. In his haste, he leaps upon her and becomes covered with blood. Flying to the closest maple tree, in the land of the sky, he tries to shake off the blood. He succeeds in getting all of it off except a spot on his breast. "That spot," says Chickadee, "you will carry as long as your name is Robin."

But the blood that he does shake off spatters far and wide over the forests of the earth below. And so, every autumn, we see the blood-red tints of the foliage. Reddest of all are the maple leaves, for trees on earth follow the appearance of the trees in the sky and the maples up there received the most blood. The sky, you know, is just the same as the earth, except that it is up there and is older.

Some time after Robin kills the bear, Chickadee arrives on the scene. Together they cut up the body, build a fire, and place some of the meat in Chickadee's pot to cook. Just as they are about to eat, Moose Bird arrives. He almost lost the trail, but when he found it again he did not hurry. He knew that it would take his companions some time to slay the bear and cook the meat, and he did not mind missing the work if he would arrive in time for his full share of the food. Indeed, he was so impressed by this policy the first time that he has never again hunted for himself. He prefers to follow after hunters and share their spoils. Today, whenever a bear or a moose or other animal is killed in the woods of the Micmac land, you will see the moose bird appear to demand his share. That is why the other birds named him "He-who-comes-in-at-the-last-moment." Probably you know some human beings who should have that name also.

Robin and Chickadee, being generous, share their food with Moose Bird willingly. Before they eat, Chickadee stirs the meat in the pot, while the other two dance about the fire. Such was the custom in the good old days, when Micmacs were brothers to all; then they felt it their duty to share their food together and to thank each other and the Universal Spirit for their present happiness.

Throughout the winter, the skeleton of the bear lies on its back in the sky. But her life-spirit has entered another bear that lies upon her back in the den, invisible, sleeping the long sleep of winter. When spring comes round again, this bear will again leave her den and will be pursued by the hunters. She too will be slain but will send her life-spirit to the den, from which she will come forth again when the sun once more awakens the sleeping earth.

And so every year the hunters pursue and capture the bear. Night after night, we tell this story beside our campfires, as we watch the Great Bear in the sky.

The origin of the north star

One time a large party of Indians was travelling in search of new hunting grounds. For many moons they wandered, finding very little game. At last they reached the banks of a big river which they had never seen before. There they had to stop, because they had no material to build boats with.

They were lost, and they were almost exhausted from lack of food. Then their head chief became very ill. They would hold a council, the sub-chiefs and elders decided. At the council they would decide how the tribe could return to their old homes.

Tobacco and pipes were brought for the council. The drummers brought out their drums, and the younger Indians began the dance.

While the tobacco was burning, a strange little being like a child came up to the Indians and said to them, "I have been sent to be your guide."

Although it was night, the people at once broke camp and started off with their guide. Preceding them with a small war-club, the little stranger led them on until daylight. Then she commanded them to rest and sleep while she prepared their food. They obeyed, and when they awoke they found a feast ready for them. Their little guide told them goodbye and promised that she would come back to them in the evening.

True to her word, she returned that evening, bringing with her a skin jug. From it she poured some liquid into a horn cup and told the people to taste it. At first they feared to do so, but the little being looked so friendly and kind that they at last obeyed. At once they began to feel strong.

"Now you are strong enough for the long journey we must make to-night," said the guide. "Follow me again."

So they followed her. Early next morning they reached a great plain.

"Here you will rest until night comes," the little guide told them. "All except you two hunters. You will come with me. I will show you where you can find plenty of game."

After going with her a short distance, the hunters saw a herd of deer.

"Kill all you need," she directed them. "I will leave you now, but I will return again when evening comes."

When the little being returned at nightfall, she reported that her chief would soon arrive among them. "He will explain to you how you can reach your own homes in safety."

In a short time the chief arrived, with a large number of his own people. The sub-chiefs and elders called a great council to meet with the strangers.

"You are now in the land of the little people," the visiting chief told them. "To guide you, I have placed a sign in the sky. It will always stay there, to be a sure guide for you whenever you are lost."

Then the little people pointed out the bright star in the northern sky. "The sun never goes there," they said. "The other stars move about, but this north star, the pole star, always stays where it is now. It will be your guide in all your wanderings. If you will follow it now, you will find your own people and your old homes. You will find plenty of game there now."

So the Indians thanked the little people and departed. Every night they travelled until they reached their homes safely. When they had related their adventures, the head chief called a meeting of all the Iroquois tribes.

"We should give this star a name," he said to them.

The people talked and talked, and finally decided to call the guiding star the Star-Which-Never-Moves. By that name it is called to this day.

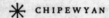

✳ CHIPEWYAN

The lover star

Once during a quarrel among the stars, one of them was driven away from its home in the heavens and was forced to descend to the earth. From one tribe of Indians to another it wandered, often hovering over their campfires when they were preparing for sleep. Everywhere the star went, people looked upon it with wonder and fear. It often lighted upon the heads of little children, as if to play with them, but the children were frightened and by their crying drove it away.

Among all the people in the world, only one was not afraid of the beautiful star. This was a little girl, the daughter of a warrior in the north country. She did not fear the star; in fact, she loved it with her whole heart and was happy in her love. The star seemed to love her also, for wherever the girl travelled with her father through the wilderness, it travelled also. When she awoke at night, the star was floating just above her head. It was so constant in its watchfulness that she never opened her eyes without being aware of its brilliant light.

People wondered at the star's devotion. They wondered even more when they saw that the girl's father never returned home from a hunting expedition without a great amount of game. "The star must be the son of the Good Spirit," people said. Ever after, they spoke of it with awe and veneration.

After several moons, midsummer came and the ripening of fruit. One day the girl went into the woods alone to gather berries. Finding that the wintergreen berries had been eaten by the birds and the deer, and seeing that cranberries were beginning to ripen, she wandered into a large swamp with her willow basket. In the tangled thickets of the cranberry marsh, she lost her way. Frightened, she cried aloud for her father, but the only answer came from the frogs and the lonely bittern. Twilight found her still lost, wandering farther and farther into the pathless brush of the swamp. At one time she waded in water up to her knees. Another time she fell into a hole and was almost drowned in the poisonous slime. When night came to the sky, she looked up, hoping to see the star that she loved. But the sky was overcast. A storm was gathering. Soon rain fell in torrents. The water rose about the frightened girl and carried her body out into the lake. She was never seen again.

As the seasons came and went, the star continued to shine above the campfires of the Chipewyans. But its light became dim, and it never remained long in one place. Always it seemed to be looking for something it could not find. "It is unhappy because of the death of the girl it loved," the people said to each other.

After more years had passed by, the star disappeared with the leaves of autumn. The next winter was cold and long. The following summer was the hottest the Chipewyans had ever known.

One night during this hot summer, a young hunter followed a bear into one of the largest swamps in the Chipewyan country. To his astonishment, he saw a small light that appeared to be hanging over the water. It was so beautiful that he followed it for a long distance, but it led to such dangerous places that he finally gave up the pursuit and returned to tell his people what he had seen.

Then the oldest men of the tribe told him this story. "The light you saw," they said, "is the star that was driven from the sky. It still is wandering over the earth, looking for the beautiful young girl it loved."

And even today that same star is near the earth. It is often seen by hunters as they journey at night through the wilderness.

Why Buffalo has a hump

Long ago, when the world was very young, the buffalo had no hump. He got his hump one summer because of his unkindness to birds.

He liked to race across the prairies for fun. The foxes would run ahead of him and tell the little animals that their chief, the buffalo, was coming.

One day when Buffalo was racing across the plains, he went in the direction of the place where little birds live on the ground. They called to him and to the foxes that he was going where their nests were, but neither paid any attention to them. Buffalo raced on and trampled the birds' nests under his heavy feet. Even when he heard the birds crying, he ran on without stopping.

No one knew that Nanabozho was near. But he had heard about the birds' ruined home, and was sorry for them. He ran ahead, got in front of Buffalo and the foxes, and stopped them. With his stick he hit Buffalo on the shoulders, hard. Fearing that he would receive another blow, Buffalo humped up his shoulders. But Nanabozho only said, "You shall always have a hump on your shoulders, from this day forth. And you shall always carry your head low for shame."

The foxes, thinking to escape from Nanabozho, ran away, dug holes in the ground, and hid themselves. But Nanabozho found them and gave them their punishment. "Because you were unkind to the birds, you shall always live in the cold ground."

Ever since then, foxes have had their homes in holes in the ground, and buffaloes have had humped shoulders.

Why Porcupine has quills

Long ago, when the world was young, porcupines had no quills. One day when Porcupine was in the woods, Bear came along and wanted to eat him. But Porcupine climbed to the top of a tree and was safe.

The next day, when Porcupine was under a hawthorn tree, he noticed how the thorns pricked him. He had an idea. He broke off some of the branches of the hawthorn and put them on his back. Then he went into the woods and waited for Bear. When Bear sprang on Porcupine, the little animal just curled himself up in a ball. Bear had to go away, for the thorns pricked him very much.

Nanabozho saw what happened. He called Porcupine to him and asked, "How did you know that trick?"

"I am always in danger when Bear comes along," replied Porcupine. "When I saw those thorns, I thought I would use them."

So Nanabozho took some branches from the hawthorn tree and peeled off the bark until they were white. Then he put some clay on the back of Porcupine, stuck the thorns in it, and made the whole a part of his skin.

"Now go into the woods," said Nanabozho.

Porcupine obeyed, and Nanabozho hid himself behind a tree.

Soon Wolf came along. He sprang on Porcupine and then ran away, howling. Bear came along, but he did not get near Porcupine. He was afraid of those thorns.

That is why all porcupines have quills today.

 CHIPPEWA

How Oriole got his beautiful feathers

Long ago when the world was young, the oriole did not have the beautiful feathers we see on him today. He was not yellow and orange, but a dull grey.

Early one morning a man who lived alone in a forest heard a bird near his wigwam. It was crying, crying softly but sadly. The Indian went outside to learn what it was and why it was weeping. He looked and looked until he saw, high in a tree, a little bird weeping.

Just then the sun began to peep over the eastern hills. The man heard the bird say, "What can I do to have such a beautiful dress as you have?"

The man saw that the grey bird was looking at the sun.

The sun smiled at the little fellow and said cheerfully, "Cheer up, little bird. You will have your wish, your beautiful dress, if you will sing gaily every morning as I come up. I will give you a dress of a golden colour, golden like my own."

The little fellow stopped crying. As he looked at himself, and as the Indian looked at the bird, a surprising change took place. His dull grey feathers began to change to gold. The bird was so surprised that he forgot the sun, forgot his duty.

The Sun reminded him. "Now if you forget what I have said, I will take your dress away from you."

So the little fellow began to sing the prettiest song he could think of. When he stopped for breath, Sun spoke to him again. "Let me tell you, my little man, that you must build your house way up in a tree, where no one can harm your family. Tomorrow morning I will tell you how to build your house. I cannot stop now, for I must go on with my other work."

The Indian was so puzzled by what he had seen and had heard that he decided to watch and listen again at sunrise the next day. Next morning he saw the bird with the beautiful golden feathers and heard it greet Sun with another gay and happy song. He heard Sun speak to the bird, but Sun spoke to the man also.

"You must never tell anyone," said Sun, "what you will learn this morning about the way this little fellow will build his house."

That is why we do not know how the oriole makes the nest that hangs like a tobacco pouch from the trees. Only the oriole knows how to build it, for the Sun told him.

This is how the oriole got his beautiful golden colour, and this is why he greets the sun with his beautiful, cheery song.

 CHIPPEWA

The origin of the trailing arbutus

Long ago, an old man, knowing he was about to die, sat in his wig-wam alone, meditating. He was wondering what he could do to confer some favour upon his people.

"What can I do for them that will make them remember me with gratitude?" he asked himself.

To help him answer his question, he called in all the good spirits. One after another they made suggestions. Presently a lovely girl came into his wigwam. Her hair was covered with white moss, her hands and feet were covered with pussy willow, her cheeks were a beautiful pink and white. A delicate fragrance filled the room as soon as she entered.

"Who are you?" asked the old man.

"I am Hope," she answered. "I keep people happy through all the long, cold winter. I have come to answer your question and to fulfil your wish. I offer myself as a sacrifice of spring. Thus your people will be blessed and will remember you forever."

The old man was content. Gradually he grew weaker and weaker, until at last his breath was completely gone. Then the beautiful maiden came close to him and covered him with leaves and moss. Among the leaves and moss she tucked tiny pink blossoms, hiding them in the folds of the old man's garments.

The next spring, his people found the trailing plant which we call arbutus. Every spring since the old man's death, the trailing arbutus has meant to the Indians a sign of spring. They greet it with great rejoicing, for it means that the cold, hard winter has gone and that soon its pink blossoms will fill the air with their fragrance.

✱ CHIPPEWA

The first white water lily

Long ago, all the people and the animals lived in peace and happiness. There was no winter, with its cold blasts and death-giving chill. There was always food for everyone, for there were many deer in the forests, herds of buffalo on the grassy plains, plenty of fruit on bush and tree. Flowers bloomed everywhere. The birds, dressed in more brilliant plumage than today, filled the air with their songs. The beasts were tame, and they came and went at man's bidding. There was no war. There was no fear of man, for no one would harm another.

By day the Indians entertained themselves with ball games and with many other games of skill and strength. In the evenings they gathered in the fields to watch the stars. The stars, they believed, were the homes of the good people who had been taken to Star Land by the Great Spirit.

One night as they watched, a star brighter than all the others shone far away in the south near a mountain peak. Every night for many nights they watched it, and they saw that it grew larger, brighter, nearer to them. They called a council and sent some of their chiefs to find the position of the bright star. The chiefs prepared for a long journey, but they soon returned.

"The star is near us," they reported. "It is hovering over the tops of some tall trees not far away. It does not look like other stars. Instead, it looks much like a bird. It must have some strange meaning for us."

So the head chiefs called another council, in order to try to find out the meaning of the unusual sight. Some people thought that it was a warning of a great disaster. Some thought that it was an omen of good. Many said that it was the star which their forefathers had regarded as the prophecy of a dreadful war. The council decided that they could do nothing but wait.

One moon passed. The star continued to hover near, its mystery yet unsolved. One night a young man had a dream. He dreamed that a beautiful maiden stood beside him and spoke to him.

"I am delighted with the land of your people," she said to him. "I like its flowers, birds, rivers, lakes, and mountains. So I have left my sisters in the Star Land above, in order to live here with you. Will you ask your wise and great men where I can live? Tell them I want to be where I can see the people at their happiest. Ask them what form I shall take in order to be loved by them."

When the young man awoke from his dream, he hastened out of his lodge and looked toward the south. There the beautiful star was glowing in its usual place. As soon as dawn arrived, he sent a crier forth to summon the men to the council lodge.

"The star we have been seeing in the south," he told them, "has fallen in love with the people of the earth and wishes to live among us." And he related his dream.

The next night a band of the finest and bravest men was sent to welcome the visitor to the earth. They presented her with the pipe of peace, which had been filled with sweet herbs. The beautiful star thanked the men, and her gracious words warmed their hearts. Together they returned to the village, and the star, with expanded wings, floated over their lodges until the dawn came.

The next night the young man dreamed again. Again the beautiful maiden appeared at his side and spoke to him.

"Ask your wise and great men where I shall live," she said, "and what form I shall take while I live among you."

The council, when summoned, suggested many places for the star's home. "On the tops of giant trees," said some. "In the heart of some flower," said others. "Let the star maiden decide where she will be happiest," said the wisest of the wise men.

At first the star chose the white rose of the mountains to be her home. But there she was so far away she could not be seen and could not often see the people she wished to live among. She went to the prairie, but there she feared the hoof of the buffalo. Next she looked for a rocky cliff, but it was so high that the children would not be able to see her. She continued until she found just the right place.

"Now I know where I shall be happiest," said the star maiden. "In the water, where I can see your canoes as they float by. The children will be my companions as they play beside the water. Even the babies will be my friends as they sleep in their cradles on the shores of the lakes."

As she finished speaking, she floated down to a lake and spread her wings on its surface. She was happy when she saw her face mirrored in its clear waters. Next morning the people were delighted to find, floating on the lake, thousands of white flowers in the midst of circles of green leaves. These were the first white water lilies.

✱ CHIPPEWA

The broken wing: an allegory

One time there were six young hawks living in a nest. When all but one of them were still too young to fly, both parent birds were shot by a hunter. The hungry brood waited in vain for their return. When night came, they were without parents and without food.

The oldest of the brood, Grey Falcon, the only one whose feathers were stout enough for him to leave the nest, took over the work of his elders. Throughout the summer he provided the younger birds with food. When the leaves began to turn yellow and red, the family began to talk of going to a warmer climate for the winter. They were just waiting to become a little stronger and a little more experienced in flying.

But one day Grey Falcon had an accident. One of his wings was broken when he pounced upon a swan. The younger ones waited in the nest for awhile, and then went in search of him.

When they reached him, he explained why he was unable to fly. "But don't let this accident keep you from going south. Winter will soon be here. It is better that I alone should die than for five of you to be miserable on my account."

"No, no!" said the younger birds, in one voice. "We will not forsake you. We will stay here and take care of you, as you took care of us before we were able to fly. If the winter kills you, it shall kill us too. Do you think we can so soon forget your kindness? It was greater than a father's, greater even than a mother's."

They found a hollow tree and managed to carry their wounded

brother to it. Before the cold and snows of winter had set in, they had stored up enough food to carry them through. To make it last better, two of the brood flew south, leaving the other three to watch over the wounded bird.

In due time he recovered from his wound, and he repaid the kindness of his brothers by teaching them to hunt. As spring advanced, and their winter stock of food was getting low, they ventured out of the hollow tree, to look for fresh things. All were successful except the youngest, Pigeon Hawk. Being small and foolish, he flew hither and thither, and always came back to the nest without anything. At last Grey Falcon spoke to him and asked him the cause of his ill luck.

"It isn't because I am small and weak," answered Pigeon Hawk, "that I do not bring home as much game as do my brothers. I kill ducks and other birds every time I go out, but just as I get to the woods on my way home, Owl robs me."

"Don't despair, young brother," said Grey Falcon. "I now feel that my strength has recovered. So I shall go out with you tomorrow."

Next day Grey Falcon went with Pigeon Hawk as far as the lake, and sat down on the shore while his young brother started after some ducks. In a few moments Grey Falcon exclaimed, "Well done!" for Pigeon Hawk had pounced upon a duck. But just as he was getting near the land with his prize, a large white owl flew down from a tree where he had been watching the hunter. He had not noticed the older brother. As Owl was about to wrest the duck from the grasp of Pigeon Hawk, Grey Falcon jumped up, fixed his claws in both sides of Owl, and flew home with him.

Pigeon Hawk followed closely, glad that he had brought home something at last, but angry at his old enemy. He flew into the owl's face as if to tear out his eyes. But Grey Falcon rebuked him.

"Softly, softly, my brother. Do not be in such a temper. Don't have such a revengeful disposition. This will be a lesson to Owl not to tyrannize over anyone weaker than he is."

So, after giving the owl good advice and telling him what kind of herbs would cure his wounds, they let him go.

Before the owl had flown from view, two visitors appeared at the hollow tree—the nestmates that had spent the winter in the south. All the brothers were happily united again. Soon each bird chose a mate and flew off to the woods.

Spring had returned, the cold winds had stopped, the streams were now open, and the trees began to show signs of new leaves.

"But spring returns in vain," said the old man who related this story, "if we are not thankful to the Master of Life who has preserved us through the winter. And all of us should show kindness to those in need or in sickness, just as did the birds in this story."

MYTHS AND LEGENDS
OF LANDSCAPE FEATURES

 SENECA

The origin of Niagara Falls

Long ago, a beautiful girl of the Seneca Indians was betrothed by her family to an old and ugly man. She did not want to marry him, but her father insisted. Knowing no other escape, she one day jumped into her canoe and pushed off into the swift-flowing Niagara River. It would be far better, she thought, to seek death in its angry waters than to marry a man she hated.

In a cave behind the rushing waters of the Niagara lived the Thunderer, the great chief of clouds and rain, and the guardian of the harvest. As friend and protector of the Seneca people, he noticed the girl's canoe approaching and saw her unhappy face. He knew that in a few minutes her boat would be dashed against the rocks. So he spread out his wings, flew to rescue the girl, and caught her just before her boat crashed to pieces.

For many weeks she lived with the Thunderer in his cave. He taught her many things. For one thing, she learned why so many of her people had been dying, why the fever-sickness was always busy among them.

"A snake monster lies coiled under the ground beneath your village," the Thunderer told her. "He creeps out and poisons the springs, because he lives on human beings. The more people he devours, the more he wants. So he can never get enough if he waits for them to die from natural causes."

"What should we do?" asked the girl. "How can we escape from the deadly snake?"

"Your people must leave their village," replied the Thunderer. "They must move nearer the great lake."

The Thunderer kept the girl with him in his cave until the death of the ugly old man among her people.

"Now you may return home," he said to her. "And tell your people all you have learned from the Thunderer."

The girl remembered all his teachings, and the people listened to her words. They broke up their homes and made a new village near the great lake. For a while all was well. No sickness entered the new village.

But after a while the old fever-sickness returned, and Indians began to die from it. The huge serpent had dragged himself after the people and hoped to kill as many in the new village as he had killed in the old. The Thunderer saw him creeping along the ground. One night as the serpent neared the creek beside the village, the Thunderer hurled a thunderbolt at him. The noise woke up all the people, but the bolt only injured the serpent. It did not kill him.

The Thunderer hurled another thunderbolt. And another. And another. At last he killed the serpent, the poisoner of the water.

The dead snake was so huge that when the Indians uncoiled it, it lay stretched out for a distance greater than twenty arrow-flights. They pushed it into the Niagara River, and watched it float down the stream.

"It looks as big as a mountain," they said to each other. "Can it get through that narrow place between the rocks?"

When the huge body reached the narrows, it could go no farther. It was wedged between the rocks. The water was forced to rise above it and to fall over it in a giant cascade. As the weight of the serpent monster pressed on the rocks, the rocks were pushed back, bent like a giant bow.

Never again did the Senecas have the fever-sickness in their village. And the giant waterfall, in the shape of a great bow that is bent, remains in the Niagara River to remind Indians of their friend and protector, the Thunderer.

 SENECA

The sacrifice at Niagara Falls

The sound of the cataract in the Niagara River was said to be the voice of a powerful spirit that lived in the waters. The last recorded sacrifice to that spirit was in 1679, when the daughter of Chief Eagle was selected as the sacrifice, in spite of the protests of La Salle.

Long ago, the Indians of the forest used to gather at Niagara Falls every year, to offer a sacrifice to the spirit that lived in that mighty cataract. The offering was made in a white canoe which was filled with ripe fruit and beautiful flowers. The canoe was paddled by a girl, the prettiest one who had just arrived at the age of womanhood. It was considered an honour to be selected as the guide of the canoe to the brink of the falls. Even the girl chosen felt complimented and honoured.

One year the maiden chosen for the sacrifice to the spirit of the cataract was the only daughter of a chief of the Senecas. Her father was the bravest among brave warriors. Her mother had been killed by an enemy tribe. Their beautiful daughter was his great joy; she was the only one who could bring smiles to his stern face.

When the chief learned that she had been chosen for the sacrifice, he did not allow a muscle of his face to move. In no way did he give any sign of the agony in his heart.

The time for the ceremony arrived. All day there were festivities beside the little river—singing and dancing and games. When evening came, all the people gathered for the sailing of the white canoe. It had already been heaped with flowers and fruit, gifts for the spirit of Niagara. The moon shone on the water, making the foam and mist from the cataract gleam with soft and silvery light. The waterfall thundered, but the people were quiet. The songs and whoops of the day-time ceremony had ceased. The people looked up the river quietly and expectantly.

Soon they saw a white canoe gliding from under the trees along the bank. Swiftly it came through the rapids above the cataract. All knew that there was no escape from those rushing waters. With seeming calmness the girl guided her canoe toward the centre of the stream. The watching people lost their own calmness and shouted at her, some with frantic yells and some with words of admiration and encouragement.

Suddenly their attention was drawn away from the girl and her canoe. They saw a second white canoe leave the shadows of the forest and shoot forth upon the river. Quickly it neared the first canoe. Soon the people on the bank recognized the man with the paddle. It was their chief, the father of the girl to be sacrificed.

With a few powerful strokes he had his canoe beside his daughter's. Father and daughter turned to look at each other as the two canoes plunged, side by side, over the thundering cataract. Together they joined the spirit of Niagara.

Some people say that they were changed into spirits of pure strength, that she is the maid of the mist, he the ruler of the cataract. To them in their home far beneath the surface of the water, the roaring of Niagara is music.

Legend of Iroquois Falls

Iroquois Falls are in the Abitibi River, in northeastern Ontario, not far from Lake Abitibi. On the eastern shore of the lake is a great rock where a spirit is said to live; whenever any noise is made in the area, the spirit growls with anger. So the Indians avoid the lake.
Several tribes of eastern Canada used to tell this story about the waterfall in the river. Similar legends have been recorded about Niagara Falls and also about a waterfall in the St. John River of New Brunswick.

Many years ago, Iroquois warriors came north to fight the Indians in the Abitibi country. On their way, they captured an old woman of the enemy tribe and took her with them as a guide. The river was new and strange to the Iroquois. They wanted the old woman to inform them which rapids they could ride through in their canoes and which ones they should carry their boats around.

When they came to white water, they asked, "Do your people chute these rapids?"

"Oh, yes. They are safe," she would sometimes say. Other times she would answer, "No, it is necessary to portage here. The current is swift, and there are many rocks."

After a while they approached the spot where the river drops more than one hundred feet. As the waterfall is immediately below swift rapids, its roar is drowned by the rushing and splashing of the white water above. And the cascade is hidden from view by a sharp turn in the river.

As the Iroquois approached the rapids above the waterfall, the leader of the party asked the guide, "Do your people chute these?"

"Oh, yes," she replied. "They are quite simple now. But as they are shallow, I had better get out of the canoe to lighten it. I'll walk to the place where we sometimes have to portage, and you can pick me up there."

So the old woman got out of the canoe and walked over the portage. The Iroquois stayed in the canoes. As they started down the rapids, the boats were caught in the strong current and were buffeted against the big rocks. Quickly the first canoe was carried around the bend. Then the men saw before them the terrifying drop of the falls. Frantically they tried to reach the shore. Frantically they yelled a warning to the people behind them.

But the warning was too late. The men could not control their boats. Canoe after canoe was swept over the brink and was dashed to pieces on the rocks below. Not a single Iroquois in the party survived to tell his people what had happened.

✳ OTTAWA

The origin of Mackinac Island

Mackinac Island rises from the straits between Lake Huron and Lake Michigan. The name has been shortened from Michilimackinac, the original name given it by the Indians who, for many generations, used the rocky island as a gathering place.

As seen from near Woody Island, it is said to "have exactly the form its name implies, that of a large turtle sleeping on the water."

Long ago when the world was very young, and all the living creatures were wandering over its surface looking for the best place to live, a large number of turtles came to the southern shore of what is now called Lake Erie. They found the land generally level, and they were delighted with the muddy waters of the lake and also with the many stagnant ponds near it. Most of the turtles liked the spot so well that they wanted to settle there.

But the leader of the band, a huge turtle, was determined to continue his journey. He was lured northward by strange lights, lights of unusual loveliness, which he had often seen moving across the distant horizon. The leader tried to persuade some of the band to go with him, but they refused. Disappointed but not discouraged, knowing that the summer was but half gone, he made up his mind to travel on alone.

He journeyed slowly, often stopping to rest and to feed along the many beautiful swamps and bayous on his way north. When the second half of summer and most of autumn had passed, he had gone no farther than a point of land which then partly divided Lake Huron from Lake Michigan. Already he had been numbed by chilly winds, but he was still determined to complete his pilgrimage. The strange lights still lured him.

On the day when he set forth upon the waters for the last part of his journey, the winds were cold and ice began to form. In a short time he could move no farther. An icy barrier had formed round him and soon he was frozen to death. He was only a little black spot on the waste of frozen waters.

The winter snows passed, spring returned, the ice melted. Again the lakes were a beautiful blue. But the shell of the huge turtle remained fastened to a tall reed. As the years went by, it grew into an island, which the Indians named Michilimackinac, meaning "the Great Turtle."

✳ CREE

Legends of the Qu'Appelle River

The Qu'Appelle River joins the Assiniboine River a short distance west of the city of Winnipeg. It flows through a beautiful valley, which in places is forested. The Cree Indians used to have many traditions and songs about it, for the echo in the valley appealed to their imagination. The first of the two traditions given below has been related in verse and set to music by Thurlow Lieurance.

The Cree name for the river is Katapaywie sepe, which means "Who calls?"

I

Many years ago, a Cree Indian girl thought that she heard the voice of her absent lover calling to her. His voice seemed to come from one of the hills overlooking the river near their village. Entering her canoe, she started off down the stream to look for him. She called and called, but no one answered. A short time after she left the village, her lover returned. At once he went in search of her, but he found no trace of the girl or of her canoe.

She was never seen again, but her voice can still be heard in the valley. When anyone calls, it answers back in sweet, sad tones. For a long time, the girl's canoe used to appear for a few minutes at twilight, on one of the beautiful lakes in the valley. If anyone tried to approach, the canoe would disappear in the soft mist of dusk.

2

Many summers ago, a young man came up the river alone in his birch-bark canoe. He was on the way to the village of his sweetheart, to claim her as his bride. In the darkness of the twilight and of the wooded slopes, he heard a voice speak his name. A strange fear came over his spirit.

"Who calls?" the young man asked.

No one answered. He heard only the ripple of the water, the wind in the trees, and then the echo of his voice asking, "Who calls?"

In a few seconds he heard the voice speak his name again, clearly and near by. It seemed to him to be the voice of his sweetheart, though it sounded more like the voice of a spirit than of a mortal.

"Who calls?" he asked again.

Again there was no answer except the ripple, the breeze, and the echo of his own question.

Lonely and fearful, he continued his journey all the night. At sunrise he drew his canoe up on the bank and went toward the lodges of his friends. As he neared the camp, he saw a number of people around the home of his sweetheart. They were singing the songs of death. Without being told, he knew that his loved one had gone to the Land of Souls.

"When did she die?" the young man asked.

"Last evening," was the reply. "Twice last evening she called your name. And then her spirit departed from this world."

The young man remembered the voice in the woods. Silently he returned to the river, launched his canoe, and was never seen again. Ever since, travellers on the river have heard a voice ask, "Who calls?"

✳ SARCEE

Buffalo Lake

Buffalo Lake is located in Alberta, southeast of Edmonton and not far from Red Deer Lake.

This tradition of the Sarcee Indians was told in 1954 by Daisy Otter. The Blackfeet of Montana relate almost the same story about Buffalo Lake. The second part of the story is similar to one that the Kootenays tell about Flathead Lake, Montana, and to one that the Nez Perce Indians tell about Snake River in Idaho.

In the early days the Sarcee tribe was big. One fall when they were in the Red Deer country, two young men went out to hunt buffalo. Quite a long distance from their camp they saw a buffalo bull standing in a dry valley.

"How can we get a close shot at him?" one young man asked the other.

"Let's chase him," answered the other. "We cannot reach him from here with our bows and arrows."

So they chased the buffalo bull and killed him. Then they began to butcher him, to get the skin and the meat.

"You cut his legs off," one hunter said, "and I will cut him open."

So the man cut off the front legs and one of the hind legs, while the other cut the buffalo open. As he finished, water began to come out of the body, just as a running spring comes out of the side of a mountain.

The men stopped their work and watched. When they saw that the stream continued to flow, they went up on a hill and sat there to watch it. Soon water covered the buffalo's body. Then it began to fill up the little hollow place where the animal had fallen when they killed it. Soon it formed a pool in the shape of a buffalo. A little stream ran out from the place that looked like the tail.

The men watched from the hill until evening. By that time the water had become a large lake, still in the shape of a buffalo. Some willow trees which had been there for a long time now stood beside the part that looked like a head. So the buffalo-shaped lake seemed to have hair.

Late in the evening the hunters returned to camp and told their people about the strange happening and the new lake. Next morning, very early, all the people went with the two men, to see the sight. Sure enough, there was a big lake, in the shape of a buffalo. A stream ran from its tail; and at the spine, where the water was very deep, the animal was deep blue.

Then the people moved on farther north to continue the buffalo hunt. When winter came and it was time to go south again, the head man of the tribe learned that the new lake was frozen over.

"Let's travel south over the new lake," he said to his people. "We can save time by going across it instead of around it."

So they packed their things on horses and on travois and started across the lake. When some of them had crossed to the opposite side, and some were on the lake, a little boy saw a bone sticking out of the ice.

"I would like to have that bone," he said to his grandmother, who was walking with him. "Will you get it for me?"

"It is the horn of a buffalo," said his grandmother.

She took her axe and began pounding the horn with it, trying to break it off.

All the people near her stopped their horses and their dogs to watch the grandmother. She pounded and pounded, there where the horn touched the ice. Suddenly a big cracking noise startled every-one, as the ice split wide open. Indians, horses, dogs—all that were on the lake fell in and were drowned. Only the people on the shores, those who had crossed over and those who had not yet started, were saved, from all that band of Sarcees.

That is how the Sarcees got divided. Those in the north became known as Beaver and Chipewyan. Those in the south kept the name of Sarcee. The Beaver Indians speak the same language, except that they talk faster than the Sarcees do.

When you pass Buffalo Lake in the evening, you can hear dogs bark-ing and children playing and shouting down in the bottom of the lake. They are the ones that fell through the ice, long, long ago.

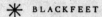 ✳ BLACKFEET

The white horses on Chief Mountain

> *Chief Mountain (9,056 feet in altitude) is a conspicuous landmark in the northeast corner of Glacier National Park, Montana. Indians on both sides of the international boundary had several traditions about it. The Blood Indians believed that Thunderbird lived in a great cavern near its summit. The Blackfeet said that Thunderbird was once overcome by a snowstorm and came down to their camp, to the lodge of their head chief. Others believed that the spirit of the west wind lived on the mountain and that the large stones which dot the prairies to the eastward are the missiles he hurled at his enemies.*

Years ago, a great chief allowed his horses to wander at will over Chief Mountain. They were beautiful and swift and strong. All their powers were marvellous because they ate the grasses that then grew on Chief Mountain and nowhere else.

Whenever the chief and his band went on the hunt or on the war-path, he left his beautiful white horses in the care of his daughter. He thought that she was the only one who knew the secret pathway leading to the top of the mountain.

But somehow a young man of the tribe learned the secret. He was angry with the girl, for he had loved her and had asked that she marry him. Rejected by the father and spurned by his daughter, he was determined to get revenge.

One night in late autumn, when the chief and his men were away hunting, the young man led an enemy band to the mountain. They knew about the chief's beautiful white horses, and longed to possess them. They had heard about the chief's beautiful daughter, and the young men wished to possess her. As soon as the rejected suitor showed them the secret beginning of the only path to the summit, they climbed swiftly. All gloated in anticipation of their reward.

When the girl saw them coming, she was mounted on her favourite snow-white horse. At first there seemed to be no way of escape for her or for the horses. She knew that there was but one way of ascent and descent, and that was held by the enemy. To be captured, or to allow her father's horses to be captured, was unthinkable.

A sudden snowstorm swept the mountain top. The girl called to the horses, pushed her mount to full speed, and led the whole band forward through the whirling snow. The enemy blindly followed, and all disappeared over the precipice.

Even today, when the Indians see snow whirling over the top of Chief Mountain, they say, "White horses ride swift and high. Hunting is good."

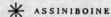 ASSINIBOINE

Ghost River

Ghost River, which is just outside the eastern boundary of Banff National Park, has a curious feature: for about twelve miles its water runs through an underground channel.

This explanation of the name of the river was given by Enoch Baptiste, of the Morley Reserve.

One time a band of Stoneys was camped at the north end of Ghost River. There were many tepees and many people. They camped close together for safety in those days, for there was fighting most of the time.

At night the Indians heard what sounded like a herd of buffalo running eastward. Someone seemed to be driving them. One evening a man said to the people around him, "I am going to find out what is driving those buffaloes."

He saddled his horse and tied it near his tepee, so that it would be ready the moment he heard the buffaloes again. About midnight he heard the pounding hoof-beats. The man jumped on his horse and followed the sound.

He pushed his horse, and after a while he seemed to be gaining on the herd. Then he saw a rider ahead of him—a man riding a grey horse. The rider was naked and had a feather in his hair. He was making the buffalo herd stampede.

The man in pursuit pushed his horse faster and faster. He wanted to see the face of the rider of the grey horse. He wanted to find out who was chasing the buffaloes. But when he rode up beside the grey horse, horse and rider disappeared. They were ghosts. No one could ever catch them.

That is why the river is called Ghost River.

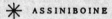 **✳** ASSINIBOINE

Banff Hot Springs

> *This tradition of the famous springs in Banff National Park was related in 1954 by Chief Walking Buffalo of the Stoney or Assiniboine tribe.*

The hot springs and the paint springs show some of the mysterious ways of the Creator. In the early days before the white man came, Indians used to hear something in those springs.

"It's a spirit," we would say.

Sometimes we would hear it singing. Sometimes we would hear it whistling, making a sound like the bone whistles we use at a Sun Dance. We would wait around, trying to see who it was and what was making the sounds. But we could never see anything in the waters.

"It's a spirit that rules the hot springs and the paint springs," people would say.

They would bathe in the springs because of the medicine in them. Then they would drop something in the water as a sacrifice, as a thank-you to the spirits for the use of their water or the use of their paint, the yellow ochre.

But since the white people came, the strength has gone out of the water. That mysterious power that comes from the spirits is there no more. Probably the white people do not pray to get well. In the old days, the Indians used to pray to the spirits to cure them of their sickness. Then they were healed by the mysterious strength of the waters.

Sunrise on Lake Louise

Lake Louise is the best known of the beautiful lakes in the Canadian Rockies. The snow-capped peaks that almost surround it rise to altitudes of 10,000 and 11,000 feet. The sunrise reflected in the lake is one of the glories of the region.

Stoney Indians, who hunted and fished in the area, used to relate this story about one of the giants of ancient days.

Long, long ago, when the world was very young, giants lived in this country. A chief of the giants was a famous hunter. Many large game animals he killed with his bow and arrows. Many birds and small game animals he caught in his traps. But he was never satisfied; always he wanted more.

One day, as he stood watching a rainbow, he had an idea: he would get the rainbow and from it he would make a giant bow for hunting. The more he watched, the more he wanted the rainbow. With it he could be a truly great hunter.

So he climbed the tallest tree on the highest mountain, reached up to the sky with his long arms, and tore the rainbow from its place. But when he seized it, the colours disappeared. The bow in his hands was colourless.

Angrily the giant threw the rainbow against the nearest mountaintop, a peak overlooking a lake. There the bow broke into pieces and the pieces rolled on down into the water. At the bottom of the lake the fragments regained their colours, and the colours spread through the water.

After a while the spirit-power in the sky made the smaller bow which we still see after a rain. Sometimes, even today, the colours of the rainbow which was shattered by the giant-chief may be seen at sunrise in the water of the lake we now call Lake Louise.

Lake Minnewanka

Lake Minnewanka, which the Indians knew as the "Water of the Spirits," is five miles east of Banff, Alberta. This story about the lake was related in the summer of 1954 by a Stoney Indian, Enoch Baptiste, interpreted by Horace Hollaway.

Northeast of Lake Minnewanka is a mountain with a high, sharp peak shaped like a tower. From a long distance you can see snow on its top, but there is never any on its side. The mountain is so steep that snow does not stay on it. Because spirits lived on top of it, Indians called it Spirit Mountain.

The near-by lake they called "Minnewanka," which means "Water of the Spirits." Whenever they travelled in the neighbourhood of the lake, they heard the voices of the spirits. As they passed by, they could see nothing that made sounds, but they could hear sounds.

One time when our people were camping near the lake, my father heard what seemed to be the beating of a drum. The noise seemed to be coming from the water. He could also hear voices down in the lake. Soon he noticed that water was coming up on the shore. It came close to the camp, and then it went back again.

Soon my father saw, near the centre of the lake, a strange creature rise out of the water. It was half fish and half human being. It had blown the water toward the shore, and then it had come above the surface. As my father stood watching, the fish-person sank back into the lake.

Other people also saw the strange creature. They were so frightened that they broke camp and never camped there again. All Indians stayed away from that water. There was no fishing or canoeing on Lake Minnewanka until white people came.

Strange creatures in other lakes were sometimes killed by lightning, but I never heard of this one being killed.

Many Indians are still afraid of the lake. A few years ago some Indian boys were working there, helping to build a dam. They did not want to work at that place, because they had heard about the strange fish-person. One of the boys was killed in a strange accident. Some people say that the accident happened because the spirits did not like to have trees near the lake destroyed.

Coyote and Shuswap Falls

Shuswap Falls are in the Shuswap River in southeastern British Columbia.

A long, long time ago, when the world was young and fresh, before hatred and greed and strife were known, Eagle, Bear, Elk, Fox, Coyote, and all the other animals and birds lived in peace and harmony together.

Coyote's home was in a lovely but lonely place far away from everyone. There he had no one to talk with, no one to play with, no one to feast and dance with. At last he became so lonesome that he decided to invite all his friends to a great feast and festival. If they had a good time, as he thought they would, he would invite them once every year.

So he set to work and built rapids in the river, rapids that ended in a waterfall. Then he made a big kettle out of stone, with legs under it, and hung it over the falls. He built a fish-trap, also of stone. Beside the waterfall he made a stone seat, where he could sit and watch the fish being caught in his trap and being cooked in his kettle. There too he could talk with his friends while seeing the sports and watching the feasting.

When he had made everything exactly as he wanted it, the buds on the fir trees were just bursting. By this sign Coyote knew that the first salmon were on their way up the rivers. So he called aloud for his friends to come and feast. His voice could be heard far and near, as it can to this day. On every hill and in every valley, his friends heard his voice. "Listen!" they said. "Coyote is calling us. Let's go."

As they called out to him along the way, Coyote recognized the voices of his friends. He knew the roar of Grizzly Bear, the howl of Timber Wolf, the snort of Elk, the hoot of Horned Owl, the cry of Eagle, the chatter of Kingfisher. He was so happy and so excited that he ran round and round, trying to catch his tail.

Soon all the animals and birds had gathered beside the river. Great was their amazement when they saw all the wonders that Coyote had built there. For half a moon they camped beside the rapids and the waterfall. They caught salmon in Coyote's fish-trap, cooked it in his kettle, feasted and danced and enjoyed all their sports. By day and by night, the first burned brightly, while Coyote visited and played and lost his loneliness.

When the time came for the festival to end, all his friends shook

Coyote's hand with grateful hearts. All promised to come again next year when the fir trees were bursting into bud. Everyone went home happy.

All this happened a very long time ago. But still the rapids and the waterfall, the kettle and the stone seat can be seen in the river where Coyote built them for his big party. And every spring you can hear the invitation call of Coyote and the answering calls of his friends.

 DOGRIB

The creation of the northern Rocky Mountains

> The Mackenzie River, which flows into the Arctic Ocean in the extreme northwestern part of Canada, was called by the northern Indians Too-cha-tes, meaning "Big Water." The stream which flows from the southwest and joins the Mackenzie near its mouth they called by a name that means "the river that flows from the country of the Big Man." Their name for Big Man was Naba-Cha.

The Big Man, Naba-Cha, was one of the very largest men who ever lived. The lodge which was his home was made of three hundred skins of the biggest caribou that could be killed on the plains that lie north of his river. The dish from which he ate his meals was made of the bark of six huge birch trees. And it took one whole moose, or two caribou, or fifty partridges to feed him every day.

Big Man was known throughout the whole North Country, for he had often made war against the tribes to the north, the east, and the south. Northward he had travelled to the mouth of Big Water to fight the Snow Men, the Eskimoes. Eastward, he had crossed Great Bear Lake to the country of the Yellow-knives. There he had seen the pure copper shining in the sands of the rivers that flow toward the Great Bear Lake and Great Slave Lake and toward the icy ocean.

Southward, he had travelled a long distance to the great plains, the country of the Crees, where he had seen many large animals. But westward he had never gone, because there lived a giant man, a man bigger than Naba-Cha.

Naba-Cha was not only big; he was wicked and very cruel. He was especially cruel to a Cree boy he had brought back from the south one time when he was on the war-path. The boy was an orphan.

without father or mother, sister or brother, to help him escape. His name was Caribou-footed.

The boy had one friend in the lodge of Big Man. That was Hottah, the two-year-old moose, the cleverest of all the northern animals. Swift he was, too. He had travelled, in one day, all the long distance from the mouth of Big Water to the home of Big Man.

Hottah liked Caribou-footed so much that he wanted to help him escape from Big Man. He knew that far to the westward, much farther west than Big Man had ever gone, flowed another river almost as long and wide as Big Water. The Yukon, it is called. West of the Yukon, he knew, lay safety for Caribou-footed. There lived Nesnabi, the Good Man.

So one day Hottah said to the boy, "We will go away. You take a stone, a clod of earth, a piece of moss, and a branch of a tree. Together we shall escape from the cruel Big Man. I will carry you on my back."

Caribou-footed gathered the things he was told to get, and soon the two were ready to leave. Hottah took the boy upon his back and carried him out to the great plains west of Big Water. But before long they saw Big Man coming behind them, riding his great caribou.

"Fling out behind you your clod of earth," said Hottah to the boy.

Caribou-footed did so, and at once there rose behind them, between them and Big Man, great hills of earth. The hills were so high and wide that it was many days before Big Man came in sight again. During those days Hottah chewed the sweet grass that grew west of the hills, and Caribou-footed ate the ripe berries.

When Big Man came in sight a second time, Hottah called to the boy, "Fling out behind you your piece of moss."

Caribou-footed did so, and at once a vast muskeg-swamp lay behind them. For days the caribou and Big Man floundered in the muskeg, while Hottah and the boy moved on toward the setting sun. When Big Man appeared a third time, Hottah said to the boy, "Fling behind you your stone."

Caribou-footed did so, and at once there rose behind them, between them and Big Man, high rocky mountains. Up to the clouds they rose, white with snow, more magnificent than had ever been seen before. It was a long time before Big Man and his caribou had crossed the mountains and appeared again to Hottah and the boy. Then they were much nearer their goal, the great western river.

"Now fling out behind you your branch of a tree."

Caribou-footed did so, and at once arose a mighty forest, with trees so thick that Big Man and his gigantic caribou could not pass between them. Big Man had to cut his way through. And because its horns had stuck in the branches, the caribou was left behind.

By the time Big Man came in sight again, Hottah had carried the boy safely across the great river, the Yukon. Away toward the west it wound, through high rocky hills, foaming as it flowed.

Big Man reached the bank of the river and, seeing Hottah on the other side, called to him, "Help me, Hottah. Help me cross this turbulent river. If you will assist me to the country that lies beyond, I will do no harm to the boy. I promise you."

Without a word Hottah went to get Big Man. But as they were crossing the great river, Hottah dropped the giant into the water. Down he was swept by the swirling rapids of the river, on and on toward the setting sun.

Thus the wicked and cruel Bad Man, Naba-Cha, was lost forever, and thus Caribou-footed was saved. And in the far Northwest, the foothills, the muskeg-swamp, the snow-capped Rocky Mountains, and the great forest remain where the Cree boy threw the clod of earth, the piece of moss, the stone, and the branch of a tree, long, long ago.

 ✳ DOGRIB

The meaning of the Northern Lights

This story is a continuation of "The Creation of the Northern Rocky Mountains."

After Hottah had dropped the cruel Big Man into the Yukon River, he returned to his young friend, Caribou-footed. From the far side of the stream the boy had watched the crossing.

"I must leave you now," said Hottah, "and return to the country where I belong. If you will follow this river, you will soon come to a big lodge. It is the home of Nesnabi, the Good Man you have heard about. Good and great is he, and he has travelled far. He has been eastward into my country. He has been southward, among the golden rivers that are lost in the mountains. He has travelled westward, to the great water that has no ending. And he has travelled northward, to the silent, snow-covered plains, where the Snow Men live.

"Like Naba-Cha, he is big. But unlike Naba-Cha, he is not cruel. He harms no one, and he will aid you."

So Caribou-footed followed the curves and bends of the Yukon River, passed through the spruce forests along its valleys, and came to the lodge of Nesnabi. The Good Man himself was standing beside his lodge.

"Where have you come from, young man?" he asked. "And where are you going?"

"Great Chief, I have come from far. I have neither father nor mother, sister nor brother. My home used to be with my own people far away in the south country. There I lived happily until Naba-Cha came and took me with him to the cruel north country, beside Big Water. There the snow lasts long, and there Naba-Cha treated me cruelly. For a long time I was unhappy with him. But Hottah, the two-year-old moose, brought me to your country, Great Chief. Now he has left me, and I am here alone."

"Young man, I have long known that you would come to me," said the Good Man. "Stay with me as long as you like. But if at the end of seven suns you wish to go farther, I will prepare you for your journey into the west country."

So for seven suns Caribou-footed stayed at the lodge of Nesnabi. At the end of that time, he said to the Good Man, "I thank you for your kindnesses, but I must leave you now and travel farther. Will you give me the preparation you promised me?"

Then the Good Man took seven arrows from his lodge and said to the young man, "These are enough to help you. But if you should shoot at any bird or animal in a spruce tree, and if the arrow should stick in the branches, take care that you do not go after it. If you do go after it, something strange will happen to you."

Soon after the young man left Nesnabi, he saw a squirrel in the branches of a red spruce tree. He raised his bow and shot one of the seven arrows. Down fell the squirrel, but the arrow stayed in the branches. Forgetting what the Good Man had told him, Caribou-footed started to climb after the arrow. As he moved upward, the arrow moved upward also. Up, up, up they went, until at last they came to the sky. The arrow passed through the sky, and the young man followed it.

Great was his surprise when he entered the Sky Country. He had expected a glorious land, where the sun always shone, where many of his own people would be living in large lodges, and where herds of caribou, moose, and musk-oxen would be roaming in great numbers. Instead, the air was damp, dreary, and cold. No trees or flowers beautified the land. No animals ran on the silent plains. No smoke from a lodge was to be seen anywhere. No hunting cry of his people or of other Indians greeted his ears.

The only pleasing thing was a great white mass that shimmered against the sky, far in the distance. It resembled a huge pile of snow when the sun shines on it in early summer. Between this great white mass and the spot where the young man stood was a winding path.

"I will follow the path," he said to himself. "I must see what lives in that shining white lodge in the distance."

As he walked along, he met an old woman.

"Who are you?" she asked. "And where are you going?"

"I am the Caribou-footed. Can you tell me who lives over there in that big white lodge?"

"Ah, I know you, young man. Long have I thought you would come here. But you have done wrong. This is no country for a young man.

"In that big lodge over there lives Hatempka. He is unhappy because he has lost his medicine belt, his great power. And until he gets it again, he will let no one be happy in the Sky Country."

"Do you know who has his belt?" asked Caribou-footed.

"Yes, it is in the tepee of the two blind women who live far beyond the lodge that shines so white and bright. No one can get it from them, I fear. But if anyone can get it, he will be given the daughter of Hatempka for his wife. She is a beautiful girl named Etanda."

Caribou-footed started off toward the tepee of the blind women, travelling as fast as he could. When he reached the place and entered he saw what he knew was the stolen belt. It was hanging on one side of the tepee. About it hung many skulls, the skulls of people who had gone in quest of the belt but had never returned.

"You are very welcome," the blind women said to the young man when they heard him in their tepee. "When you are ready to leave us, tell us, so that we may bid you goodbye."

But Caribou-footed was watchful. He noticed that, behind her back, each of the old women had a copper knife, long and sharp. One woman sat on one side of the door, the other woman on the other side.

"I understand them," he thought to himself. "When I am ready to leave, they will try to kill me. But I shall fool them."

He noticed a bag of bones and feathers lying in one corner of the tepee. He tied a string to the bag and then pulled the string over the pole above the door.

To the women he said, "I am going now. Remember that I am old and fat, and that when I leave, I make much noise."

At that moment he pulled the string, and the bag of bones and feathers moved toward the door. At once the two old blind women stabbed with their copper knives. Striking only feathers, each knife passed through the bag and into the woman on the other side of the door. They killed each other.

Seizing the medicine belt, Caribou-footed went back to the shining white home of Hatempka.

"Great chief," he said to Hatempka, "you can now be happy. I have brought you your belt with the healing power. I claim as my reward your daughter, the beautiful Etanda. Give her to me, to be my wife, and I will return at once to my own country."

"Much happiness you have brought me, young man," replied Hatempka. "You have saved my people. Now the sun will shine again. Now the caribou, moose, musk-oxen, and bear will live again in our country. Once more we shall see the smoke of many lodges. Once more we shall hear the voices of many hunters.

"Yes, take my daughter, my beautiful Etanda. But do not go away. Stay with me and be a great man after me."

So Caribou-footed remained in the shining white home of Hatempka. He became the great chief of the Sky Country when Hatempka was no more.

And in the far north country, when the northern lights flit across the sky, the Indians bow their heads and say, "The fingers of Caribou-footed are beckoning us to the home beyond the sky. Soon some of us will pass to that great country where he has found a home for us, far, far away."

✳ SLAVEY

The origin of the Mackenzie River

Long ago, before there were any people in the land of the Slavey Indians, Great Slave Lake was much larger than it is today, and no river flowed from it to the north.

At the eastern end of the lake lived a giant, tall as a pine tree. His clothing was made of the skins of immense elk sewed together. His spear was a fir tree hardened in fire and tipped with the copper he found near Great Slave Lake.

Hungry one day, the giant went out hunting. After a while he found the house of Beaver—not the small house of the small beaver of today, but the immense house of the huge beaver of the days of old. After great effort the giant broke down the house. Out ran a female beaver and her young.

The giant killed the young beavers, but the mother escaped. Carrying one of the dead cubs on his shoulder, on the point of his spear, the giant pursued the mother beaver. She hurried across the water and he along the shore, until they reached the west end of the lake. There a wall of rock seemed to stop them. But Beaver made a hole through the rock and pushed herself through it. The water of the lake followed her. In the new river, Beaver was swept downward, far out of the reach of her pursuer.

The giant kept on following, however, until he reached the mouth of Bear River. There he was so hungry and so weary that he stopped to eat. Taking the cub from his shoulder, he made a fire and cooked it. So it was the giant of Great Slave Lake that started the fire which continues to burn, even today, in the beds of lignite along the Mackenzie River, near the mouth of Bear River.

And it was because of the courage and the strength of the immense beaver that, long ago, the Mackenzie River was released from Great Slave Lake and made its way to the Arctic Ocean.

 ✱ ESKIMO

The smoking mountains of Horton River

The Horton River flows into the Amundsen Gulf from the north western area of the Northwest Territories.

When the world was very young, the first human beings were never alone. They were always surrounded by spirit people. These spirit people lived like human beings; in fact, they were human, but they were invisible. Their bodies were not for our eyes; their voices were not for our ears.

Whenever the human people of the far north country travelled and pitched camp, they would begin immediately to build their snow huts. Then around the snowdrifts they would see the snow blocks begin to move, being lifted out of the drifts by invisible hands. By invisible hands the snow blocks were piled together into a snow house that seemed to grow out of itself. Occasionally someone might see the glitter of a copper knife, but that was all.

They were clever, these spirit people. And they did not object when human people came into their houses, which they arranged just like the houses of human beings. All their belongings were invisible, and people could trade with them very profitably. If anyone wished to buy something, all he needed to do was to point to it and show what he was willing to give for it. If the spirit people agreed to the trade, the object lifted itself up and moved toward the man who wanted it. If they did not agree, the object stayed where it was.

So the first people were never alone, whether they stayed in a village or travelled on a long journey. Always they had small, silent, invisible spirits about them.

But one day during a halt in a journey, a human person seized his knife and cried out, "What do we want with these people who are always right on our heels?"

With these words he shook his knife in the air and thrust it in the direction of the snow huts that had at once made themselves. No one heard a sound, but everyone saw that the knife became covered with blood.

From that moment on, the human people saw no sign of the spirits. Never again did they behold the wonderful sight of snowdrifts forming themselves into snow huts when they made camp. Forever they lost their silent, invisible guardians. The spirits had disappeared inside the mountains. There they lived, to escape from one who had mocked them and wounded their feelings.

That is why, to this day, smoke comes from the mountains near Horton River, from the enormous fires flaming inside them, beside which the spirit people do their cooking.

 LILLOOET

The great rock in the Fraser River

To the Indians who lived along the Fraser River in British Columbia, a tall granite rock near the foot of Big Canyon was a warning. As the following story explains, the rock reminded them that the first salmon caught at a village did not belong to the person catching it; it was to be honoured with religious ceremonies. The Spirit of Salmon would feel so honoured by the ceremonies that it would send plenty of salmon up the river to the people.

These First Salmon ceremonies were conducted solemnly, according to ancient ritual, and the entire village took part in them. At their conclusion, the chief declared the salmon season open.

Today, white people call the granite rock Lady Franklin Rock; when the explorer's widow tried to go up the Fraser in search of Sir John, the rock blocked the passage.

One year, a long time ago, the salmon were late in coming up the Fraser River. After a long and dreary winter, the supply of dried fish that had been prepared the summer before was exhausted. Roots and berries were slow in maturing. Game was scarce in the surrounding area, and because of enemy tribes, hunting in other places was unsafe. The people in the present village of Yale were in great need of food.

A certain woman named Sta-eel was in distress because her little ones were starving. One day when her husband was away hunting in the mountains, Sta-eel took a sweep-net down to the river to see if she could catch a salmon. She had little hope, for no salmon had been reported by the Indians along the lower river. But she dipped her net. A second time and a third time, she dipped it. The fourth time, to her great surprise and joy, she caught and landed a fine salmon.

She knew the tribal law, the tribal custom, concerning the first salmon. But she quickly concealed her catch in the bushes, and when darkness came she carried home the first salmon of the season. In secret she boiled it and fed it to her children. Mother and little ones devoured it hungrily.

As they were eating the last bites, lightning flashed and thunder rolled. Black clouds darkened the sky. A furious wind whipped the branches of the trees and the waters of the river.

The medicine men knew that someone had offended the spirits, perhaps the spirits of the salmon and of the river. Solemnly they began their chants, hoping to appease the wrath of the spirits and insure the coming of the salmon. But the chants met no response. The storm grew worse. The wind became stronger and stronger. The waves on the river became larger and larger. The people watched in terror.

Suddenly Sta-eel, at the door of her tepee, was picked up by the whirling wind and carried high into the air. Startled, her neighbours saw her in the air, then saw her drop into the midst of the river. There the angry waves seized her body and hid it beneath them. Still watching the river, the people saw a large granite rock quickly rise from the spot where the woman had disappeared. Soon it towered a great height above the rushing waters surrounding it.

Then the medicine men and other people of the village learned from Sta-eel's children what their mother had done. Everyone understood what had happened. The woman's body had been changed into a rock as a punishment and as a warning to any other person who might be tempted to disobey the law of the tribe.

Whenever the Indians of today see Sta-eel's Rock, they remember that the first salmon of the season should be greeted with general rejoicing and with reverent ceremony.

And whenever they observe the seven streams that flow down the mountainside near the great rock and near Yale, British Columbia, the Indians remember that the streams are the tears once shed by the seven children of Sta-eel.

✳ SQUAMISH

A legend of Siwash Rock

*Travellers entering the harbour of Vancouver notice a tall, grey rock
beneath Prospect Point, which is at the edge of Stanley Park. Close
up, one sees that the monolith resembles an erect human figure,
although a tuft of green shrubbery is on its summit. White people
call it Siwash Rock.*

*Squamish Indians call it T'elch. To them it symbolizes unselfish,
noble-spirited manhood. They have several legends about the rock, one
of which E. Pauline Johnson has made known in her Legends of Vancouver.*

*The following story of its origin came from Chief Matthias Kapalana
of the Squamish Indians.*

T'elch was a noble of the Squamish tribe, famed for his good deeds.
His constant care was to help others. His wives also were generous-
hearted and unfailing in their desire to be of service to their people.
The three lived under Prospect Point, in a rocky cave that was closed
by a stone door.

Whenever T'elch set out his lines for cod and sturgeon and halibut,
whenever he trapped salmon in some near-by stream, he did not
stop when he had enough for his own family. He kept on until he
had plenty of fish for the poor of his tribe. Similarly, when his wives
gathered berries and dug for roots in what is now Stanley Park, they
always planned to get enough for the needy. When they stripped
the cedar bark from the big trees and beat it and shredded it and
wove it into soft garments, they always laid by a stock from which
to aid people in distress.

T'elch had no enemies. He was respected and loved by all, and his
voice carried weight around the council fires. Everyone knew that his
opinion was given without prejudice. Everyone realized that he was
unselfish and that he wanted to do what was best for the whole tribe.

T'elch and his wives lived in the early days, when the world was
very young and the Changer was working his wonders on the earth.
The Great Chief Above sent the Changer from tribe to tribe, to give

to each person he saw whatever that person wished most. Hearing of this generosity to people among the neighbouring tribes, the Squamish excitedly awaited the coming of the Changer among them.

Men and women could think of but little else than the coming of the Changer. Watchers were set on the headlands to signal the approach of the mighty chief. He would come, they thought, with all the ceremony suitable to a messenger of the Great Chief Above, and the Squamish people planned an entertainment in keeping with the importance of the event.

Days and weeks passed without a sign of the coming of the Changer. These were anxious days—days of work and vigil, nights of fear that he might pass their village in the darkness. Men and women grew secretive. Friends no longer confided in each other, for each was holding fast to the wish that he hoped to have fulfilled, and dared not trust knowledge of it to another.

The harmony of village relations was so disturbed that the chiefs became worried. At last Chief Kapalana called a meeting of all the people.

"It is foolish," he said, "for you to be so secretive. Perhaps all of you are wishing for the same thing. Would it not be better for each of you to discuss your wish? Then we can arrange to ask the Great Chief Above for those things most helpful, not only to the individual, but to the tribe as a whole."

The people thought the chief's plan was sensible and agreed to it. Only one person invited to the meeting had not been there. That was T'elch. His absence caused some anxiety, and so several of the more important chiefs went to his home to find out why he had not come.

"What are you going to ask from the Changer?" inquired the chiefs.

"Nothing," replied T'elch.

"Nothing!" exclaimed his visitors in amazement. "Surely you are going to ask for something!"

"Why should I? The Great Chief Above has been very good to me. He has given me all that I want and has permitted me to obtain more than I really need, so that I may help the poor."

The chiefs looked at him in wonder for a while, and then one ventured the question, "But surely you will meet the great Changer when he comes?"

"No," replied T'elch, "I will not meet him. There will be plenty of people to bother him without my doing so."

"But if you do not meet him," suggested the one who had asked, "he may become angry and refuse to give anything to any of our people."

T'elch was silent for a moment and then said slowly, "Ah, that is different. If it will help others to get what they want, then I will gladly meet the good Changer when he comes."

And so it was settled. In order to make himself worthy of the honour of meeting the agent of the Great Chief Above, T'elch started to cleanse his mind and body. He fasted, in order to purify himself inwardly, and he took long swims in the cold sea-water to purify his body. So that his thoughts might not be distracted while purifying himself, he daily shut his two wives in the cave and closed the rock door.

One day when he was swimming, a canoe bearing four men approached. It was an ordinary canoe, and T'elch paid no attention to the strangers until one of them spoke.

"Greetings, swimmer. Who are you?"

"I am T'elch."

"And where do you live?"

"Over there at the point, in a cave with my two wives."

"And why are you purifying yourself?"

"To make myself worthy of meeting the good Changer when he comes to give each person the thing he wants most."

"Oh! And what are you going to ask from the Changer?"

"I am not going to ask him for anything," replied T'elch.

"You are not going to ask for anything! Why not?"

"Because I don't need anything. The Great Chief Above has been good to me. He has given me more than I need for myself, so that I am always able to help other people."

"But surely," persisted the man in the canoe, "you want something that some other person owns?"

"Oh, no," T'elch replied quickly. "Let others enjoy what they have. I do not wish to deprive them of their possessions."

For a moment the men in the canoe had a whispered conference. Then the one who had done all the questioning addressed T'elch again.

"I am the Changer. In our journey around the world, we have met no one but you who has been free from selfishness. We want you to stand, for all time, as an imperishable monument, so that those who look upon you will realize that they too should be unselfish."

As the Changer spoke, T'elch grew taller and changed to stone, to become an everlasting monument and inspiration to his people.

And behind the closed stone door in the rocky cave at Prospect Point, the two wives still wait patiently for the return of T'elch the Unselfish.

HAIDA

A story of the eagle crest

> *Many of the stories of the Indians of the north Pacific coast are concerned with the crests, or clans, to which a family belonged. Formerly there were two principal clans, or brotherhoods: the Raven and the Eagle. Each of these was divided into a number of smaller crests, all named after some animal or bird or fish.*
>
> *Eagle, like Raven, is often placed at the top of the carvings on totem poles. Here is one of the stories told by families belonging to the Eagle crest.*

Long ago a boy and his mother made their home with his uncle, a chief. The uncle did not like the boy and made his life so miserable that he decided to leave the house forever.

After wandering for a while, the boy was found by three women. One of them was the daughter of the head chief of the Eagles. Seeing him sorrowful and woe-begone, she asked him, "What is the matter, my boy?"

So he told her all his troubles.

"Come with me to my father's house," she said, when he had finished his story.

She led him into the woods and to a town, which was up on a tree. This was the town of the Eagles, and a large number of young birds were flying about. The woman took the boy to her home and presented him to her father, saying, "Father, I have found a nice husband."

The old chief was greatly pleased to see such a nice-looking son-in-law. The boy quickly became a young man, and he delighted in doing things to please his father-in-law. If the old chief wanted anything, off the young man went and got it for him.

One day the old man said he would like to have a piece of whale's flesh. So the young man dressed himself in a suit of the old chief's feathers and flew out to sea until he found a number of whales. From one he cut a piece, and then returned to the town of the Eagles.

The old chief was greatly pleased. And the young man was so delighted because he could fly that he was always on the wing. He wished to have a suit of feathers for himself. So he and his wife decided to ask the old father. When he heard their request, he went immediately to a box, and from it took enough feathers to make the son-in-law a full-grown eagle.

Some time later, the old chief asked the young man to get some more whale meat for him. So he dressed himself in his new suit of feathers and started forth. In a short time he returned with an entire whale.

While over the sea this time, the young man saw so many fish everywhere that now he spent his entire time flying among them. He left home early and returned only after nightfall. One day the old chief decided that he should warn his son-in-law of possible danger.

"If ever you come across Ahseak, the devil fish, do not take hold of it. Do not even touch it, for it may harm you."

Some time later, while flying around and not thinking of Ahseak, the young man saw a strange object floating below him. Curious, he flew down and took hold of it. It seized his hand and pulled him down under the water. There it held him, so that he was unable to get up, one arm only remaining above the sea.

Next day all the young eagles went out to search for the missing one. After flying about for some time, they thought of Ahseak. When they reached his place and saw the upheld hand, they wondered what it could be. One eagle after another took hold of the hand and tried to pull it out of the water. But as fast as they did so, they too went under, until not one was left. All formed a line under the water. Only the arm of the last eagle remained in view.

When none of the family returned, the mother eagle, the old chief's wife, went in search of them. She suspected Ahseak and went to his place in the ocean. When she saw the upheld arm, she knew at once what was wrong. Now Ahseak had no power against her. Without fear she took hold of the arm and pulled. One after another the young eagles came above the surface of the water, the son-in-law last.

As each of them came up, the mother eagle passed her hand over him a few times and restored him to life. When she had recovered all of them and made them well and strong, she only said, "What are you all doing here? Go home and never be seen here again."

And so they did, each of them a wiser young eagle.

The origin of mountain goats

The figure of a mountain goat carved on a totem pole signifies nobility. It is shown as a head with two horns. The story of this totem as explained by the Cowichans of Vancouver Island is as follows. It seems to refer to the end of the Ice Age.

Totem poles were carved and erected by the Indians along the north Pacific coast, from Vancouver Island to Alaska.

Our people once lived farther south than we do now, along the shores of Puget Sound. They were called the *Whull-e-Mooch*, which means "people who live on Puget Sound."

Long ago their country and the sea beside them became covered with snow and ice so thick that the heat of summer failed to melt them. Our fathers did not like so much cold, but they did not know where to go. They were afraid to go south because of a tribe much larger and stronger than they. North of them were even more snow and ice.

One time Raven came among them and learned about their trouble. He turned all of the snow and ice into mountain goats, and sent them to make their homes in the caves in the highest mountains.

"The goats will find plenty of food in the mountains," said Raven to the people. "And their flesh will make good food for all of you. You won't want to eat fish all of the time. And from the hair of the mountain goats, your women can make clothing and blankets."

And so Raven sent the snow and ice from the lower country. Then the climate became warmer and the land drier, along Puget Sound and as far as the people wished to travel. So they moved north to where we, their children, now live and where our fathers lived before us.

The spirit sacrifice

Several examples of human sacrifice among the Iroquois and Hurons were recorded by the Jesuit missionaries of the seventeenth and eighteenth centuries; usually the victims were captives who were burned in order that the victors might continue to have success in war.

The Chippewas occasionally sacrificed a virgin by placing her on a scaffold and presenting her "to the Great Spirit in order to obtain a prosperous success in war." Once in an Iroquois village a girl, made beautiful with ornaments, was led to the place of sacrifice, to satisfy a man's dream. "But when they thought him about to deal the death-blow, he cried out: 'I am satisfied; my dream requires nothing further.'"

The scene of the following Chippewa story was the St. Mary's River, which flows from Whitefish Bay in Lake Superior into the north end of Lake Huron. At St. Mary's Falls, the river descends about twenty feet a mile.

One summer, many years ago, there was a terrible plague among the Chippewas along Lake Superior. In some villages, every person had died of this dreadful sickness. The only band that had escaped was the one whose hunting-grounds lay on the north shore of the St. Mary's River. Their principal village stood on a bluff overlooking the great lake, at the head of the falls.

In the middle of the summer all the chiefs and warriors of the tribe assembled in this village for a grave council. For many days they offered sacrifices to the spirits, they chanted, they prayed to the spirits to keep the sickness from them. But every night they received messages from other bands that the disease was sweeping over the land, like the fires of autumn over the prairies. Signs in the skies also warned the wise men that this band too would soon be stricken by the plague.

On the last night of the council, they were in despair. They knew that the plague had been sent upon the earth by the spirits, as punishment for some wrong-doing. They knew too that only one thing would soften the anger of the spirits: the sacrifice of the most beautiful girl of her tribe. She should seat herself in her canoe, throw away her paddle, and allow her boat to float toward the falls.

Next morning, the council chose the beautiful girl for the sacrifice, believing that the good of the tribe was more important than the life of one person. When they announced their decision, a wail of sorrow broke upon the air. The maiden selected was greatly loved in the village, the only child of a widowed mother. But the girl herself accepted the decision calmly, without a sign of grief.

The girls and women of the village flocked round her and made her beautiful for the sacrifice, so that she would be welcome to the spirits. They dressed her in her best robe and adorned her hair with the most beautiful shells and feathers they could find. Around her neck they placed a string of brightly-coloured wampum beads.

As the day waned toward sunset, the hour set for the ceremony, the gloom of the people deepened. Their murmurs seemed to mingle with the roar of the waterfall. As the sun moved slowly toward the horizon, bright-coloured clouds gathered about it, and the waters of the lake were a deeper blue than ever before.

At the proper time, everything was ready. The old chiefs and the wise men silently and sadly conducted the girl toward the river-bank and her canoe. She was still calm, but her friends were wailing. Once during a pause in their lamentations, a strange echo came from over the waters. What did it mean? The echo was followed by a strange silence. The wailing women were quiet. Even the old men listened with fear, and the girl paused before stepping into her canoe. Then all heard another echo, louder and clearer than before.

All eyes were turned to the spot across the lake where the sound seemed to come from. They saw only a speck on the big lake. When the sun dropped below the horizon, the speck proved to be a small canoe. It seemed to come from the very spot where the red ball had touched the water. The strange sound was a song coming from a mysterious figure in the canoe. Rapidly, without paddles, the boat approached the people on the shore. In it they saw a beautiful being, a spirit in the form of a girl dressed in a snow-white robe. She was standing in the boat, her arms folded, her eyes fixed upon the sky. Now the listeners could understand the words of her song:

> I come from the Spirit-Land
> To soften the wrath of the spirits.
> I come to stop the plague
> And save the life of the beautiful girl.

On the spirit canoe came, following its path toward the mighty rapids in the river. Silent with astonishment, the Indians continued to watch the spirit girl. While they looked, the boat and its passenger moved into the white water and the foam. Soon it was lost to them forever.

And so the plague was lifted from the Chippewa nation, without the loss of the beautiful daughter of the widowed mother.

Today, all along the St. Mary's River, many lilies bloom in the summer, larger and whiter lilies than any found elsewhere. The Chippewas say that they spring from the body of the beautiful and mysterious spirit who saved them from the dreadful sickness, many years ago.

✳ MICMAC

The Little People

A belief in dwarfs, "the Little People," was held by most North American tribes. There are scattered references to them in many myths and legends; the Little People are often said to have done the picture-writing and painting on the rocks, and to keep the paint fresh; they were thought, by some tribes, to have strong spirit-power and so were greatly desired as guardian spirits.

One of these dwarfs seems to be very similar to Robin Goodfellow of British folklore.

Here are some Micmac traditions about the Little People.

The Little People are human beings, but very small. They live in caves, or they burrow in the ground. You may sometimes hear their footsteps in the forest on a still day, though they themselves are rarely seen. They generally remain quiet during the day but come out at night to revel and dance, to do mischief and perform wonderful deeds. If you should happen to offend them and they give chase, you must run for the nearest brook; if you succeed in reaching the further bank, you are safe. The Little People do not like to wet their feet.

One of them seems to be rather fond of fun, and he enjoys a joke at the expense of other people. Invisible, he comes prying around when you are busy, snatches up something that you are continually in need of, and slips it away. After he has enjoyed your embarrassment for a while, he slips the object back. Then lo! To your astonishment, it is before you, in plain sight.

Once in a while, in the forest, you will come upon stones piled together so as to make a little house. If you move them and go away, when you return later you will find them placed just as they were before you touched them. You will also observe many tiny footprints; if you follow them, they will lead you to a hole in some rock. If you really see these little people and associate with them, they will make you small like themselves. But you will not notice the change, and you will return to your normal size as soon as you leave them.

One day, long ago, when a girl was bathing in a river, she noticed a curious object floating down on the current. As it came closer, she saw that it was a tiny canoe paddled by an equally tiny man. Curious about him, she took the canoe in her hand and carried it home with her.

Her parents, when they saw the little man, were alarmed.

"Take him back at once!" they exclaimed. "Take him back where you found him, and let him go."

Crying with disappointment, the girl left the wigwam, but she played with the little man for some time before she carried him back to the stream. She set the canoe adrift at the very spot where she had picked it up, and then stood watching it. Coming to a rapid, it seemed to be in great danger of being swamped. Very much alarmed, the girl ran toward the rapid, but the little man guided the canoe skilfully through the white water and into the smooth stream beyond.

Before passing out of sight, the dwarf promised her that he would come back again. So every day she went down to the river to look for him.

One day when picking berries with some other girls, she saw a dozen tiny canoes coming up the river. In the first one was the little man she had played with on his earlier visit. He proved to be the head chief of a band of Little People. The dwarfs landed on the bank of the stream, and cooked a meal there. When they had finished eating, they said to the Micmac girls, "We will take you across the river in our canoes if you wish to go."

The girls laughed. "How can we go in canoes so small that we can pick them up in our hands?"

The Little People coaxed, but the girls only laughed again. At last the head chief asked his former captor to step into his canoe. Willing to humour him, she did so. To her astonishment, the moment she put her foot into it both canoe and chief grew as large as any canoe and chief of the Micmacs. But to her companions on the shore, she appeared very small.

At last she persuaded the girls to step into the other canoes. The instant they did so, she saw them have the same experience she had had: the boat and the paddler seem to grow large, each girl seemed to become small. The Little People took the whole group across the river. As soon as the girls stepped ashore, the canoes and the crew shrank to their former size and floated on downstream.

The Little People and the greedy hunters

The Little People who lived in the early world left their carvings to beautify rocks and cliffs and caves. And they helped the early Indians. Small though they were, the Little People were so strong that they killed many of the monster animals that were dangerous to man. "Our mission is to help you," a pigmy once told an Indian hunter. The bones of extinct animals found in their travels, the Indians believed, were the bones of the monsters that had been destroyed by the Little People.

The following legend of the Senecas, called a true story by the man who told it, reveals a little about the pigmies and also an attitude toward greediness and waste expressed in the stories of several North American tribes.

One time a party of hunters went on a hunting expedition to a region far from their homes. There they found game plentiful, and they killed many animals. In order to preserve and take home with them the skins and furs of these animals, they threw away large amounts of the meat.

When the hunters had finished preparing the hides in that region, they moved on farther north. There game was scarce. They found so little that they were soon in need of the meat they had thrown away. At last they were so hungry that they were near starvation.

After a while one of the Little People came among them.

"You are being punished because of your wastefulness and greed," he said. "You know that you should not kill so many animals and that you should not throw away their flesh."

"What must we do in order to obtain food now?" asked the hungry hunters.

"You must give up all the skins and furs you have collected and prepared for use," replied the little person. "If you do not give them up, you will have to starve."

The hunters talked among themselves and then asked, "How much time will you give us to discuss the matter?"

"When you have made your decision, just tap on a rock. Some one of my people will hear you and come for your answer."

For a long time the hunters discussed the matter, for they did not want to part with the hides. At last they decided to ask the Little People for better terms. So they tapped on a rock, and one of the pigmies appeared before them.

"If the amount of food you give us is small," said the hunters, "we will starve rather than accept your terms. For if we do not have enough food, we shall be unable to reach home. And we are in strange country. Give us a guide to show us the way to our own land."

"I cannot grant your request unless my people give their consent," answered the little man. "But I will bring you enough food to relieve your present hunger."

He then led them to a large cave, in which the Indians found some food and he told them to remain there until the Little People gave them permission to leave.

Next day the pigmy came back with a cheering message.

"You have been forgiven for your greed and your wastefulness," he told the hunters. "My people have decided to provide you with food, without forcing you to give up your furs. You are to remain in the cave until someone calls for you."

About midnight, when the men were wakened, they were surprised to find themselves in their first camping place. When they told their Seneca friends about their experiences, they ended with the statement: "We were brought back by our friends, the Little People."

The hunters used those words whenever they told the story, and they never forgot the lesson the Little People had taught them.

✳ M I C M A C

The water fairies

> *This story from the Micmac Indians of Nova Scotia has some interesting parallels with the old Danish folktale that Matthew Arnold used in his poem "A Forsaken Merman" and also with "The Mortal Who Married a Merman," from the Coos Indians of the Oregon coast.*

Far within a thick forest a young man lived with his parents and older brother. One day while walking along the shore of a lake, he saw a group of beautiful young women playing ball. He was so pleased by their beauty that he moved quietly near and watched them at their play. They looked different from any girls he had ever seen, for they were dressed in the costumes of the old days.

At last one of them saw him and cried in alarm, "Look out!" None of them had ever seen a man before and so, frightened, they dived into the water and disappeared from his view.

The young man was greatly disappointed, for they were so pretty that he wanted to capture one of them. Thinking that they might return, he planned how he would conceal himself. First he broke from its stem a peculiar leaf that has a kind of cover over its top, probably the jack-in-the-pulpit, and placed it on a rock near the lake. Then he made himself very small and hid in the leaf.

After a while he heard the girls come out of the water and begin again their game of ball on the shore. They were near him and yet too far away for him to reach them. Hoping to attract their attention, he jumped up and down in the leaf and moved nearer them. Just as he was about to seize one of them, she saw him and cried out as before. Again the water fairies dived into the lake and disappeared. Again the young man was discouraged, but soon he was more determined than ever to win one of them for his wife.

While trying to think of a new way of hiding, he saw a bunch of reeds growing near the water. He broke off one of them, saw that it was hollow, and hid himself within it.

A third time the water fairies arose from the lake and continued their game of ball. Again they came near the hiding place of the young man, but again something alarmed them and they all ran toward the water. This time, however, the young man seized one of them before she could disappear. She begged him to let her go. "I am married," she said, in response to his plea. "But if you will let me go, I will bring my younger sister to you tomorrow."

He released her, and she kept her promise. Next day she returned with her beautiful young sister, who willingly followed the young man to his wigwam.

After their first child was born, the young wife said that she wished to see her father and mother again. The husband consented, saying that he would like to go with her. So they travelled to the lake, the mother carrying the baby in a case on her back. At the shore, she walked straight on into the lake. At first, her husband was afraid to follow, but she persuaded him to go with her, even under the surface of the water.

Soon things began to look very much as they did in the upper world. After a while they reached a large village in the midst of a wooded country of great beauty.

"My father is chief here," the wife explained. And she led her husband to his lodge, where they and the child were warmly welcomed.

The chief and his wife had the form of fish below the waist, of human beings above. The father was the ruler of the many kinds of fish living in the village.

For some time the little family from the above world lived pleasantly in the village, but at last the man wanted to return home. He and his wife had not gone far when they were pursued by a huge shark. For a while they thought that they could escape its grasp, but later the wife's strength began to fail her. She took from her back the case in which she carried the child and fastened it on her husband's back.

"Do not wait for me," she said, "but save yourself and the baby. Go straight toward the sun, and you will reach the shore at the point where we left it. I will try to follow you."

The man did as she directed, and so reached the lake shore. With the child he sat there, waiting, for a long time. But his wife did not appear. At last he knew that she must have been captured by the shark, and so he went sorrowfully home.

✳ CHIPPEWA

The cannibal giant

Giants appear frequently in North American mythology. Some of them are human in form, some bird, some animal. Usually they are males, and most of them are cannibalistic.

On the shores of the Lake of the Woods stood an Indian village. One summer day, after a heavy rain had passed over the country, a Giant suddenly appeared in the village. He was as tall as the tallest hemlock, and he carried in his hand a club which was longer than the longest canoe.

"I come from a country in the far north," he said to the people of the village, "and I am tired and hungry. You must bring me all the wild rice and game that you have. Even that may not be enough to satisfy me."

His orders were obeyed, and all the people of the village gathered to see him enjoy the food that was brought. But when he had eaten every morsel, the Giant said that he was still hungry. With one blow of his huge club he killed all the people who had treated him with kindness. Only one person escaped—a little boy who happened to be sick in one of the wigwams.

During the night, the Giant ate a number of the dead bodies, and then he disappeared. He had not discovered the little boy. In a few days the child was well enough to move about, and as he went from one lodge to another, he was made unhappy by their emptiness. He remembered all his relatives and friends, and thought bitterly of the Giant Cannibal.

For many years he lived alone. First he lived largely on such birds as the partridge. But as he grew older, he became a successful hunter who often feasted on deer and buffalo. He grew to be a strong man, but a very lonely one. Every time he thought of the Giant who had destroyed his people, he thirsted for revenge.

As time passed, the hunter became more and more lonely and discontented. He decided to fast and to ask the spirits to give him power to find and destroy the Giant Cannibal. Taking pity on him, the spirits sent to his aid a troop of one hundred men, from whose backs grew the most beautiful wings he had ever seen.

"We know all about the Giant," they said, "and we will help you find him and kill him. He is very fond of the meat of the white bear. If you will give a bear feast, the Giant will come and ask you for some of the choicest parts."

They agreed that the feast should take place in a large natural wigwam, formed by the locked branches of many trees. As soon as they had decided upon the day for the feasting, the hundred strangers disappeared, and the hunter started toward the north in search of a bear.

He killed a bear, prepared the feast, and, at the time agreed upon, the strange people with wings returned. First, all danced and sang, for the feast was a joyous one. When the bear soup was filling the wigwam with a pleasant odour, all heard a heavy tramp in the woods. In a short time the Giant appeared, attracted to the place by the smell of the food. He rushed in like one who knew nothing about fear, but when he saw the winged people he became quiet.

"May I join you in your feast?" he asked the hunter.

"You may join us if you will go to the nearest stream emptying into the lake and bring back a large rock that you will find there."

The Giant was angry at the request, but the people with wings made him afraid to disobey. He did as he was bidden, although the thong he used to hold the rock on his back cut a deep gash in his forehead.

Not yet satisfied, the hunter now said to the Giant, "Before we admit you to the feast, you must bring to the wigwam a gill-net that will reach across the widest stream."

So the Giant obtained a huge net from a mammoth spider that lived in a cave, and brought it to the hunter.

Pleased but still not satisfied, the hunter said, "One more thing is necessary before we can admit you to the feast. You must come dressed in a robe of weasel skins which still have on them all the teeth and claws."

In due time the Giant obtained the weasel skins, made the robe, and appeared at the wigwam wearing it. The feast then began, and it lasted for several days and nights. The hunter, the strange people with the wings, and the Giant danced and caroused together as if they were the best of friends. The Giant was delighted with the singers and praised them before all the company. He did not know that in his bowl of soup the hunter had placed a bitter root that would deprive him of all his strength.

On the last night of the feast, the Giant became so tired and stupid that he asked permission to sleep awhile. That was just what the hunter wished. In the centre of the lodge the strangers spread the weasel-skin robe, and the Giant lay down upon it. He rested his head on the stone he had brought from the river, and over him was spread the net he had brought from the mammoth spider. Quickly he fell into a deep sleep, while the others continued their revelry.

Each of the one hundred men with wings seized his war-club, and all formed a ring round the sleeping Giant. Together they danced the dance of revenge. At a signal from the hunter, everyone gave the sleeping figure a heavy blow with his war-club. Then the spirit-men disappeared into the air, and the weasel skin was transformed into a host of small animals. Hungrily they feasted upon the body of the Giant, and by morning there was nothing left of him but his bones.

These bones the hunter gathered into a heap and burned to ashes. Then he threw the ashes into the air. Immediately he was surrounded by all the beautiful birds that now fill the world.

In this way the Giant Cannibal was destroyed, and his body was turned into birds, some of which are used as the food of man.

✱ IROQUOIS

The punishment of the witches

The Indians of the eastern woodlands told many tales about witches, many of which are similar to European witch stories. Indian witches were men as well as women.

Such tales were not prevalent in the tribes of other areas, though witchcraft was practised by evilly disposed persons among them.

One time a man suspected that his brother's illness was caused by witches. Wanting to find out who they were and where they met, he went to an old woman and said to her, "I want to be a witch."

"If you are very much in earnest," she replied, "you may become a witch. First, you must go to your sister and point at her. She will be taken sick and after a while she will die."

Then the old woman directed him where to meet her in the woods that night, if he still wanted to become a witch. The man went to his sister, reported to her what the woman had said, and made a plan with her. At the proper time she was to pretend that she was ill and was to tell people the pretended cause of her illness.

When night came, the brother started for the place where he was to meet the old woman. As he walked along, he now and then broke off a leaf or a bit of underbrush. Suddenly he saw the old woman he was to meet spring into a tree in front of him and cling to it. When she turned to face him, she was a huge panther, with sharp teeth, long claws, and glaring eyes. As she spat and snarled at him, he was terribly frightened, but he pretended to have no fear. When she came down the tree as an old woman, she asked, "Did I frighten you?"

"Oh, no," he answered, "I was not at all afraid."

As they walked on together, he again broke off twigs and leaves from the underbrush, here and there.

After a while they came to an open place in the woods, where were gathered many old men and women, and some young women too. The man was surprised at some he found there. In the middle of the clearing was a fire, and over the fire hung a little kettle, not much larger than a teacup. Over it hung a bunch of snakes, from which blood slowly dropped into the kettle. From time to time all the witches drank some of the blood. Pretending to drink, the man looked carefully about him. He found that the people had taken various shapes and were doing many strange things.

"What would you like to be?" they asked him.

"A screech owl," he replied.

So they gave him the head of an owl and told him to put it on later. "When you wear it," they said, "you will be able to fly like a bird." Then when he showed that he was able to imitate the cries and movements of an owl, they said, "You will be a witch chief."

With the owl's head on his head, the man seemed to lose control of himself. He flew over the trees to the house of his sick brother, just as the meeting broke up. The witches went off in various forms —as foxes, wolves, panthers, hawks, and owls.

When the man came to his brother's house, he flew to the roof and made sounds just like an owl. All the people in the house were frightened. Then the man took off the owl's head, came down from the roof, and went into the house. He pointed at the dog, instead of at his sister, and the dog sickened and died. The man's sister pretended to be sick, as they had agreed, and the witches came to see her. They mourned for her, and everywhere they went they talked about her illness, just as if they had not intended her death.

Next day the man gathered together all the warriors of the village and told them what he had seen. After discussing the matter, they agreed to get their weapons and to follow him. That night he led them through the woods, finding his way by the broken underbrush. When they reached the spot where he had been the night before, the meeting of the witches had begun. They had officers and orators, and one of them was making a speech.

"If you kill any people," the orator was saying, "you will go to heaven, and the Good Spirit will reward you well. You really will save your victims from much evil if you kill them, for if they lived they might become bad. If they die now, they will go to the Good Spirit."

The warriors listened for a few minutes. Then the leader gave a signal, the men rushed in, and soon they had killed all of the witches.

Next day the man's brother recovered from his sickness.

✳ CHIPPEWA

The story of Lone Bird, the woman in the moon

> The following legend was recorded in 1848 by the distinguished archaeologist Ephraim Squier; he heard it beside a campfire on the shore of Lake Superior, related by George Copway, an educated chief of the Chippewas. In another version, the girl is called Sweet Strawberry.
>
> The story has a unique combination of two themes frequent in folktales: the origin of the face in the full moon and the "son-in-law test."

Many snows in the past, before white people invaded the lands of the Indians, the Chippewas were great and strong. And they were as numerous as the leaves on the maple trees. They hunted the buffaloes on the prairies of the West, they trapped the beaver in the lakes and rivers, they hunted the deer in the forests around the Great Lakes, they caught the fish in the streams that flow from the mountains toward the rising sun. They were feared and respected by their enemies and loved by their friends. The Good Spirit, the Master of Life, was pleased with his children, and his children were happy.

In those long ago years, there lived on the shores of the big water now called Lake Superior a beautiful girl whose name means Lone Bird. She was the only child of her father, Dawn of Day, and of her mother, She Eagle. Lone Bird was as graceful as a birch tree, and her voice was like the song of a stream at twilight. She was tall and slender, and no daughter of the tribe had such beauty of face.

From all the villages of the Chippewa nation came the young men to seek the favour of Lone Bird and ask to bear her from the lodge of her father. But she looked coldly upon all of them. In vain they recited to her their success as hunters and their bravery as warriors. In vain they brought choice gifts to the lodge of Dawn of Day. The heart of Lone Bird was like the ice of winter, and the young men had to return home, lonely and sad.

Dawn of Day, realizing the coldness of his daughter, tried to bring some warmth into her heart. He praised the skill and the bravery of the young men he knew and trusted; he reminded her that no maiden in the tribe had so noble a group of lovers from whom to choose a husband.

But when her father ended his speech, Lone Bird laughed and said to him, "Do I not have my mother to love me? Do I not have my father to protect me and care for me? What need have I for the young men? Why should I choose a husband?"

Dawn of Day made no answer. But next morning he went forth from his lodge, called the most trusted young men of the village to him, and told them the plan he had made during the night.

"At a certain time that I shall announce later," he said to them, "all who wish to wed my daughter will gather here on the shore of the lake. Here you will run a race. The one who proves to be the fleetest of foot shall win my daughter and carry her to his lodge."

At the father's words the hearts of the young men filled with joy. Eagerly each youth prepared himself for the race. Hopefully each prayed for fleetness of foot like the deer.

The news of the contest to be held spread through all the villages of the Chippewa nation. And so, on the morning which Dawn of Day set for the race, a great crowd of people gathered at the appointed place on the shore of Lake Superior. Everyone wanted to see who would win the beautiful Lone Bird.

The old men were there, for they were to judge the race and award the prize. Mothers were there, to encourage their sons. Their daughters were there, to see the young men and to be seen by them. And of course, the young men were there, painted in the best manner and plumed with the feathers of the turkey and the eagle.

Only one person of the tribe was missing—Lone Bird. She sat in the lodge of her father and mother, weeping.

All was ready for the contest. The bounds of the race were set, and the judges gravely took their places. The young men lined up at the starting point, their muscles quivering, their hearts beating with excitement. The instant the signal was given, they dashed forward.

Soon two runners were far ahead of the others. They were Bending Bow and Who-Strikes-the-Game, both of whom had loved Lone Bird for a long time. Each was as fleet as a deer, as swift as the wind. Neither could surpass the other. And when they came to the end of the course, the judges could not tell which of the two was the winner.

So Bending Bow and Who-Strikes-the-Game ran again, and again they came in side by side. A third time they ran. A third time the judges could not announce a victor.

"This time, let them jump," someone suggested.

But when they jumped, neither could surpass the other the breadth of a hair.

"Let them show their skill in hunting," someone suggested.

So next morning Bending Bow and Who-Strikes-the-Game hunted in different parts of the forest. On their return, each of them threw down at the feet of the old men the skins of twenty bears he had slain.

Then was the heart of Dawn of Day troubled, for he saw in these incidents the hand of the Good Spirit. He returned to his lodge in silence, wondering what he should do. There he found Lone Bird with head bowed to the ground, her eyes red with weeping. Her father's heart was touched, for he loved his beautiful daughter.

He lifted her gently and said to her kindly, "Why do you weep, my daughter?"

"Why do you wish to cast me from you?" she replied. "Is not the home of Dawn of Day large enough for his only daughter?"

Again his heart was touched. "Never," he promised, "shall Lone Bird leave the lodge of her father."

Then he returned to the people still gathered beside the lake. "The contest is ended," he said to them. "Bending Bow and Who-Strikes-the-Game have done well, but it is the will of the Good Spirit that my daughter shall not leave me."

"It is the will of the Good Spirit," repeated the old men.

And so the people returned to their villages and to their homes. The contests were ended.

The summer and the autumn passed, and the winds of winter blew across the lake. When the snows began to melt, Dawn of Day went to the sunny slope of a hill to make maple sugar. Lone Bird went with him and helped him gather the sweet juice in vessels made of birch-bark.

One day when the smoke was curling up slowly from her father's fire, she seated herself on a flat rock and looked round. The sun was warm and bright, the world was beautiful, but the heart of Lone Bird was sad. She thought of her father and mother, of their grey hair and their slow steps. She knew that old age and death were not far from them.

"What will become of me when they are gone?" she asked herself. "I have no brother or sister, no sister's children to be like my own."

For the first time in her life she felt alone and lonely. Looking down on the early spring flowers blooming at the edge of snow-banks, she noticed that the blossoms were in pairs, two on a stem. Each flower seemed to add beauty to the other. Birds busy with nest-building reminded her that they too always lived in pairs. At that moment she heard the high-pitched tootling of a flock of geese over the lake. Turning her head, the girl saw them alight on the water and then glide away—in pairs.

"Neither flowers nor birds live alone," Lone Bird said to herself.

Her observations made her feel more alone than ever. She remembered her coldness to the young men who had wished to woo her. She recalled her father's kindly chiding and his attempts to choose between Bending Bow and Who-Strikes-the-Game.

"But I still do not want any of the young men," she said to herself. "I am all alone. Alas! Why did the Good Spirit fill the hearts of birds with a love denied to me?"

For a long time the girl sat there on the rock above the lake, wrapped in her sad thoughts. When she rose to go, it was evening and the full moon was making a silver path on the water. Lone Bird looked longingly at the bright ball in the sky. Stretching forth her arms toward it, she exclaimed aloud, "Oh, how beautiful you are! If I had someone like you to love and to be loved by, I would no longer be lonely."

The Good Spirit heard the voice of Lone Bird and quickly carried her up to the moon.

While she had sat upon the rock, her father had finished his work. Not seeing her, he had decided that she had returned home, and so he too had gone. Not finding her in the lodge, he came back to the place where he had made the maple sugar. From there he called his daughter's name, again and again. But no voice answered him.

Sad and anxious, he lifted his eyes toward the sky, toward the moon shining so brightly. There he saw his daughter in the arms of the moon. Comforted by the sight, he grieved no longer. He knew that his daughter would always be cared for tenderly.

Many, many snows have come and gone since the days of Lone Bird and her father, Dawn of Day. Their people have become few, and they are weak. Strangers occupy their old hunting grounds, and the graves of their fathers are unhonoured.

But the flowers still bloom when spring comes to the lake country. The face of Lone Bird can still be seen in the moon, and she still looks down upon her people as they tell her story by the light of the lodge fires.

 CHIPPEWA

Blessed by a serpent

> For information about the concept of Indian religion that forms the background of this story and of the next two, see "The Guardian Spirit Quest," in the second section. The purpose of the fasting and the vigil was to obtain one of the spirits of nature as a personal guide and protector who gave the individual special abilities or powers.
>
> These tutelary spirits were sometimes thought of as the spirits of the animal people of the mythological age.

This is the story of a man who was helped by the blessing he received when he fasted.

When a boy fasts, he does not eat for ten days, except a little at sundown when the sun cannot see him. He sleeps all the time, waiting for some spirit to come and bless him, so that he may be protected through life.

When the young man of this story fasted, he was blessed by a serpent, whose spirit told him that he would never be killed. Next morning, when the older man who had instructed him came to see him, the young man related what he had dreamed.

"That's a very good blessing," the old man said. "Accept it, for the serpent will take good care of you."

The young man was helped by this blessing until he became a very old man. Then the spirit of the serpent deserted him.

Once when the man and his three sons were living near a lake, he said to them, "We are going to be attacked by the Mohawks, for they have discovered us. We will place a boat near the shore, so that our women may escape across the lake during the night. There are one hundred of these Mohawks, and we are only four. But we will come through this fight alive, because of my fasting. The serpent told me all about this attack when he blessed me during my fast.

"The day after tomorrow we will send the women away. In about three days from now we shall have to fight."

So his three sons placed all their boats along the lake, and the women escaped. When the third morning dawned, the old man arose ready to fight. Three times he gave the war-whoop.

All day long these four men fought the one hundred Mohawks. Not one of the four was killed, for they were not seen by the enemy. The men were protected by the spirit of the serpent.

When night came, the old man took sick.

"We must escape, for I am ill," he said to his sons. "Follow me."

The three sons followed their father and, under the water, they walked across the lake. When they came up on the other side, the Mohawks saw them and started to pursue them. The young men took turns hiding themselves and fighting the enemy, while their father went on ahead. When they had killed all of the warriors who had followed them, they caught up with their father near a bay.

They all got into a birch-bark canoe and went out into the lake. When they were out a little distance, the father began to sing his song, turning his boat round and round as he sang.

After he had finished, they went on again. By paddling all night, they landed on the other side of the lake at daybreak. There they joined their women.

This was one man's blessing—to know, three days in advance, just what was going to happen. Some people are blessed so that they can see distant things and persons. They build a little hut and throw their shirts into it, and the person they want to see appears inside the hut.

In these ways, and others, the people who have fasted are blest.

✳ CHIPPEWA

The dream of Little Raven

The following personal experience was related, through an interpreter, to J. G. Kohl, a German traveller around Lake Superior in 1855. Before beginning the reminiscence, the old Indian filled his pipe and smoked it to the very end; this was done in order to make peace with the spirits that would hear the story.

This story happened to me when I was a small boy. I was so young that when I was standing and my father was seated on a mat, we were the same height. It was autumn, and harvest time. I had gone with my father to gather wild rice.

One day when we were hard at work, all of us busy husking the grain and filling our canoes, I heard gun shots in the distance. They came first from our village, and were replied to from the neighbouring village. The shots meant that someone in our village had died.

As soon as I heard them, I stopped working for I felt sad and mournful. "My mother is dead," I thought to myself. Soon we saw the messengers hurrying toward the lake where we were gathering our harvest. They brought with them the sad news of the death of my mother.

With heavy hearts we buried her. I wanted to go alone into the forest, to weep out my grief in solitude. But my father, uncle, and four sisters would not let me go alone, and they watched me closely when they saw how sad I was.

One time when my father and uncle were away, I sprang away from my sisters and ran into the forest as fast as I could. When I was a safe distance from the village, I began to weep loudly and to call for my mother. As I cried, I ran farther and farther into the forest. At last I climbed a tall tree, where I wept until no tears were left within me. Exhausted by my grief and by my running, I remained there in the tree.

Suddenly I heard a voice near me and I saw a black form hovering over me. "Who are you?" the voice asked. "And why do you weep?"

"My name is Little Raven," I replied. "And I weep because my mother is dead."

"Come with me," said the person in black. And she took me by the hand.

Through the air, we took one step to the next tree, a white pine. When we stepped on the top of it, it trembled and bent, and I feared it would give way under us.

"Fear not," the stranger said, "but step firmly. The tree will bear us."

Then she put out the other foot, and with the second step we reached the top of a tall young birch. This tree also shook greatly and bent down, and again I feared that we would fall to the ground.

"Fear not," my companion said again. "Step firmly. The tree will hold us."

We took a third step through the air and came to the foot of a tall mountain. But what had seemed to me to be three steps was, in reality, three days' journey. During the nights we had rested on the tops of the trees, and many forests and prairies already lay behind us.

When we had climbed the mountain and stood on its top, my guide asked me, "Do you know this mountain?"

"No, I do not."

"It is the mountain of the Stag's Heart."

Then she waved her hand. The mountain opened, and we saw, through a long narrow ravine, the sunlight shining brightly at the other end. We went through the rift at the far end, my companion gliding along before me. At the other end of the ravine we walked out into the light and the sunshine. In the centre of brilliant sunshine was a house.

"Go in there," my companion said to me.

The door opened and I walked inside, but my guide remained outside. Indoors, the light was so dazzling that I covered my eyes with my robe. I trembled with fear and curiosity. At last a voice from the back of the room began to speak to me.

"Little Raven, when I saw that you were sorrowing for your mother, I sent for you. You are very welcome in my home. Look around you. You can now see how I live and how things are with me."

When I became used to the light, I looked round me. At first I saw nothing but a lamp hanging in the middle of the hut, which gave a brilliant light. It was the Lamp of the Sun. The Sun himself was sitting behind the lamp. It was his voice that I had heard. Now he said to me, "Look down!"

When I looked down through an opening in the floor, I saw the earth far below us—the forests, the mountains, the Big Sea water, and the whole round of the world.

"Now look up!" said the Sun.

When I looked up through an opening in the roof of the house, I saw the whole curve of the heaven above, and the stars so close that I could grasp them.

After I had looked and looked, at the earth below and the stars above, the voice of the Sun spoke again. "Now look straight forward. What do you see? Do you know the one you see?"

I looked and I was frightened, for I saw my own image.

"Remember," said the Sun, "that you are always near me. I see you every day, and I watch over you. I know what you are doing, and whether you are ill or well. So be of good cheer.

"Now look out to your right and to your left. Do you know the four persons that surround you? They are a gift that I, the great source of life, make to you. These four are in you. They will come from you. They are your four sons. Your family will grow in numbers. You will live for many years, and your hair will become like mine in colour. Look at it."

So I looked on the white locks of the Sun Spirit. They shone like silver, like the moon trail on the water. A feeling of joy came over me, knowing that I should have so long and happy a life.

"In remembrance of your visit to me," continued the Sun, "and for a good omen, I give you this bird, which soars high above us. And I give you this white bear with the brass collar.

"Now I must tell you farewell. The woman I sent to bring you to me will lead you home. She is waiting for you."

And giving me the two gifts, the Sun Spirit sent me away. These gifts were spiritual gifts, not the actual creatures themselves. That is the kind of gift an Indian receives in his vision. Ever since my dream, the spirit of the eagle and the spirit of the bear have been my protecting spirits.

When my companion and I descended to the earth, the height seemed to me immeasurable—far greater than when we had climbed up to the house of the Sun. We spent one whole night descending. Early in the morning we reached the earth, when one half the sun's disk had risen above the horizon. As we stood on the last fir tree. at dawn, we saw a black dog running past.

"That dog you will give to me," said my companion. "Next spring, sacrifice it to me."

I promised her that I would. After she let me down from the last tree above our own forest, she spoke again. "Four persons will come directly to fetch you, but do not follow them if they try to seize you with naked hands. If they have leaves of the lime tree in their hands and seize you with them, it is good. Follow them.

"Now farewell, Little Raven. I will leave you here where I found you."

Shortly after my guide started back, I heard voices under me, under the tree where I had cried myself to sleep.

One voice said, "I am going here to seek him."

Another voice said, "I am going there."

I felt too weak to turn around and see who was speaking.

Suddenly I heard a voice cry, "What is that up in the tree? A boy? Yes, yes! Come here, my sisters! I have found our brother!"

The voices belonged to my sisters. They had come out to find me after I had run from the lodge.

"But he dreams a deep dream," said the oldest of my four sisters. "Do not touch him with naked hands. Pluck leaves from the lime tree and cover your fingers with them, before you take him down."

And so they covered their hands with lime leaves, took me from the tree, and carried me home. I was so weak and ill that I could eat nothing for three days. My sisters took care of me, and in time I began to eat like the others and I recovered.

I have never forgotten my dream. When I have caught young eagles in my traps, I have let them go, in memory of my vision. I took as my token the image of the white bear with the brass collar. I have scratched it a hundred times on my pipes, I have sewed it in my blankets, I carved it from a piece of wood and carried the carved image always in my medicine bundle.

All that the spirit of the Sun promised me has come to pass. I married and brought up four sons. I have lived a long and good life, and my hair has grown white like the silver hair of the Sun Spirit. I am now one hundred years old.

Every autumn, at the time of the rice crop, I dream of my mother. I see her and speak with her, and I dream that I am walking along the path of the dead. Soon, I know, all that I dream will come to pass.

✴ ASSINIBOINE

The vision of Chief Walking Buffalo

For many years, visitors at the annual Banff Indian Days have seen Chief Walking Buffalo's yellow tent at the campground, and in the parade they have seen him wearing a buffalo head and horns. Many have heard the friendly, kindly address with which he closed the programs.

When he was about eighty-two years old, he told the following story of a vision he had in his youth that influenced him all his adult life. He was one of the last "medicine men" of the Stoney Indians.

When I was a child, I had dreams, but I never thought much about them until I was grown. Then I remembered that a buffalo had talked to me in all those dreams. And I realized that the buffalo's purpose on earth was to save life. I remembered that human beings depended on the buffalo for food and for many other things they needed.

In one of my dreams, the buffalo showed me what I should do. The Great Spirit, God, was using him to talk to me, to tell me how I should live in order to help people.

"You are to be helpful to human beings," the buffalo of my dreams told me, "as helpful as we have always been. You must be strong, and feel strong, so that you can help others. The Great Spirit put you on earth to help other people, just as he put the buffalo on earth to help human beings."

When the spirit voice gave me that message, I had just come out of the paint springs where the yellow ochre is. I was then purified in body and in spirit.

"The paint spring," the voice told me, "represents a buffalo tent. You will have a buffalo-skin tent, and you will paint it yellow."

Then the buffalo in my dream showed me the designs I should paint on my yellow tent. I should paint a range of mountains and a row of tepees at the foot of the mountains. All the tepees should face the west. I should paint a circle to represent the sun, and the figure of a buffalo to indicate my name.

Then in my vision I saw myself running around a circle of tepees, while several buffaloes watched me from the top of a near-by hill. When I got around the circle, I felt like a buffalo.

The voice spoke to me again. "Roll on the ground."

So I rolled on the ground.

"Shake yourself like a buffalo that has just rolled on the ground." When I shook myself, several things fell from my body to the ground.

Those things were ammunition thrown at me by the people living in the painted tepees on my tent. The ammunition did not penetrate my body. It represented evil words, unkind words, desires to hurt me and kill me. Such things would have no effect upon me.

Then the buffaloes who were watching me had a scalp dance. They sang a song about a victory they had had. They said to me, "You can use an old buffalo head, a buffalo skull. Hold it by the horns. When you do, it will give you power.

"If ever you lose your strength, if you ever need us, act the way I have told you. That is, roll on the ground shake yourself, and then take hold of the horns on your buffalo skull. We will give you spirit-power. You can use your spirit-power to help other people, even to save human lives.

"You are to use this skull in the Sun Dance lodge. Put it beside the Sun Dance pole. Use for the centre pole no tree except the Balm of Gilead tree. It represents the tree of life. Make a nest in the fork of the tree. It will represent the home of human beings. In the Sun Dance lodge you will pray to the Great Spirit."

And so the buffalo has been the source of my strength. It has given me the power to heal sick people. Just as the buffaloes were helpful to everyone, regardless of the tribe, so I have always tried to help everyone. That is why I now want to be helpful by trying to bring peace among all peoples.

This is the end of my vision and of the message of the buffaloes I saw in my dreams, but I want to tell you more about the Sun Dance.

The Sun Dance is a truly religious ceremony. It is not held every year or even every two years. A person may vow that if a loved one who is sick recovers, he will gather the people together in the Sun Dance. Or perhaps the Great Spirit tells a man that the people should get together and pray, in order to prevent a bad thing from happening. The Great Spirit has given that man the power to foretell future events.

The man who is to bring the people together for the Sun Dance has to make a vow that he has led an honest, good life for six months before the dance is held and that he will lead it for six months afterward. Only if he keeps that vow will the Great Spirit answer his prayer.

"Whatever good thing you ask," the spirit says to the man, "you will receive it. If you ask for mercy and strength, you will receive it."

The Great Spirit is with the sun. The clouds, the winds, the water, the animals—all are the servants of the Great Spirit. The sun looks after everything—the herbs in the ground, people, animals—everything. It is ruler of health and strength, of all things that feed human beings.

Everything in the Sun Dance lodge has a meaning. The four poles overhead symbolize the four corners of the earth, the four directions. The twelve upright poles are part of the Mystery. They may refer to the twelve tribes of Israel or to the twelve apostles, or to the twelve virtues in the Indian religion—right speech, right action, and the others. As I said, they are part of the Mystery.

The banners you asked about, the banners you saw attached to the Sun Dance pole, are gifts to nature—gifts to the sun, the wind, the clouds, the water. The people are grateful. They give gifts to nature, because nature gives them everything. Then they give gifts to people —to their guests and to the needy among their own people.

In a vision, somewhat like the vision of my youth, the Great Spirit has told someone when to have the Sun Dance. It was the great religious ceremony of all our people of the plains.

✱ MALECITE

"Let us bury the hatchet"

Long before the white men took our country from us, the worst enemies of the Malecite tribe were the Mohawks. Their war parties used to portage from the St. Lawrence to the head of the St. John River and then journey down the St. John until they came to our villages. In the darkest nights, when there was no moon, they would attack our settlements—burn our camps and tomahawk our women and children.

Early one morning, many moons ago, one of our young men went out in his canoe and paddled up the St. John River until he came to the mouth of the Muniac River. He planned to spear some fish. While paddling along, he thought he saw smoke rising from the river's bank, near where the little stream flows into the main stream. Pushing his canoe ashore, he carried it into the woods and hid it behind a fallen pine. Then he went through the forest until he came nearly opposite the mouth of the Muniac. There he hid behind a clump of wild cherry trees.

Peering through an opening in the trees, he saw a party of Mohawk warriors, five hundred or six hundred strong. They were making a breakfast off the bodies of several dogs, in order to stir the war spirit in their blood.

The Malecite young man had seen enough. Cautiously as a fox and silently as the night, he slipped back to the place where he had hidden his canoe. Hastily he carried it back to the shore, and began paddling toward his home village as rapidly as possible.

The day was just breaking as he arrived, and he had hurried so fast that he could hardly lift his canoe ashore. Entering the first house he came to, he was stunned to learn that all the warriors of the village except five were away from home on a fishing trip. There was no time to send for them. If anything was to be done to save the lives of the women and children, it must be done at once. His news had terrified the people; the women were crying and the children were shrieking.

The young man gathered the five warriors on the grass beside the river and said to them: "Brothers, the savage Mohawks thirst for our blood. Already they have had their war-feast. I have seen the heads of the dogs they have eaten. Are you willing to die to save our women and children?"

Each of the five bowed his head and said, "A ha!" which means "Yes." Quickly the young man outlined a plan. "Now let us be off," he said, "to meet the swift feet of the Mohawks!"

With three canoes, two men in each, they went up the St. John River to the mouth of the Muniac. They hugged the opposite shore as they neared their enemies, who were still camped where the fisherman had seen them. The men heard the hoot of an owl in the forest. They saw storm clouds hovering over the woods. Then they lighted a few fires, so as to make it appear that a party of Malecites were camping on the opposite bank.

Shortly after the break of day, the six men carried their canoes through the woods, across the bend in the river, and placed them in the river again. They then poled upstream boldly, in full view of their enemies, but beyond the reach of arrows. As soon as they were out of sight of the Mohawks, they landed, took their canoes on their shoulders again, carried them across the point, put them in the water, and poled upstream again. For three days the six men continued these movements, so that a canoe or two were always passing in front of the enemy. The Mohawks became very uneasy and soon concluded that the Malecite warriors were as numerous as the leaves on the trees.

Holding a council, the Mohawk elders decided that they would have a powwow with the Malecite warriors. So they sent an interpreter in his canoe to the middle of the river to ask for a parley. As soon as they heard the request, the six men shoved their canoes into the water and joined the interpreter. It was arranged that six men from the Malecites should cross the river to the Mohawk camp and begin to plan for a lasting peace between the two nations.

Early the next morning, the six Malecite warriors painted themselves with the red earth found in that region and ornamented themselves with eagle feathers. Then they calmly paddled to the Mohawk camp.

"We are the delegates from an army of one thousand warriors," their spokesman told the council. "If you do not leave the river at once, our men will cross over and take every scalp-lock in your band."

A good deal of angry talk followed. At last a very old Mohawk warrior arose and said, "Brothers, my sun is nearly set. I look now for rest and quiet. In peace, I would seek the happy hunting grounds of our fathers. Let us bury the hatchet. Grant me this favour, and I die content."

Rising as one man, all replied, "We will. We will. Let peace be made. Let us bury the hatchet."

So, going down to the mouth of the Muniac River, all of the Mohawk warriors and the six delegates from the imaginary force of Malecite warriors ranged themselves close to the St. John River. There one Mohawk and the six Malecites dug a deep hole in the bed of the stream. In it they buried a stone hatchet and covered it with one of the huge boulders which the water had brought down from the distant mountains.

There the hatchet has remained ever since, undisturbed. Never since that morning has a band of Mohawk warriors descended our river to trouble our people.

An eclipse of the sun

> Traditions of several tribes reveal the alarm caused by an eclipse. The Hurons used to shoot arrows into the air, in order to drive away the enemies that were making war on the sun or the moon. During an eclipse of the sun, the Quinaults of the Washington coast used to make noises in every possible manner, in order to frighten away Fisher, who was eating the sun.
>
> The Senecas had the following tradition.

In the days of our grandfathers, the Senecas had enjoyed peace for many moons, but at the time of this story the young men were burning to go on the war-path. Pretending a peaceful visit, a band of them went into the land of the Mohawks and carried away some of them as captives.

When they had returned to their homes, they sent back one of the Mohawks with this message: "You will find your maidens in the wigwams of the Senecas, and your young men captives in the village."

Mohawk warriors then came to the Seneca village, reproached them for breaking the long peace, and announced that the Mohawks would attack them and destroy the entire Seneca tribe.

But the Seneca chief replied, "Young men should not be reproached for deeds of bravery. You will now be seized and bound. If your warriors come too near our village, you will be slain."

The envoys were then bound. Soon they heard the Mohawk war party approaching and saw the Seneca village preparing for battle. When the Mohawk warriors arrived, the leader of the captives, fearless of death, urged them to destroy the Senecas. "We are ready to die," he said.

Just as the Seneca guards were raising their tomahawks to strike the death blows, one of the captive girls gave a cry and pointed to the sun. "See, see, my brothers! The Great and Good Spirit hides his face and will not look upon the battle of his people. He will go away and leave them in darkness if they burn the villages and if, with their poisoned arrows, they send the hunters and the women and children on their long journey before their time.

"Look, my brothers! The sun has seen the Mohawk maidens happy in the lodges of the Senecas, and he will not look upon them in misery and death. He hides his face. He hides his face!"

A black disk moved forward over the face of the unclouded sun.

All the people, both Mohawks and Senecas, were terrified and thrown into confusion. The guards released their prisoners and fell at their feet. Even the old chiefs and the wise men hid their faces. As the sky grew blacker and blacker, warriors on both sides asked forgiveness from the others and promised everlasting friendship.

But through the terrible gloom and fright came a ray of hope in the voice of the oldest wise man of the Senecas. His voice rang forth, so that all heard it and listened in silence.

"My children, I speak to you with the voice of the past, but my eyes are looking into the future. The Great and Good Spirit, the Good Brother who was on earth long ago, is angry with his children below. He would have them live in peace. He has drawn the door of his wigwam before his smiling face. His children will see him no more unless they smoke the pipe he gave their fathers long ago. I have spoken. Will the children of the Good Spirit hear and heed my voice?"

From chief to chief in the council circle the pipe was passed anxiously. Anxiously all the people watched the sun. As the old man ceased talking, the light of the sun gradually increased until it shone with a clear brilliance.

Thus the Good Spirit opened again the door of his lodge. Thus he made the Seneca and the Mohawk people willing to live side by side in peace and harmony. Soon thereafter they joined the league of all the Iroquois tribes.

✷ ONONDAGA

Hiawatha and the wizard

The name of Hiawatha has become familiar through Longfellow's epic of Indian life, The Song of Hiawatha. In the poem, the deeds of the supernatural personage Nanabozho, mythical hero of the Chippewas, are blended with the deeds of Hiawatha, legendary hero of the Iroquois. Longfellow's identification of the two heroes was due to a confusion in one of his sources—which, in turn, may have been due to a confusion in the minds of the Iroquois of the nineteenth century. Either they or a recorder of their stories did not distinguish between Hiawatha and Teharonhiawagon, a mythical personage of Iroquois traditions similar to the benevolent Nanabozho and almost identical with the "Good Brother" of Huron-Wyandot mythology.

Hiawatha was an actual person—a reformer, lawmaker, and prophet of the Mohawk tribe of the Iroquois nation. Dekanawida was a similar hero of the same period, also among the Iroquois. In time, after much storytelling, historical persons and incidents became enveloped in a mist of legendry, very much as did the British chief Arthur of the fifth or sixth century.

> Dekanawida was said to have been born of a virgin mother and to have miraculously escaped death three times in his infancy; in one version of the story, his grandmother was directed in a dream to call him Dekanawida "because this child will reveal to men-beings the Good Tidings of Peace and Power from Heaven, and the Great Peace shall rule and govern on earth."
>
> Hiawatha's struggle to persuade Atatarho, crafty tyrant of the Onondaga tribe, to cease his warfare and join the League of the Iroquois was transformed into the following legend with super-natural incidents. The story here has been greatly abridged from the original.
>
> The names of the main characters are pronounced "Ä-ta-tär'-hō," "Hē-a-wă-tha," and "Dē-kän'-a-wee'-da."

In the times of our forefathers, our people unbanked many council-fires without being able to do any business. Atatarho, the wizard and tyrant of the Onondagas, brought all plans to nothing. At last the chiefs met in secret and chose a secluded spot where they hoped to hold a public council.

But Atatarho, by means of his spies, learned the time and the place of the council. Sure that the purpose of the chiefs was to find ways of curbing his power, he resolved to be present. Arriving at the place before the others, he sat down facing the lake, with head bowed, silent but forbidding.

After many people had arrived and had fastened their canoes near where Atatarho was seated, he arose and, in a loud voice, called to those who were still out on the lake. "Hurry! Hurry, or you will soon be destroyed! A wind is coming, and it may soon cause you all to drown."

Then the people saw the approaching storm, which had the fury of a hurricane. All those that had not landed were buffeted by the wind and drowned in the lake.

"Again Atatarho has defeated all our plans," said the chiefs to one another. "He brought on this storm by his wizardry."

A second time the chiefs chose a place and a time for a public council. A large number of people assembled and built their tepees near the lodge of their great chief, Hiawatha. But they found that Atatarho was there also. All the people were depressed, for they feared his vengeance and his blood-thirstiness. He had already caused the death of many people, including the wife and all but one daughter of Hiawatha.

When Hiawatha's only living daughter started into the forest to gather firewood, Atatarho watched her. As she looked skyward, he shouted, "Look up! Some living thing is falling. What is it?"

All eyes were turned upward, and they saw a beautiful creature flying down toward the place where the girl was gathering wood. At once she started for her lodge, and so met the people who were rushing to see the flying object. In the tumult, she was knocked down and was trampled on by the onrushing mass of people. When her body was picked up, she had been trodden to death.

Hiawatha was torn with grief. "It has gone ill with us," he said. "All my family have been taken from me. Atatarho has caused the death of each one, and he has again spoiled our plans for a council. It is now fitting that I leave and go among other people. I will start now. I will go directly south."

Then he entered the forest and, going south, crossed the Onondaga Mountain. Soon he reached a lake and travelled along its shore. When he came about midway of its length, he saw a great flock of ducks floating on the water. Hiawatha called out to them in a loud voice, "Attend to this matter, you floating boats."

At once the ducks flew up, taking with them all the water of the lake. Going a short distance into the dry lake bed, Hiawatha saw many shells of various colours. These he gathered and placed in a skin bag that he carried. When the bag had been filled, he returned to the shore of the lake, sat down, and strung the shells on skin strings, arranging the colours in patterns. He called the shells wampum.

Placing the wampum in his pouch, he again took up his journey, naming places as he travelled. After a long time he came to a cabin and entered it.

"What has happened to you, Hiawatha?" asked the owner of the cabin. "Why do you wander aimlessly? You are worthy of the highest homage, of the greatest respect."

"Atatarho is mad," replied Hiawatha. "He is angry and he rages. My children have died because of him. When he destroyed my third daughter, I came away. I was angry and troubled."

"In what kind of place does Atatarho live?" asked his host.

"From his lodge, smoke rises until it touches the sky."

"I will inform the chiefs," his host replied. "Perhaps they may have something to say concerning it."

Then Dekanawida, for it was he who lived there, asked Hiawatha to stay with him. And he laid the matter before his council to learn its judgement.

After discussing the subject for some time, the chiefs decided to go to the house of Atatarho. But first they made their preparations. Having no wampum, they began to string common shells on threads of skin. Then Hiawatha took from his pouch the wampum he had gathered from the lake bed.

The council members gazed upon the wampum-strings, the first they had ever seen, and they were greatly pleased. "We will use these in our work. They will be of great benefit to us."

"Hereafter we shall always use wampum in our councils," said Dekanawida, as he thanked Hiawatha. "It shall endure for all time."

"Now we must go to the lodge of Atatarho," said the chiefs of the council when they had placed the wampum in parcels. "We will straighten and reconstruct his mind, so that he may again have the mind of a human being."

That night two spies appointed by the council started out on their journey to the land of Atatarho. When they reached the end of the clearing surrounding the council house, they transformed themselves into crows. As they passed over the tops of forests, they watched carefully for the smoke they had been asked to find. After a long search, they found a smoke rising like a huge pillar, to the very sky. At the edge of the forest near it, they took again their human forms, and walked toward the long-house from which the smoke arose.

Entering it, they asked at once, "Does Atatarho live here?"

"Sh!" whispered the astonished people in the house. "It is death to anyone to speak louder than a soft whisper when in the presence of the wizard." And they pointed to the shape that was Atatarho.

The two spies looked and were struck speechless and motionless. The hair of Atatarho consisted of writhing, hissing serpents. His hands were like the claws of a turtle. His feet were like a bear's claws in size and were twisted like those of a tortoise.

Quickly the two spies left their place, resumed their crow forms, and flew back to Dekanawida, Hiawatha, and the other chiefs.

"We found the smoke," they reported. "The thing we saw was horrifying. Atatarho is not a human being. He is a demon." And they described what they had seen.

Again the chiefs resolved to go to the lodge of Atatarho, to reconstruct his mind and make it the mind of a human being.

"If we can accomplish this great work, we shall be fortunate and shall reap benefits from it," said Dekanawida.

On their journey the chiefs sang the Six Songs, the sacred songs that they would use as they worked on Atatarho's mind. When they reached the edge of the forest in which stood the lodge of the wizard, they sent a messenger to the chiefs, the members of the council of that land.

"Tell them to meet us at our fire, at the edge of the woods, beside the thorny underbrush."

So the resident chiefs met the visiting chiefs at their fire at the edge of the woods. After greetings and explanations, the newcomers began to sing the Six Songs.

When they had finished, they said to the resident chiefs, "We will begin with the mind of Atatarho. We will cast his ungovernable temper deep in the ground. He will then meditate in peace and contentment. His hair of living serpents we shall change from its snakehood. His hands and his feet we shall change to those of a human being. Let us go now to his house."

When they reached the place and entered, they too were horrified at the sight, just as the spies had been. But Dekanawida, undaunted, said, "We are now here. Chiefs, unwrap your wampum."

When they had done so, the leader said, "Now let us sing the Six Songs."

Atatarho had heard the singing when the men were at the fire at the edge of the woods, beside the thorny underbrush. And immediately a change had come over his mind. Now he listened attentively and even showed some pleasure. Then he raised his horrid head, something he had never been known to do. Dekanawida rejoiced.

"It gave me great pleasure to hear the singing of the Six Songs," said the wizard.

Rising, Dekanawida said to him, "The mind that belongs to your body is not that of a human being. We have come to straighten it out."

Then he sang a song three times and gave Atatarho a string of wampum. "This song shall hereafter belong to you alone. It is called 'I use it to beautify the earth.'"

Knowing that the mind of Atatarho had experienced a change, Dekanawida continued, "We intend also to make your body straight and natural. Your feet are misshapen."

Then he passed his hand over the wizard's feet, and they at once were natural in size and shape. Dekanawida handed him another string of wampum and said, "We will now restore the shape of your hands. They shall be like those of men."

He passed his own hands over the misshapen hands, and watched them change to a natural shape. Then giving Atatarho another string of wampum, he spoke again. "It was not intended that men should have snakes in place of hair."

Dekanawida brushed the snakes away, saying, "Your head from now on shall be like that of a human being." And then he gave Atatarho another string of wampum.

Thus they reconstructed the mind and body of the wizard Atatarho and made him into a natural man. He became a good leader of his people.

The Iroquois League of Nations

The greatest achievement of the two statesmen Hiawatha and Dekanawida was the founding of the League of the Iroquois, also called the Confederacy of the Five Nations. The chief purpose of the union was to bring about peace among the five Iroquois tribes and between them and neighbouring nations.

The five tribes in the original League were the Cayuga, the Mohawk, the Oneida, the Onondaga, and the Seneca. The date of its organization is uncertain; the year 1390, the mid-fifteenth century, and the last decade of the sixteenth century have been given as approximate dates by equally good authorities. By 1722 the Confederacy had been joined by the Tuscarora, another tribe speaking the Iroquois language, and was henceforth known as the Six Nations.

The following account of the founding of the League of the Iroquois is abridged from the one given by an Onondaga chief and fire-keeper on the Reserve of the Six Nations, Ontario, in 1888; it is really a continuation of "Hiawatha and the Wizard," from the same source. In the full versions of the history (see Parker and "Traditional History" in the Bibliography), both narratives are a preface to the constitution and laws of the Confederacy.

In the version given here, Dekanawida did most of the talking. In other traditions, he is said to have had an impediment in his speech and so asked Hiawatha to be his speaker at the council and in conferences with tribal chiefs. Dekanawida first showed his great ability in his youth by making a stone canoe that would float; and in that white stone canoe he departed at the end of his life, from the Council of the Great Peace.

The legend is full of symbolism.

When the chiefs had finished the work of straightening the mind and body of Atatarho, they rejoiced greatly.

"Now that we have redeemed Atatarho," they said, "everything will proceed in a harmonious manner. It is now our duty to work, first, to secure to the nations peace and tranquillity."

"Yes," said Hiawatha, "we must now work for the good of all the nations. We must establish laws for all and must work to get them accepted. Are there not nights when there is danger that one person may kill another? We must set this matter right. We must have a league of nations, so that all may live in peace and tranquillity, undisturbed by the shedding of blood."

"In the first place," said Dekanawida, "the chiefs must be patient, long-suffering, and courageous in the cause of right and justice. This applies to the chiefs and to the war-chiefs. And we must carry this Law around and show it to all nations. We will call it the Great Law, the Great Law of Justice. Today all the tribes, without exception, hate the Iroquois nation. Everywhere battle-axes are crossed and men are slaughtering one another.

"So we have put the evil of warfare from the earth. We have cast it deep down in the earth. Into one bundle we have gathered the causes of war. and we have cast this bundle away. We even uprooted a tall pine tree and thus made a very deep hole in the earth, at the bottom of which runs a swift current of water. Into this current we have thrown all the causes of war and strife. Our great-grandchildren shall not see them, for we have set back the tall pine tree in its former place.

"Under this great tree we shall rest, for its shade will be pleasant and beautiful. All the nations will look upon the law, and all will like it and desire it. Never again shall we be in fear. All tribes will then dwell in peace and tranquillity, for they will have given their allegiance to the Great Law. They will give wampum to confirm their words; and for future generations they will record their vow in wampum. All will rejoice, for we have formed ourselves into a union, into one round and compact body.

"More than this," continued Dekanawida in his address to the council, "we have erected a tree which has put forth a Great White Root running toward the sun-setting. Another root goes toward the sun-rising. A third goes toward the mid-sky, a fourth toward the place of cold. These are the Roots of the Law of Natural Men, the Indians. On these the tree stands and spreads forth its branches.

"On the top of the tree sits a bird, the eagle. Its eyesight is unequalled by any other, and it keeps a lookout in all directions. If it should see anything approaching which will be our death and destruction, it will inform us.

"A council-fire in behalf of the Great Law shall be kindled for all nations. Such a fire shall be lighted for the Cherokee nation south of us. Another shall be lighted for the Hurons west of us. There all shall learn about the Great Law, and all shall adopt it as their own. We shall kindle such a fire also for the Seven Nations living toward the sun-rising, so that they can work in behalf of this law. Then they can light council-fires for the same purpose among the nations that live farther toward the east than they do. This is our great purpose —to put an end to all strife and war, to promote peace and tranquillity throughout the land."

Dekanawida then ceased speaking.

The Seven Nations did light such fires for the tribes living still farther toward the sun-rising. All accepted the Great Law and worked together for the good of all Natural Men. Then some of the Iroquois went toward the mid-sky, visiting the Cherokees in behalf of the Great Law, and a council-fire was lighted for them. These men then went toward the sun-setting, where they kindled similar fires for the Tobacco Nation and the Wyandots. All these nations received the Great Law with rejoicing.

When the Iroquois messengers returned from their journeys to distant nations, they said, "We have completed our task. Nevermore will anyone hear it said, 'There lie the bodies of persons who have been slain.' That is what we have accomplished. We have persuaded men to work in the Law to secure to all the nations peace and prosperity—all the benefits of living in peace."

"May what we have done endure forever!" said Hiawatha. "There may be some tribes, at a distance, who will not be willing to accept the Great Law, but we shall not be responsible. We have offered it to them, to the nations living along any of the Great White Roots of the Great Law. And we have laid our heads on these Roots for mutual protection."

"It may be," said Dekanawida, "that after a lapse of time, some person may come along and will see one of these roots, beautiful beyond comparison. It may be that he will raise his hatchet and strike the root. Blood will flow from it and all of us shall feel it. Then we shall know that he who has struck his hatchet into the Root does not wish to receive the Great Law. Then we will see the back of the retreating culprit. Before he has gone very far, something supernatural will happen to him, for blood will come from his mouth."

The men of the council indicated their approval.

"We have now completed this part of the matter," said Dekanawida. "Permit me to urge you, my chiefs, to apply yourselves diligently to all the responsibilities that you have undertaken. Perform every duty faithfully, for to you are entrusted the preservation and the settlement of all things.

"Let us now make tokens and symbols for rulers to wear, so that whoever sees you and them will say, 'These are chiefs.'"

When the men of the Council of the Great Peace had completed this task, Dekanawida spoke to them for the last time.

"Now my work is done. Let my name never be mentioned as an official of the League. No one shall be appointed to succeed me, for other men can now advise you. Having founded the League of the Iroquois, a work that no other person could have done, I shall be seen no more by any man."

Crossing through the Iroquois country, Dekanawida came to Onondaga Lake and paddled across it toward the setting sun. On the far side of the lake he left his canoe. There he lies buried in a grave lined with branches of hemlock, and his body is covered two spans deep with hemlock boughs.

Hiawatha and the other chiefs at the council sadly watched their leader until he disappeared from their view. Then they turned to the duties left undone. After deciding who should be the members of the council in the different nations of the League, they carried the Great Law to them, along with the symbols of chieftainship.

In this law, the chiefs of the Great Peace Council set forth these six principles as the basis of all good government: sanity of mind and health of body; peace between individuals and between groups of persons; righteousness in conduct, in thought and in speech; equity and justice—the fair settlement of rights and obligations; physical strength, as shown in military force or civil authority; spiritual power—of the people, of their institutions, and of their rituals.

"It shall be an enduring custom," said the men of the council to the people they visited, "that at certain times the councillors shall re-examine the Great Law, the Constitution of the League. It should not be permitted to become out-of-date. It must be studied regularly."

Everywhere the chiefs went, people liked the Great Law so much that they took this vow: "We shall forever refrain from all the things that kill human beings, because we desire that there shall be continual peace. We shall join our hands so firmly that if a tree should fall on them they would not be separated. We shall now have but one soul, but one head, and but one tongue, so that the nations of the world shall be of one mind."

Before the chiefs banked the council-fire, they decided that all that had been done to bring about the Great Peace and the League of the Iroquois should be recorded in wampum belts. On wampum belts also was recorded the Great Law, so that it would endure forever.

✷ PASSAMAQUODDY

The Wabanaki League for Peace

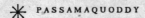

The five Wabanaki tribes—the Passamaquoddy, the Abnaki, the Micmac, the Malecite, and Penobscot—had a federation with each other and also with the Iroquoian Six Nations. The word "Wabanaki" means "those living at the sunrise" or "children of the dawn country"; so they are evidently part of the people referred to by Dekanawida as "the Seven Nations living toward the sun-rising." The Pennacook and the Mahican may have been the other two Algonquian-speaking tribes of the "Seven Nations."

In their wampum records, the Passamaquoddy preserved the traditions regarding both of these unions for peace.

Many bloody battles had been fought, many men, women, and children had been tortured by constant and cruel wars, when some of the wise men began to think that something must be done, and done quickly. They accordingly sent messengers to all parts of the country, some going to the South, others to the East, and others to the West and Northwest. Some even went as far as the Wabanaki. It was many moons before the messengers reached the farthest tribes.

When they arrived at each nation, they notified the people that the powerful tribes of the Iroquois had sent them to announce the tidings of a great council for a treaty of peace. Every Indian who heard the news rejoiced, for all were weary of the never-ending wars. Every tribe sent two or more of their wisest men as representatives to the great council.

When all the delegates had assembled, they began to discuss what was best to do. All of them seemed tired of their evil lives.

The leading chief addressed the council in these words: "As we look back upon our blood-stained trail, we see that many wrongs have been done by all our people. Our bloody tomahawks, clubs, bows and arrows must be buried. They must be buried for all time."

The council decided to make a general treaty of peace, a treaty of peace between all the nations there gathered together. And they set a day when the ceremonies should begin. For seven suns a strict silence was observed, during which each delegate meditated on the speech he should make to the council. Each person also tried to discover, in his own mind, the best means for avoiding wars. These days were called the Wigwam of Silence.

After seven days, they held another wigwam, which was called the Wigwam of Oratory. Each delegate made a speech in which he related the history of his nation. He told about all the hardships and cruelties that his people had suffered during the wars. Each speaker ended his address with words like these: "The time has now come when we must think about our women and our children, our crippled men and our old warriors. We must have pity on them, for they have suffered equally with our strongest and bravest warriors."

When all the speeches had been delivered, the council decided to erect an extensive fence, and within the fence to build a large wigwam. In this wigwam they would build a big fire. They would have a whip made and would place it in the hand of a father who would be the guard of the large wigwam. If any person did wrong, the father would punish him with the whip. Every person within the fence must obey all the orders of the father, who would be not only guard but also fire-keeper. It would be his duty to see that the fire in the wigwam never went out.

The fence symbolized a treaty of peace for all the Indian nations that took part in the council. There were fourteen of these nations, in which there were many tribes. All these were to go within the fence and dwell there. If any should do wrong, he would be liable for punishment with the whip at the hands of the father.

The wigwam within the fence symbolized a universal house of all the tribes, in which they might live in peace, without disputes and quarrels. They would be like members of a family.

The big fire in the wigwam symbolized the warmth of the brotherly love developed in the people by the treaty. The father ruling the wigwam and keeping the fire always burning was the Great Chief who lived at Caughnawaga. The whip in his hand represented the Wampum Laws. Disobedience to them was punishable by the consent of all the tribes mentioned in the Great Treaty.

After the Council had drawn up the Great Law and had it recorded in wampum, they made lesser laws and had them recorded also. Every feast, every ceremony, had its own law, its own ritual preserved in the wampum.

"All these records are to be read aloud, in every tribe, from time to time," the council decreed. "If this is done, the peace that we have made will endure forever."

The council also made boundaries around the hunting grounds, so that each tribe knew where it could hunt without being attacked by another tribe.

In former days, the members of the Wabanaki nation and the members of the Iroquois Six Nations had waged bloody and unceasing war with one another. But after the meeting of the Great Council, after the making of the Great Law, the Wabanaki lived as one nation, at peace with all the Iroquois tribes. There was no strife within the nation, and there was no war with their neighbours. All presented a united front for peace.

✳ SENECA

The Seneca peacemaker

"*According to tradition, the powerful Senecas were not anxious to enter the league [of the Iroquois], but were told they should be the west door, and through them all messages in that direction should come.*"

The hero of the following legend is said to have been a "grandfather"—probably a forefather—of Red Jacket, a famous Seneca chief and orator of the late eighteenth and early nineteenth centuries. The story was recorded about 1848.

There was a time when all the Indian tribes were at war with the great Seneca nation, whose hunting grounds were the forests surrounding Lake Ontario. So fearful had the Senecas become of their many enemies that even the bravest warriors never left their wigwams without bending their bows in readiness. And little children were not permitted to gather berries or hickory nuts, even in the woods near their homes.

The head chief of the Senecas at that time was named Always Awake. He was a good man, devoted to his people. Sorely grieved by their unhappiness and uneasiness, he pondered and pondered about what should be done. He knew that his father had been a cruel chief, feared and hated by his people, but he believed that it was not right for his generation and the younger ones to be made miserable for crimes committed by others.

At last he had an idea: he would try to secure an everlasting peace with all the enemy tribes. So he prayed to the Good Spirit, "Tell me in a dream what I should do to bring about peace in the world."

This was his prayer one night as he went to bed, and in spite of his name, Always Awake fell into a deep sleep and had a dream. In his dream a spirit voice spoke to him these words: "In the direction from which come the warm winds of summer, distant from your village a journey of one moon, there stands a large mountain. On its summit live a few people from all nations of the earth except the Seneca. The place is called the Mountain of Refuge. It is so sacred that its soil has never been wet with human blood; the people who live there are favourites of the Good Spirit, for they are the peaceful lawmakers of the world.

"You can secure everlasting peace," the spirit continued, "only by visiting the sacred mountain. But the distance is great, and your enemies along the way will make your journey very dangerous. By travelling at night, however, and sleeping in the daytime, you may be able to reach there. You are free to make the attempt. Everything depends upon the earnestness of your desire for peace."

The spirit left, and the good chief awoke. For a long time he lay thinking about the strange vision, wondering whether he should undertake a journey with so many hazards. At last he determined to start. He did indeed find the path long, and it was so rugged that he became very weary. Often he had to satisfy hunger with only roots and berries. Often he narrowly escaped death at the hands of his enemies.

But at length he reached the Mountain of Refuge, and there he was warmly welcomed. When he told the people about his great desire for peace throughout the world and about his dream, they honoured him with a shout of approval. They called a council at once, and it decided to summon a great council, composed of the head chiefs of all the nations in the land. The subject proposed by the Seneca chief, the idea of a universal and everlasting peace, was so important, they thought, that it should be discussed by the leaders of all the tribes.

So the people on the Mountain of Refuge sent forth their swiftest runners in all directions—to the nations near the sun-rising, to those toward the sun-setting, to places below the mid-sky, and to the place of the cold. The chiefs of all these nations gathered at the time and place agreed upon, to find the best way of making an everlasting peace.

After many speeches and much discussion, they worked out a plan acceptable to all but a few chiefs present at the great council. They formed themselves into a confederacy. They became a united group of tribes, pledged not to wage war with each other, pledged not to carry war to distant nations not represented in the council. With one exception, the nations of the wilderness became like one nation, one people.

Chief Always Awake, on his journey back to his home, felt very happy. He was never in danger, though he travelled in the daytime. All along his way, his trail was lined with bonfires of rejoicing, and in every village where he stopped, he was feasted with the best of game. People were weary of war and joyous that the great chief of the Senecas had made a path to a peaceful world.

The only chiefs at the great council who would not join the League were from the Osage nation. Because of their wickedness in refusing to co-operate, the Osage people have not been favoured by the Good Spirit, and they have been disliked by their neighbours.

Only one moon after Chief Always Awake came back to his village, he died and was buried on the shore of the beautiful Lake Ontario. His work was done. Ever since the time of the chief and the great council on the Mountain of Refuge, the Good Spirit has permitted his people to live unmolested on the land inherited from their fathers. And the nations that united in the League continued to live in peace until the white men crossed the great waters and taught them the vices that have almost wiped them from the face of the earth.

A Chippewa dream of peace

A British folklorist recorded this tradition among the Chippewas in 1925–26. About it she wrote, "I know no parallel of this."

Many years ago, an Indian prophet predicted that the world would come to an end during the next winter.

"The snow will fall until it covers all the trees of the forest," he said.

While he was talking, his two young sons began to fight. Their father punished them, saying, "You should be silent while I am telling people what is going to happen."

That night, in a vision, a spirit came to the prophet and offered to take him to the four layers of heaven above. There they came to a great lodge, in which the spirits were seated. The spirits rebuked the prophet.

"We heard you telling your people that the world is coming to an end, because of a great fall of snow," they said to him. "Do you see that box, half full? It means that many years will pass by before the world ends. Our judges have agreed to extend the time for hundreds of years.

"Now go back to your people and tell them what you have seen and heard in the lodge in the four layers of heaven. Tell them to do away with all the bad medicine they use to kill one another. Tell them they must all love everyone as if they were a family.

"Build a big lodge in your village, big enough for the whole tribe. Gather there twice each year, in the spring and in the fall, for a big feast. Smoke the pipe of peace and dance together as brothers. Then you will be blessed by the spirits."

When the prophet awoke, he told his people his dream, and they did as the spirits directed. Ever since, the Chippewas have held the Ogemah dance in the spring and in the fall, as a reminder of the vision and of the spirits' desire that they live in peace with each other and with all people.

The first Europeans

This tradition' was recorded in 1855 from a Chippewa of the Bear clan. The Chippewas referred to their country as an island.

For a long time before this story began, my people had lived on a small promontory on Lake Superior. It is called the Point of the Old Village.

One night one of my grandfathers, a prophet of the tribe, had a dream which had a strange effect on him. For days he busied himself very earnestly, as a result of this dream. He fasted, he took sweat baths every day, he shut himself alone in his prophet lodge.

His penance was so thorough, so unusual, that the people of the village were curious. What was about to happen? Was there to be a great famine or an unusually successful hunting season? Was there to be a serious war with the Sioux? Or was something else of equal importance about to take place?

At last when the prophet had considered everything carefully, and after he had the whole story of his dream clear in his mind, he called together the other prophets and the chiefs of his people. He had astonishing news for them.

"Men of strange appearance have come across the great water," he told them. "They have landed on our island. Their skins are white like snow, and on their faces long hair grows. These people have come across the great water in wonderfully large canoes which have great white wings like those of a giant bird. The men have long and sharp knives, and they have long black tubes which they point at birds and animals. The tubes make a smoke that rises into the air just like the smoke from our pipes. From them come fire and such terrific noise that I was frightened, even in my dream."

Half a day it took the prophet to tell his dream. He described the sails and the masts of the ships, the iron corslets, the guns and cannon. The other prophets and the chiefs listened in amazement. When he finished speaking, all agreed at once that they should prepare a fleet of several canoes and send it eastward along the Great Lakes and the great river. There at the big water, their messengers should find out about these strange people and, on their return home, should make a report to the tribe.

Canoes were made ready for the long journey, and trusted men were selected. For many suns and several moons they travelled over the waters of the lakes and down the great river, through the lands of friendly tribes. These people knew nothing yet of the white strangers, for they had no gifted dreamer and prophet among them.

At last the travellers from the Point of the Old Village came to the lower part of the great river. One evening they found a clearing in the forest, where even the largest trees had been cut down quite smoothly. The Indians camped there and examined the stumps closely. Giant beavers with huge, sharp teeth had done the cutting, the men thought.

"No," said the prophet. "These trees were probably cut by the long knives I saw in my dream. The white strangers must have camped here."

His companions were filled with awe, and with terror also. Using their own stone-headed axes, they could not cut down such large trees or cut anything so smoothly. Then they found some long, rolled-up shavings that puzzled them, and also some pieces of bright-coloured cloth. The shavings they stuck in their hair and in their ears; the cloth they wound around their heads.

Wearing these decorations, the travellers went on. Soon they came to the camp of the strangers. The men had white faces and bushy beards, just as the prophet had said. They had long knives, thundering fire-tubes, and giant canoes with white wings, just as the prophet had said. Now we know that these first white men were Frenchmen.

When the travellers had finished their visit, they made the long journey back to their home on Lake Superior and reported what they had seen. They were excited, and their story excited all the village. Everyone crowded round, to see the things the men had brought back: the shavings, the pieces of wood cut with sharp tools, the gaily-coloured cloth. This cloth was torn into small pieces, so that each person might have one.

To impress other chiefs and other tribes, the Chippewas followed an old custom. In former days they had bound the scalps of their enemies on long poles and sent them from one tribe to another; now they fastened splinters of wood and strips of calico to poles and sent them with special messengers.

And so these strange articles were passed from hand to hand around the whole lake. In this way the people of Lake Superior gained their first knowledge of the white men from Europe.

The dream of the white robe and the floating island

When there were no people in this country but Indians, before white people were known, a young woman had a strange dream. She dreamed that a small island came floating in toward the land. On the island were tall trees and living beings. Among them was a man dressed in garments made of rabbit skins.

In those days it was the custom, when anyone had an unusual dream, to consult the wise men of the tribe, especially the prophets and magicians. So the girl related her dream and asked what it meant. The wise men pondered but could make nothing of it. On the second day after the girl's dream, however, something happened that explained it.

When they got up that morning, they saw what seemed to be a small island that had drifted near to the land and become fixed there. There were trees on the island, and what seemed to be a number of bears were crawling about on the branches.

All the Micmac men seized their bows and arrows and spears, and rushed down to the shore to shoot the bears. But they stopped in surprise when they saw that the creatures were not bears but men. And what had seemed to be a small island with trees was really a large boat with long poles rising above it. While the Indians stood watching, some of the men on the ship lowered a strangely built canoe into the water. Several of them jumped into it and paddled ashore.

Among those in the strange canoe was a man dressed in white. As he came toward the shore, he made signs of friendship, by raising his hand toward heaven. He talked to the Indians in an earnest manner, in a language they did not understand.

Now people began to question the girl about her dream.

"Was it an island like this that you saw in your dream?"

"Yes."

"Is the man in the white robe the one you saw in your dream?"

"Yes, he was."

Then some of the prophets and magicians were greatly displeased—displeased because the coming of these strangers to their land had been revealed to a young girl instead of to them. If an enemy had been about to make an attack upon them, they could have foreseen it and foretold it by the power of their magic. But of the coming of this white-robed man, who proved to be a priest of a new religion, they knew nothing.

The new teacher gradually won his way into their favour, though the magicians opposed him. The people received his instruction and were baptized. The priest learned their language and gave them the prayer-book written in ornamental mark-writing.

 MICMAC

A chapel built without hands

> The Sanctuary of Sainte Anne de Beaupré, about twenty-two miles from the city of Quebec, has drawn pilgrims for three centuries. According to tradition, the first chapel there was built by some Breton sailors who suffered a violent storm on the St. Lawrence River in 1650. During the night they vowed that if they were not destroyed by the tempest they would build a chapel to Saint Anne on the spot on which they first touched land. The next morning they landed on the shore of Beaupré, where they honoured their vow.
> The following Indian tradition was recorded about 1869, by a Protestant missionary who worked among the Micmacs for forty years.

Once upon a time a French ship, manned by Frenchmen, was cruising on the ocean. A violent storm arose, which became so furious that all hope of saving the vessel was abandoned. She had sprung a leak and was rapidly foundering. The captain then called all hands together and informed them that there was no hope but in God. He commanded them to fasten the hatches and hatchways, and invited them to go to the cabin and unite with him in prayer. This was done. The captain read from the prayer-book and they all followed in earnest supplications.

Soon they noticed that the water was no longer rising in the ship. After a while she stopped rocking and lay perfectly still. The captain, taking an auger, bored a hole in the side of the vessel. No water came in. He bored another hole lower down. Still no water came in. He tried a third time, boring in the bottom of the vessel. Still no water. The hatchway was now removed, and to their surprise, the men saw no water.

Looking shoreward, they found that they were close to a forest. And near at hand was a large stone chapel with a cross on the top of the steeple. The heavy door was closed. The ground leading to it was paved with broken flint-stones.

Then all the men left the ship, with the captain at their head. At his direction, they took off their shoes, rolled up their trouser-legs, and walked over the sharp pavement on their bare knees. As they approached the chapel, the door opened to them of its own accord.

When they entered the stone building, they saw no one, and no one entered after them. There the men remained fasting and praying until they all died. But the captain of the vessel, before his death, wrote out all the details of their experience and left his journal for the benefit of those who might come later.

Soon afterward, people who lived in the area passed by and were astonished. There stood the chapel they had never seen before, and in the water near-by was a strange vessel. Entering the chapel with reverence and awe, they found the dead crew, the dead captain, and the writing he had left.

At once these people began to use the chapel for prayer and worship, as they do unto this day. The ship decayed after a while, but a model of it was constructed and hung on the outside of the chapel door. There it remains.

After the country passed into the hands of the English, Protestants tried to burn the chapel, but it would not burn. They filled it with hay, which they set on fire; but though the hay burned readily and rapidly, the fire made no impression on the chapel. The people tried a second time. They filled the chapel with shavings and chips and set fire to them. These burned as the hay had burned, and a few marks of smoke were left on the walls and ceiling. But the chapel stood intact. The people made no further attempt to destroy it.

Wonderful miracles are performed at the chapel. The blind receive their sight, the deaf hear, and the lame walk. A pile of crutches and canes left by those who have been cured of their lameness is silent evidence of the miraculous power of the chapel that was built without hands. A white dove hovers over the altar.

Children of the moon

Many years ago, a chief who lived along the Pacific Ocean was one day walking on the beach. He was on his way to a forest, to look for a suitable tree to make into a canoe. On the shore he saw a small round log that seemed to have been washed up by the waves. It was quite smooth, without any bark, and one end was bigger than the other. Around the middle was something black and hard. As he examined the log, he found that the hard piece was loose and could be easily taken off.

When it lay in his hand, he thought, "I believe I can cut with that."

So he hammered it with a large stone, broke it, and flattened it into a straight piece. When he tried to cut with it, he found that it would go entirely through a piece of wood. He was delighted. He could use it in making his canoe. With a leather thong he fastened a wooden handle to it and so made a good knife.

"This is my secret power," he said to himself. "I will tell no one that I have this power."

He found a good cedar tree, felled it, and began to build his canoe. Inside and outside, he made it so smooth with his new knife that his friends wanted to know how he was making it. The man only laughed and replied, "My spirit has given me great power."

"Let us see the sign of your power," his friends asked.

But the man refused, and he would not work while they were watching him. So after a while they left him alone.

One day when the man was out hunting, he lost his power. He searched and searched but could not find it. He would not ask his friends to help him, for he was afraid they might find it and keep it. Grieving, he lost interest in everything. He could not eat and he could not sleep. At last he decided he did not want to live longer, and so he climbed the mountain behind the village, planning to die on its summit.

When he reached the top, he turned round to take one last look at the ocean. He saw the moon rising in the distant sky. On the moon-path, a few minutes later, he saw a beautiful big canoe, bigger than any he had ever seen. It had large white wings, like a giant sea-gull flying.

"The moon's canoe!" the man exclaimed. "The children of the moon must be coming down to the earth. Something unusual is going to happen. Will all of us die, or are our enemies coming to attack us?"

As he watched, marvelling and wondering, the big canoe slowly moved out of sight. And the man forgot that he had climbed the mountain in order to die there, alone. He hurried down the mountainside, jumping from rock to rock. Breathless, he rushed into the village. "I have seen the canoe of the moon!" he shouted.

People laughed at his message. They laughed at the story he told them. "You have been dreaming," they said. "Some spirit has been deceiving you."

But the very next morning, when they awoke, they saw in their own bay the beautiful big canoe the man had described to them.

"Now you know that I told you the truth," he said. "Come. Let us visit the moon's children in the canoe."

But the people were afraid.

"Let us call a meeting of the council," they cautioned. "Our wise men should decide what we should do."

The council talked and talked. At last they decided to select twelve men, clean in body and in heart, who should go to visit the moon's children. So they made ready one of their large war canoes, and the twelve young men stepped in. As the boat pushed off, the man who had first seen the moon's canoe jumped in. So great was his curiosity he could not wait for a report from the others.

The young men paddled round the giant canoe, finding it longer and higher than they had realized.

"How can we get on it?" they asked each other.

Then they saw that long pieces of something like cedar-bark rope were dropped down the sides of the big canoe. Above, hands were motioning them to take hold of the ropes and climb up. The men did so. And when they were inside the boat, the chief of the children of the moon came to greet them. His face was white, his eyes were blue like the summer sky, his hair was like grass when it is yellow.

He looked friendly and made signs to them not to be afraid. When the Indians obeyed his motion to sit down, the children of the moon placed in their hands some bright, shining dishes. In each were bones and blood. With signs, the men were told to eat from the dishes.

The Indians shook their heads and talked among themselves. How could they eat blood and bones? But one of the moon's children took a piece of bone, dipped it into the blood, put it into his mouth and ate it. Then one of the Indians, more daring than the others, followed his example. He smiled and licked his lips.

"Good! Good!" he said to his companions. "Eat it!"

So they all fell to and ate with relish. They had never tasted anything like that food.

When they had finished eating, the moon's people passed their fingers over the Indians' clothes, which were made of sea-otter furs. They seemed to like the feel of the fur so much that one of the young men suggested to the others, "Let us make them a present of our clothes."

So all of the Indians took off their fur garments and laid them down in front of the strange white men. With signs they indicated that the furs were gifts for the moon's children.

Seeing a flock of ducks flying overhead, one of the white men took a long stick and pointed it at the birds. Something made a terrific noise. The Indians were startled by the sound, and when they saw smoke pouring out of the long stick, they fell on their faces in terror. Then they heard a thud on the floor of the boat—a dead duck had fallen near them!

In wonderment, the Indians asked to see the fire-stick. Then they asked to have it. With signs the white men agreed to trade the fire-stick for furs.

Some of the Indians then went down the ropes to their own canoe, paddled back to shore, and told their people of the strange things they had seen. Back they came to the giant canoe, loaded with bundles of sea-otter skins. These they laid down by the fire-stick, which they used as a measure.

Taking the furs, the white men gave them the fire-stick and showed them how to use it.

"Now we have something better than bow and arrows," they said among themselves. "Now we can kill all the bears we want."

The chief of the white men gave them the shining dishes, saying, "You may take these to your people." The Indian chief hung them up in his lodge, where they shone brightly, just like the moon. Over and over again, the twelve young men told the story of their visit to the wonderful canoe, where they saw the wonderful children of the moon.

That was the first time any of them had seen white men or tin dishes, the first time they had handled a gun or tasted molasses and biscuits.

Captain Cook's discovery of Nootka Sound

In the spring of 1778, Captain James Cook, English mariner and explorer, spent a month at Nootka Sound, on the west coast of Vancouver Island. In his journal is a description of his dramatic meeting with the Indians, who approached his ship in many canoes. In Captain John Meare's Voyages (1790) is a sketch of Chief Maquinna and Chief Callicum at Nootka.

More than a century later this Indian tradition was related by Chief George of Nootka Sound. The Muchalats were a subdivision of the Nootka tribe.

One day Chief Maquinna and Chief Nanaimis, looking out over the water, saw the tops of three sticks against the horizon. As the chiefs and their people stood watching, the sticks grew bigger and bigger and rose out of the water. At first people thought that a new island was appearing, but the objects seemed to be moving, coming closer to the shore.

"It is some kind of canoe, a big canoe with white wings," said Chief Maquinna. "See! It is going quickly and making great waves."

"Lightning-snake must be moving it," someone said. "It is moving so fast that Lightning-snake must be pushing it under the water."

As the boat came nearer, all the men and women on the shore grew very much afraid. Some of them thought that it was magic. Others thought that it was a salmon that had been changed by magic into a strange canoe.

But the two chiefs said, "It is the work of Quaots, the Great Power. Quaots is sending it to us."

Nearer and nearer sailed the ship.

"My advice," said a warrior called Towkin, "is that everyone go into hiding. And I think that the women should be separated from the men for at least ten months. Before we go into hiding, let us hide everything that we own."

People listened to Towkin, for he was a brave warrior who had killed at least ten men. But as he finished speaking, a woman appeared with a whalebone rattle in each hand. She was a doctor who had power over salmon. Wearing a cap and apron of red cedar bark, she sang a song with the words, "It must be a salmon turned into a boat."

Then the people launched a canoe with three strong young men as a crew and the woman doctor sitting in the middle. The men paddled out to see the ship, which was sailing straight for the harbour on Bligh Island. The woman hailed the strange boat and called out, "Hello you, you spring salmon! Hello you, dog salmon! Hello, cohoe salmon!"

Then a second canoe came with another woman doctor. She hailed the strange boat in the same manner. Chief Nanaimis, taking two of his best beaver skins out of his storage chest, put off toward the ship in his canoe, with ten strong men.

"Hello, you!" called the chief of the strange big boat. "What is your name?"

"My name is Nanaimis," answered the Indian chief. "I am a chief of the Muchalats. What is your name?"

"I am Captain Cook."

Then he went into a little room on the big ship and soon came out with blankets under his arm. He asked Chief Nanaimis to come up on his ship, but the chief replied, "No, I would rather stay in my canoe."

Then Captain Cook asked him to shake hands and offered him a gift of two black blankets. Nanaimis saw that he was not an enchanted salmon but a man, a man with fair skin. The chief then opened the box he was sitting on in his canoe, took out the two beaver skins, and gave them to the captain. He accepted them with pleasure.

Chief Maquinna also put off in his canoe and had his men paddle to the strange ship.

"I am Maquinna," he said. "I am a chief of the Muchalats. My village is a little way off there, near the entrance to the inlet. It is a good, safe harbour. I want you to come and stay with me next year. You will be well treated."

Then Maquinna gave Captain Cook a fine sea-otter skin. In return for that gift, the white chief offered Maquinna his hat, which was decorated with gold braid.

People watching from the shore saw that the strangers meant no harm, and so they danced a wolf dance on the sandy beach. Captain Cook and his men stayed with our people for several days and nights, trading with us and exploring the coast.

The address of Pontiac

Pontiac, an Ottawa chief of the eighteenth century, was the military leader of several tribes. In the general attack upon the British forts along the Great Lakes in the 1760's—an attack usually referred to as the Conspiracy of Pontiac or as Pontiac's War—he led the tribes against Fort Detroit. After the peace treaty of 1766, he remained friendly with the British.

On April 27, 1763, Pontiac addressed the warriors assembled from many bands and different tribes. He was "plumed and painted in the full costume of war." After rousing their thirst for war and vengeance, he related the following story. Its origin, wrote the historian Francis Parkman, is uncertain. It may have come from the Delaware prophet whose teachings are a part of the story, or it may have been "the offspring of Pontiac's heated imagination, during his period of fasting and dreaming."

It is thought that Pontiac told the story wherever he went to arouse the Indians against the British. The story seems to have been influenced by Christian teachings.

A Delaware Indian who was eager to learn wisdom from the Master of Life resolved to journey to the master's home up above. Not knowing anyone who could tell him the way, the man hoped to find out in a dream. So he purified himself and fasted. As he hoped and expected, he was rewarded with a vision. In his dream it was revealed to him that if he would but begin his journey, he would find a trail that would take him all the way to the lodge of the Master of Life.

Telling no one his purpose or his goal, the man took his gun, his powder-horn and ammunition, and a vessel in which to cook his food. For some time he walked, in high hope and confidence, along an easy trail. On the evening of the eighth day, at sunset, he stopped as usual on the bank of a stream, at the edge of a little prairie. As he was making camp in this pleasant spot, he saw at the other side of the prairie three wide and well-trodden paths. All of them entered the woods opposite him.

Though surprised and very curious, he continued to prepare his shelter for the night, and he lighted a fire. While he was cooking his supper, darkness fell, but the three paths were more clearly visible than before. The man would have been frightened if he had not recalled his dream and his great purpose.

"One of those three trails surely leads to the home of the Master of Life," he said to himself.

Unable to rest, almost unable to eat, so great was his curiosity, he left his camp and his fire and took the widest of the paths. Until the middle of the next day he followed it without seeing anything to halt him.

But while stopping to get his breath, he suddenly noticed a bright flame coming out of the ground in front of him. Excitedly he started forward, but when the fire grew larger, he was so alarmed that he turned back and took the wider of the other two paths.

After following it as long as he had followed the first one, he was stopped by a similar curiosity—a flame springing out from under the ground. So the man returned and took the third path. On it he walked for one whole day without seeing anything strange.

But all at once, as he emerged from the forest, a mountain of dazzling whiteness burst upon his sight. He stopped in amazement, and then went forward to examine it. Surely the Master of Life had his home on this beautiful mountain. But he saw no sign of a trail, and the ascent looked forbiddingly difficult.

At this moment he saw a woman seated on the mountainside. She was a person of wondrous beauty, and her garments were whiter than freshly fallen snow. She spoke to him in his own language.

"Yes, the way to the Master of Life is on this mountain. But to ascend it, you must leave here your clothing, your weapons, and your food. No one will harm you. Wash yourself in the river which I am now showing you, and then ascend the mountain."

The man did everything as he was directed, but still he saw no path. The mountain was steep and as smooth as unrippled water.

"How can I climb so steep a mountain?" he asked the woman.

"If you really wish to see the Master of Life, you must use only one foot and one hand as you climb."

After much trouble, the man succeeded in reaching the top. The woman disappeared, and he was left alone. Three strange-looking villages were in sight, far better looking than any he had ever seen. As he approached the best-looking one, the gate to it opened and a handsome man dressed all in white came toward him. The man took the Indian by the hand and said kindly, "I shall satisfy your wishes by leading you to the presence of the Master of Life."

Soon they arrived at a place more beautiful than anything the Delaware had ever seen. Speechless with surprise, the Indian gazed at the splendour about him. The Master of Life took him by the hand, bade him be seated, and then addressed him with these words:

"I am the Master of Life, whom you wish to see. Listen to what I tell you, both for yourself and for all the Indians.

"I am the Maker of heaven and earth, of the trees, lakes, rivers, men, and all else. Because I love you, you must do my will. And you must avoid what I hate. I hate that you drink as you do, until you lose all reason. I hate that you fight one another. I wish you to take only one wife and keep her until death.

"When you go to war, you sing the medicine song, thinking that you speak to me. You deceive yourselves. It is to the Evil Spirit that you sing and speak. He induces you to do evil, and for want of knowing me, you listen to him. You must avoid the conduct that I hate.

"The land on which you live, I made for you, not for others. Why do you permit the whites to dwell upon your lands? Can you not do without them? You might live as you did before you knew them. Before they arrived, did not your bow and arrow maintain you? You needed neither gun and powder, nor any other object. The flesh of animals was your food, their skins your clothing. But when I saw you inclined to evil, I took the animals into the depths of the forests, that you might depend upon the white people for your needs. If you will again become good and do my will, I will send the animals back to you.

"But these red-coated men who have come to trouble your possessions—drive them away. Wage war against them. I do not love them. They do not know me. They are my enemies. They are your enemies. Send them back to the lands I have made for them.

"Here is a written prayer which I give you. Learn it by heart. Teach it to all the Indians, to the men, women, and children."

"But I cannot read," said the Delaware.

"Then give it to the chief of your village when you have returned to the earth. Tell him that I ask him to read it and to teach it to you and to all the others of his band. It must be repeated every morning and every evening.

"Do all that I have told you and announce it to all the Indians as coming from the Master of Life. Let them drink but one draught of fire-water, or two at most, in one day. Let them have but one wife, and stop running after other men's wives and daughters. Let them not fight one another. Let them not sing the medicine song, for when they do they speak to the Evil Spirit.

"Drive from your lands those dogs in red clothing. Do not sell that which I have placed on the earth as food. When you need anything, pray to me. In short, become good, and you shall want nothing. When you meet one another, bow and give one another the hand of the heart.

"Above all, I command you to repeat, morning and evening, the prayer that I have given you."

The man promised to do the will of the Master of Life, and also to urge it upon all the Indians. "The Master of Life shall be satisfied with us, I promise you," he said.

Then the beautiful woman guide came and led him to the foot of the mountain. "Put on your clothes," she said, "and return to your village."

His return surprised his friends very much, and they asked him where he had been. But as he had been told to speak to no one until he had seen the chief, he went at once to the chief's lodge. To him he delivered the prayer and the laws entrusted to him by the Master of Life.

✳ COWICHAN

Simon Fraser, chief of the "Sky People"

> *Simon Fraser, of the North West Company, had built trading posts at Stuart Lake and Fraser Lake, in what is now northern British Columbia. In 1807 he was directed to explore the Fraser River, a long and turbulent mountain stream that flows from the north into Georgia Strait near the present city of Vancouver. Not far from the mouth of the river, hostile Indians forced the Fraser party to turn back.*
>
> *This tradition of the coming of Simon Fraser and his men was related by an hereditary chief of the Cowichan Indians. He had heard the story from Staquisit and others who were at the village of Kikait when the explorers reached it. Kikait was across the Fraser River from the present site of New Westminster. The story is given as if Staquisit were speaking.*

I was there when Simon Fraser came. All the people were so frightened that they called out and ran around, not knowing what to do. Some picked up their bows and spears. Others just stood still and looked. They saw that some of the people in the canoes were like those who had come from the sea earlier in the white-winged canoes. They were not like any other people that lived on the river, or like those who came when the salmon ran thick in the summer. Some of them had pale faces; others had big beards. All wore strange clothes. They were the Sky-people, we thought. They stopped out on the river in their canoes for a time, and then they came ashore.

We looked at them closely, and saw that the eyes of some of them were blue like the sky, and others were grey like the clouds. Yes, they must be the Sky-people. Their faces were light in colour, but were not painted. We touched their clothes. They felt strange—not like blankets made from dog's hair, or from skins, or from cedar bark.

Whattlekainum, one of our sub-chiefs, tried to talk to them, but they had strange tongues. The chief of the Sky-people then made signs and we understood. He was on his way to the sea, but he would come back again. Then he went away.

When the canoe of the chief of the Sky-people started down the river, one of his men took what looked like a crane, put the legs over his shoulder, blew on the head of it, and made his fingers dance on the bird's bill. Strange sounds were made. Some said it was not a crane, but sticks. The noise that the man made went up the river and came back, and we thought that there were more Sky-people coming.

At this time the Musqueam Indians, who had a village at the mouth of the river, were at war with the people at Point Roberts. When the Musqueams saw the strange canoes coming, they thought that their enemies had crossed over by the way that the Semiamus came to get salmon, and they got ready to fight. When they saw that the men i the canoes were strangers, the Indians did not shoot. But they were so unfriendly that the Sky-people did not go any farther.

The next day the Sky-people came back to Kikait, and they all came ashore. Some of them took out small sticks with knobs on them and put them in their mouths. Then they took out bags and made fire; they put the fire to the end of the sticks, and smoke came out of their mouths. We thought that they would burn up, but when this did not happen, we knew that they must be supernatural.

Then the chief of the Sky-people showed us what we thought was a big stick. He cut and peeled some small willows and put them up, one of them crossed over the other. Then he went back some distance and pointed the big stick at the twigs. We nearly died from fright, for fire came from the big stick and it made thunder, and the smaller sticks fell over. Everyone was frightened.

The white chief talked to Whattlekainum, and made him understand that he could use the thunder-stick. He said, "If you can knock over the small sticks, when they are set up again, you can have the thunder-stick."

Whattlekainum, who was not afraid of anything, said he would try. Twice he pointed the big stick, and only a flash came. Then the strange chief did something to the thunder-stick. This time when Whattlekainum pointed it, it made thunder, but it knocked him back and he fell down. He did not want to touch it any more.

Before they came to us, the water had made some of the goods in the canoe wet; so the Sky-chief had them taken out and spread out to dry. When our young men saw the great treasures, they became excited. There were daggers, not made of bone or stone, but of metal like those of the Songhees, that they had secured from the tribes on the outer sea. There were ropes there, too, not made of cedar bark or skin, and—oh, lots of things we would like to have.

Some of the young men watched.

The strangers stayed all night. When it was dark, they had the strange music again, and one of the men danced. Before they came down the river, we were told later, they had stopped at Chilliwack; when the music was made there, they all danced. It was so good that the people all wanted to dance with the white men.

In the morning when the Sky-people made ready to depart, some things were missing. The white chief became angry. Some of his men searched among the people and found the articles our young men had stolen. They took the things from the young men and kicked them. That was bad. It is all right to kick a woman, but not a warrior. It makes him ashamed. When the visitors left, the young men got ready to follow and kill them that night when they stopped. We knew where their camp would be—opposite Mount Lehman.

When Chief Whattlekainum heard their plan he said, "No, do not try to hurt the Sky-people; you cannot kill them, for they are supernatural. They come from the sky. There are as many of them as there are stars. If you try to kill them, more will come and they will kill us all. You saw how they took fire into their stomachs and were not burned; you saw the thunder-stick. No, you must not do what you plan."

Some of the old men said the words of Whattlekainum were good. But the young men who had been kicked looked black. Then the chief said, "I know you feel ashamed because you were kicked. I feel sorry for you, so I will remove the shame. I will make you presents."

And Whattlekainum gave away all his own belongings to the young men to keep them from killing Simon Fraser.

✳ OKANAGAN AND SHUSWAP

The first white men and the revenge of Chief Nicola

When Marie Houghton Brent was a little girl, about 1880, she was chosen as the grandchild to memorize the speech which her great-great-grandfather had made to the first white men he had seen. She had to repeat it to her grandfather, Chief Nicola, many times, for her duty would be to transmit the speech to the next generation.

Her grandfather, son and successor of the Chief Nicola in the following story, was recognized as the head chief of the Okanagan *nation and as the most prominent chief in the interior of British Columbia. Fortunately for the white people, he was their good friend and had great faith in Queen Victoria and in the Queen's laws. In 1875–76, when sub-chiefs and their people were planning to attack white settlers who, they felt, were encroaching on their lands, Chief Nicola favoured a peaceful policy and was strong enough to prevent serious hostilities. Undoubtedly he was influenced by his grandfather's speech, which he had had to memorize in his boyhood.*

The narrative following the speech (which was recited by Mrs. Brent in 1955) was recorded between 1887 and 1890 by G. M. Dawson, of the Canadian Geologic Survey. The great-great-grandfather's name was given by Dawson as Pila-ka-mu-lah-uh, by James Teit as Pelkamulox. It means "Revolving Earth." Dawson's version was the one Mrs. Brent heard in her childhood in the Okanagan country. The two white men in the story were Finan MacDonald and Legace, fur-traders of the early nineteenth century.

Pelkamulox did a great deal of travelling, for his time. He often visited the different bands of his own people and also his neighbours and relatives, the Shuswaps and the Spokanes. Almost every year he hunted over in the buffalo country, east of the Rocky Mountains. On these hunts, the people of his area banded with the Kalispels, Spokanes, and Kootenays, sometimes also with the Nez Perces and the Coeur d'Alenes, for protection against the Blackfeet.

The last time he went on a buffalo hunt, he travelled as far as Helena, Montana. There he met a party of white men, the first white men he had ever seen. He thought they were beautiful—not human beings, but good spirits that had come from somewhere to do good for his people. He wanted to take them home with him, but for some reason he could not at that time. He did guide two of the white men west over the mountains to the Colville country and introduced them to the chief, who was a friend of his.

"Take care of these men while I am gone," he said to the chief. "I will be back to get them."

He asked the chief to promise that the white men would not be harmed. He asked the white men to promise that they would stay there with the Colville chief until his return. Then he made a speech to them, in the presence of the chief and of his own followers:

"You are my white children, and I do not want to lose you. I want you to live in my territory. I have a big country, big enough for all of us. I have plenty of everything—enough for all of us, for our children, and for our children's children.

"Our mountains are green and full of fruits. We have many roots for food. We will show you which ones to eat and which ones not to eat, so that you will not be poisoned. We have grouse and many other birds for the hunt. We have plenty of deer for meat and hides.

We have all kinds of fur.

"As long as the waters run and until yonder hill is no more, you and I will stay there, your children and my children. From my waters, I drink, you drink. From my fruits, I eat, you eat. From my game, I eat, you eat.

"You are my white children."

Leaving the two white men with the Colville Indians at Kettle Falls on the Columbia River, Pelkamulox returned to his own country. Late in the autumn, he made winter camp at Penticton. With him was his young son Nicola and the boy's mother.

Fond of telling stories, Pelkamulox entertained the tribe with his account of the white people, their doings and sayings and the strange things they possessed. Wherever he went, he was the centre of attraction, welcomed and feasted by the people. A band of Shuswaps invited him to their camp between Okanagan Lake and Great Shuswap Lake. There it took him a month to relate all he knew about the white men.

Then he was invited to two other Shuswap camps on the Great Lake. After spending a month at each of them, he was asked to go to Kamloops, where Chief Tokane welcomed him warmly. By this time, summer had arrived and Pelkamulox had had no time to prepare for a buffalo hunt. So he accepted Tokane's invitation to spend the season at the Shuswap fishery on the Fraser River, at the foot of Pavilion Mountain. There the travelling storyteller had new opportunities to tell about the wonderful white people.

At one of the feasts which Chief Tokane gave in his honour, Pelkamulox met a chief of the Lillooet band and was invited to visit his camp. The Lillooet chief sent invitations to several camps along the Fraser River and along the lakes behind Lillooet, to come to Fountain and hear the marvellous tales told by his guest from Penticton. So Pelkamulox had new audiences of eager listeners.

But one evening, when he had nearly finished his recital, a chief from Seton Lake arose and asked to speak.

"Do not believe this man," said the Seton Lake chief. "He says he is telling us true stories, but they are not true stories. There are no human beings with white skins, none who have eyes blue like the waters of the lake and light hair that curls like shavings from a white pine tree. There are no human beings who cover themselves with woven material which keeps them warm and yet does not make their movements clumsy. There are no moccasins that can keep the feet from being pricked when a man walks over cactus."

Chief Pelkamulox looked angry, but courtesy kept him silent until the speaker had finished.

"No weapon can kill a bird while it is flying," continued the chief from Seton Lake. "Nothing can be hurled so far or so fast that the eye cannot follow it. There is no weapon which can kill animals as far away as across the river. There is none that makes a noise like thunder and at the same time makes a smoke like fire. And there is no animal which men can ride safely and be carried faster than the swiftest buffalo can run.

"All these statements are lies. Pelkamulox should not be listened to by men and warriors."

Insulted and angered, Pelkamulox reached for his bow and arrows. But the Seton Lake chief was too quick for him. Two arrows left his bow before Pelkamulox could reach his weapons. Mortally wounded, he was carried to his lodge, and there he soon died. Before his death, he asked his wife and young son to promise that Nicola, in time, would avenge his death.

Years passed by. When Nicola grew to manhood, he became a chief of great importance among his people. And he was trusted by a white man who had a fur-trading post at the head of Okanagan Lake. One winter the white man had an unusually good season of getting furs from the Indians. Before he left in the spring to take his pelts to the coast, he cached the remainder of his goods and left them under the protection of Chief Nicola.

Finding everything safe when he returned to the post in the autumn, he rewarded Nicola with some tobacco and pipes, with ten guns and a supply of ammunition. The young chief already had a horse which had been given him by white traders at Fort Walla Walla.

Now was the opportunity Nicola had been waiting for, all the years he had been growing up and proving his strength. During the winter, he trained his best young men in the use of guns. He persuaded other Okanagan bands, the Shuswaps, and the Thompson River Indians, to join him against the Lillooet band on Seton Lake. They made the attack suddenly, in the midst of the salmon season, when the Lillooets were busy fishing.

The noise of the guns terrified them, as did the appearance of Nicola, on horseback, riding from place to place to direct the attack. Panic-stricken by the deadly effect of the guns, the survivors tried to flee. Over three hundred of them were killed, and many women and children were taken prisoners.

Nicola's revenge was complete. On their return from the battle, he gave a big feast for his warriors and their friends. In order to have meat for all, he drove a large herd of elk into an enclosure, where his men killed them with spears. The antlers of the animals killed at that time were piled in two large heaps, where they remained for many years. They were a constant reminder that Chief Nicola had obeyed his dying father's request.

The first white men and the first missionary

These traditions of the first contacts between Stoney Indians and white people were related in 1954 by Eliza Hunter, at the age of seventy-two.

One detail in her story is a recorded fact. The first missionary to reach Rocky Mountain House, a post of the Hudson's Bay Company, was the Reverend Robert Rundle. When he arrived on February 22, 1841, he wrote: "I found several Indians at the fort, and shortly after my arrival another party arrived from the plains. Great warmth of feeling was expressed by them on seeing me. . . . Whilst I was saluting them, some kissed me; others, after shaking me by the hand, passed both hands over part of my dress, uttering at the same time a kind of prayer; and others gave me their left hand because it is nearest the heart."

Rundle Mountain, near Banff, was named for this missionary in 1859.

A long time ago, only Indians lived in Alberta. No one knows who put them here or how they got here. They lighted their fires by striking flint rocks together.

One time a Stoney Indian travelled far to the east and was hunting near the sea. There he saw two white men who had come across the ocean. They were cutting logs to build a house. The Stoney man looked at them and wondered what kind of people they were. They were the first white men he had ever seen.

When he came near them one of the white men made a motion to shake hands with him. Then he made a sign that meant he wanted the Indian to go home with him. In the white man's house the Stoney was given something to eat, but he did not like the smell of white people's food. He ate nothing but bread. He did not like the other things he was offered.

After they had eaten, the white men gave the Indian an axe, a knife, and a shotgun. They taught him how to shoot with the gun. At first he was so frightened by the noise that he fell down on the ground. In the sign language, the white man said to him, "You can kill an animal with that."

They invited him to bring his people to the place where the white men were living. Then the Stoney started home. On his way he shot an animal with his gun, butchered it, and took it with him. His people were very much surprised when they saw the axe and the knife and the shotgun.

"What is that?" they asked. "And where did you get it?"

He told them about the strange-looking white men he had seen. "They were very friendly," he said. "They want us, all of us, to go where they are."

Many people went back east with him. The white people were pleased to see the Indians and were very friendly. They gave axes and knives to the men and cloth to the women. Then the Indians cut logs to help the white people build their houses.

After about a year all the Indians came back to the West—the Stoneys, the Blackfeet, and the Sarcees. White people also came west. After a while, some white people settled at Edmonton. Later, others settled at Rocky Mountain House, near where the Stoneys lived all the time.

One night a Stoney had a dream. In his dream a voice said to him, "A white man is coming to Rocky Mountain House. He will tell you about a Great Spirit you have never heard about. He works for that Great Spirit."

Not long afterward, the Indian men went to Rocky Mountain House to get knives and bullets for hunting and to get clothing for the women. When they came back, they said to the old men and to the women, "The man who works for the Great Spirit is at Rocky Mountain House. His name is Rundle."

The man's dream had come true.

Next day all the Stoneys went to Rocky Mountain House to see the missionary—all the men and all the women. He taught them about God. As soon as they heard this preacher, the Stoneys believed in God. They quit all their sins and followed his teachings.

Ever since then, the Stoneys have been Christians. They don't want to do wrong things. They are always friends to everyone. They love all the tribes in the world. They want to have everlasting life.

Sources

Indian stories and storytelling

Swanton and Jenness (a); Hewitt (c), pp. 50 and 66; Hale, pp. 179–80; Jameson, II, 159–60; Kinzie, pp 367–68; Gilman, II, 23–24; Kohl, pp. 87–88; Cheadle and Milton, p. 119; Parker (b), pp. 50–55; Paget, p. 100; Barbeau, pp. 5–6; Curtin, p. vi; Chamberlain (c), p. 141; Jenness (a), p. 192; McLean (b), p. 296; Johnson, p. 220.

The creation myth of the Hurons and the Iroquois

Hale, pp. 180–82; Smith, pp. 76–77; Cusick, pp. 1–9.

Nanabozho of the Chippewa

Squier (b), pp. 394–95; Brinton, pp. 3–4; Chamberlain (b); Gilman, II, 113–15; Lanman (a), pp. 107–9; Kohl, p. 515; Charlevoix, II, 41–45; Hamilton, p. 310; Hoffman, pp. 210 and 213; Henry, pp. 212–13; Hewitt (f).

The beginning of the Cree world

Tyrrell, pp. 85–88.

The beginning of the Haida world

Hill-Tout (a), pp. 700–1.

Other supernatural beings

E. F. Wilson (a), pp. 185–87; Rand (a), pp. 283–86; Hagar (c), p. 104; Speck (a), p. 30; Jack (a).

The big snow in the northland

Robert Bell, pp. 26–29, and Jamme.

The story of the great flood

Harris, pp. 10–12.

How Deer got fire

Hunt, pp. 894–96.

Who was given the fire

Deans (a).

Coyote and the salmon

Teit (a), pp. 26–28, 104–5; (b), pp. 3, 9, and 12.

Coyote and Old Man

Teit (a), pp. 48–49, 109–10.

Why the salmon come to the Squamish waters

Hill-Tout (b).

The animals climb into the sky

Franz Boas, BAE MS No. 1933 (2).

Glooscap and his four visitors

Rand (c), pp. 253–58.

The origin of stories

Curtin, pp. 70–75.

A message from the Happy Hunting Grounds

Sanborn, in Leland, pp. 200–5; Smith, pp. 51–53.

A boy's vigil and the first robin

Schoolcraft, pp. 221–24.

The origin of the trailing arbutus
    Blackwood, pp. 341–42.

The first white water lily
    The Red Man, V, 340–41.

The broken wing: an allegory
    Schoolcraft, pp. 233–37.

The origin of Niagara Falls
    Smith, pp. 54–55.

The sacrifice at Niagara Falls
    Skinner, I, 61–63.

Legend of Iroquois Falls
    Davidson, pp. 266–67; Speck (a), pp. 26–27 and 76.

The origin of Mackinac Island
    Lanman (c), pp. 192–93.

Legends of the Qu'Appelle River
    McLean (a), p. 179; Paget, pp. 162–64.

The white horses on Chief Mountain
    Staunton, MS.

Sunrise on Lake Louise
    "Legend of Lake Louise."

Coyote and Shuswap Falls
    Marie Brent, personal letter and newspaper clipping.

The creation of the northern Rocky Mountains
    James M. Bell, pp. 80–82.

The meaning of the Northern Lights
    James M. Bell, pp. 82–84.

The origin of the Mackenzie River
    B. R. Ross (Fort Simpson, 1861), BAE MS 170 (in part).

The smoking mountains of Horton River
    Ostermann, pp. 60–61.

The great rock in the Fraser River
    Hughes; Dodd (letter).

A legend of Siwash Rock
    McKelvie.

A story of the eagle crest
    Deans (b), pp. 34–37.

The origin of mountain goats
    Deans (b), p. 57.

The spirit sacrifice
    Headnote : Jesuit Relations, XLII, 153–55; Michelson (b).
    Story : Lanman (d), pp. 127–28.

The Little People
    Rand (a), p. 6; Hagar (b), pp. 170–72.

The first white men and the revenge of Chief Nicola
    Dawson, pp. 26–28; Teit (c), pp. 265–73.

The first white men and the first missionary
    Headnote : Quoted in McRae, pp. 155–56.

Bibliography

Abbreviations used :

> AA, *American Anthropologist*
> BAE, *Bureau of American Ethnology*
> JAFL, *Journal of American Folklore*
> MAFS, *Memoirs of the American Folklore Society*

BARBEAU, C. M. *Huron and Wyandot Mythology.* (Canada, Geological Survey, Memoir 80; Anthropological Series No. 11.) Ottawa, Government Printing Bureau, 1915.

BEAUCHAMP, W. M. (a) "Iroquois Notes," JAFL V (1892), 223–29.

——(b) "Onondaga Notes," JAFL, VIII (1895), 209–16.

——(c) "Onondaga Tale of the Pleiades," JAFL, XIII (1900), 281–82.

BELL, JAMES M. "The Fireside Stories of the Chipewyans," JAFL, XVI (1903), 73–84.

BELL, ROBERT. "Legends of the Slavey Indians," JAFL, XIV (1901), 26–29.

BLACKWOOD, BEATRICE. "Tales of the Chippewa Indians," *Folk-Lore* (London, 1929), pp. 315–44.

BOAS, FRANZ (ed.) *Folk-Tales of the Salishan and Sahaptin Tribes,* MAFS, XI (1917).

BRINTON, DANIEL. "The myths of Manibozho and Ioskeha," *Historical Magazine, and notes and queries concerning the antiquities, history and biography of America,* New Series, II, No. 1 (July 1867), 3–6.

CHAMBERLAIN, A. F. (a) "The Thunderbird among the Algonkians," AA, III (1890), 51–55.

——(b) "Nanibozhu amongst the Otchipwe, Mississagas, and Other Algonkian Tribes," JAFL, IV (1891), 193–213.

——(c) "Tales of the Mississaguas," JAFL, II (1889), 141–47.

CHARLEVOIX, PIERRE. *Journal of a Voyage to North America,* ed. LOUISE P. KELLOGG. 2 vols. Chicago : The Caxton Club, 1923.

CHEADLE, WALTER B. *and* MILTON, WILLIAM F., VISCOUNT. *The North-west Passage by Land.* London : Cassell, Petter, and Galpin, [1865].

CLARK, ELLA E. *Indian Legends of the Pacific Northwest.* Berkeley : University of California Press, 1953.

CONNELLY, WILLIAM E. "The Wyandots," archaeological report, 1899, being part of Appendix to the *Report of the Minister of Education,* Ontario (Toronto, 1900), pp. 92–123.

CURTIN, JEREMIAH. *Seneca Indian Myths.* New York: E. P. Dutton & Co., 1923.

CUSICK, DAVID. *Sketches of Ancient History of the Six Nations.* Lewiston, N.Y.: 1827.

DAVIDSON, D. S. "Some Tête de Boule Tales," *JAFL*, XLI (1928), 262–75.

DAWSON, GEO. M. "Notes on the Shuswap People of British Columbia," in Royal Society of Canada, *Proceedings and Transactions . . . for the Year 1891*, Vol. IX, Sec. II (Montreal, 1892), pp. 3–44.

DEANS, JAMES (a) "How the Whullemooch Got Fire," *American Antiquarian*, VIII (1886), 41–43.

——(b) *Tales from the Totems of the Hidery*, ed. OSCAR L. TRIGGS. (Archives of the International Folklore Association, Vol. II.) Chicago, 1899.

FEWKES, J. W. "A Contribution to Passamaquoddy Folklore," *JAFL*, III (1890), 257–80.

"The First White Water Lily," *The Red Man*, V (April, 1913), 340–41.

GILMAN, CHANDLER. *Life on the Lakes.* 2 vols. New York: G. Dearborn, 1836.

HAGAR, STANSBURY. (a) "Micmac Customs and Traditions," *AA*, VIII (1895), 31–42.
——(b) "Micmac Magic and Medicine," *JAFL*, IX (1896), 170–77.
——(c) "Weather and the Seasons in Micmac Mythology," *JAFL*, X (1895), 101–5.
——(d) "The Celestial Bear," *JAFL*, XIII (1900), 92–103.

HALE, HORATIO. "Huron Folk-Lore," *JAFL*, I (1888), 177–83.

HAMILTON, JAMES CLELAND. "Famous Algonquins; Algic legends," *Royal Canadian Institute, Toronto: Transactions*, VI (December 1899), 285–312.

HARRIS, MARTHA D. *History and Folklore of the Cowichan Indians.* Victoria: The Colonist Publ. Co., Ltd., 1901.

HENRY, ALEXANDER. *Travels and Adventures in Canada and the Indian Territories.* New York: I. Riley, 1809.

HEWITT, J. N. B. (a) "A Sun-Myth and the Tree of Language of the Iroquois," *AA*, V (1892), 61–62.
——(b) "Legend of the Founding of the Iroquois League," *ibid.*, 131–48.
——(c) "Introduction to Seneca Fiction, Legends and Myths," *BAE, Thirty-fifth Annual Report, 1910–11*, 1918, pp. 37–819.
——(d) "A Constitutional League of Peace in the Stone Age of America. The League of the Iroquois and Its Constitution," *Annual Report of the Smithsonian Institution for 1918* (Washington, 1920), pp. 527–45.
——(e) "Nanabozho," in Hodge, *Handbook . . .*, pp. 19–23. See below.
——(f) "Wampum," *ibid.*, pp. 904–9.

HILL-TOUT, CHAS. (a) "Haida Stories and Beliefs," *Report of the 68th Meeting of the British Association for the Advancement of Science, 1898* (London, 1899), pp. 700–8.
——(b) "Myth of Salmon Coming to Squamish Waters," *Museum and Art Notes*, IV (Vancouver, 1929), 62–64.

HODGE, FREDERICK W. (ed.) *Handbook of American Indians North of Mexico.* 2 vols. (BAE, Bulletin 30.) Washington, Govt. Print. Off., 1912.

HOFFMAN, WALTER J. "Pictography and Shamanistic Rites of the Ojibway," *AA*, I (1888), 209–29.

HUGHES, J. C. "A Bit of Indian Folk-Lore," *Overland Monthly*, I (1883), 351–54.

HUNT, GEORGE. "Myths of the Nootka," BAE, *Thirty-first Annual Report, 1909–10,* 1916, pp. 888–935.

JACK, EDWARD. (a) "Heroic Deeds of Glooscap," *JAFL,* I (1888), 85.
——(b) "Maliseet Legends," *JAFL,* VIII (1895), 193–208.

JAMESON, ANNA. *Winter Studies and Summer Rambles in Canada.* 2 vols. New York: Wiley and Putnam, 1839.

JAMME, G. E. "Dogrib Legend of the Flood," *The Coast,* XI (1906), 180–81.

JENNESS, DIAMOND. (a) *The Indians of Canada.* 2nd ed. (National Museum of Canada, Bulletin 65; Anthropological Series No. 15.) Ottawa, n.d.
——(b) *The Sarcee Indians of Alberta.* (National Museum of Canada. Bulletin 90; Anthropological Series No. 23.) Ottawa, J. O. Patenaude, 1938.

The Jesuit Relations and Allied Documents. Ed. by R. G. Thwaites. 73 vols. Vol. XLII. Cleveland, Ohio: The Burrows Bros. Co., 1899.

JOHNSON, ELIAS. *Legends, Traditions and Laws of the Iroquois, or Six Nations, and History of the Tuscarora Indians.* Lockport, N. Y.: Union Printing Co., 1881.

KINZIE, JULIETTE. *Wau-bun, or "Early Day" in the North-west.* London: 1856.

KOHL, J. G. *Kitchi-Gami: Wanderings Round Lake Superior.* London: Chapman and Hall, 1860.

LAIDLAW, GEORGE E. (a) "Certain Ojibwa myths," annual archaeological report, 1914, being part of Appendix to the *Report of the Minister of Education,* Ontario (Toronto, 1914), pp. 77–79.
——(b) "Ojibwa myths and tales," 6th paper, thirty-third Annual Archaeological Report, 1921–22, *ibid.* (Toronto, 1922), pp. 84–99.
——(c) "Ojibwa myths and tales," 7th paper, thirty-fifth Annual Archaeological Report, 1924–1925, *ibid.* (Toronto, 1927), pp. 34–80.

LANMAN, CHAS. (a) *Adventures in the Wilds of the United States and British American Provinces.* 2 vols. Philadelphia: J. W. Moore, 1856. Vol. I.
——(b) "Indian Legends," *Magazine of History,* II (1906), 356–58.
——(c) *Ibid.,* III (1906), 115–16; 192–93.
——(d) *Ibid.,* XVII (1913), 127–28.
——(e) *Ibid.,* XVIII (1914), 149–50; 221–23.

LEACH, MARIA (ed.). *Funk & Wagnalls Standard Dictionary of Folklore, Mythology, and Legend.* 2 vols. New York: Funk and Wagnalls, 1949.

"Legend of the Canoe," *Native American,* II (1910), 6.

"Legend of Lake Louise," *Alberta Folklore Journal,* II (1946), 7.

LELAND, CHAS. *The Algonquian Legends of New England; or Myths and Folk Lore of the Micmac, Passamaquoddy, and Penobscot Tribes.* Boston and New York: Houghton, Mifflin & Co., 1884.

MCCLINTOCK, WALTER. *The Old North Trail or Life, Legends and Religion of the Blackfeet Indians.* London: Macmillan, 1910.

MCKELVIE, B. A. *Legends of Stanley Park.* N.p., n.d.

MCLEAN, JOHN. (a) *The Indians of Canada: Their Manners and Customs.* 4th ed. Toronto: 1907.
——(b) "Blackfoot Indian Legends," *JAFL,* III (1890), 296–98.

MCRAE, ARCHIBALD O. *History of the Province of Alberta.* [Calgary?]: Western Canada History Co., 1912.

MICHELSON, TRUMAN. (a) "The Piegan Tales," *JAFL*, XXIV (1911), 238–50.

——(b) "Maiden Sacrifice among the Ojibwa," *AA*, n.s. XXXVI (1936), 628–29.

MOURNING DOVE. *Coyote Stories*. Caldwell, Idaho: The Caxton Printers, Ltd., 1933.

OSTERMANN, H. (ed.) *The Mackenzie Eskimos, after Knud Rasmussen's Posthumous Notes*. (Report of the Fifth Thule Expedition, 1921–24. Vol. X, No. 2.) Copenhagen, Gyldendal, 1942.

PAGET, AMELIA. *The People of the Plains*, ed. DUNCAN CAMPBELL SCOTT. Toronto: W. Briggs, 1909.

PARKER, ARTHUR C. (ed.) (a) *The Constitution of the Five Nations, or the Iroquois Book of the Great Law*. (New York State Museum, Bulletin No. 184.) Albany, The University of the State of New York, 1916.

——(b) *Seneca Myths and Folk Tales*. Buffalo: Buffalo Historical Society, 1923.

PARKMAN, FRANCIS. *The Conspiracy of Pontiac and the Indian War after the Conquest of Canada*. 2 vols. (1851.) Everyman's Library ed., 1908.

PRINCE, JOHN. (a) "The Passamaquoddy Wampum Records," *Proceedings of the American Philosophical Society*, XXXVI (1897), 479–95.

——(b) "Some Passamaquoddy Documents," *Annals of the New York Academy of Science*, XI (1898), 369–75.

RADIN, PAUL. *Some Myths and Tales of the Ojibwa of Southeastern Ontario*. (Canada, Geological Survey. Memoir 48; Anthropological Series No. 2.) Ottawa, Government Printing Bureau, 1914.

RAND, SILAS. (a) "The Legends of the Micmacs," *American Antiquarian*, XII (1890), 3–14.

——(b) "Glooscap, Cuhkw and Coolpurjot," *ibid.*, pp. 283–86.

RAND, SILAS. (c) *Legends of the Micmacs*. New York and London: Longmans, Green & Co., 1894.

RAVENHILL, ALICE. *Folklore of the Far West*. Victoria: 1953.

RUSSELL, FRANK. "Athapascan Myths," *JAFL*, XIII (1900), 11–18.

RUSSELL, JASON. "A Legend of the Senecas," *Progressive Teacher*, XXXVIII (September, 1929), 2.

SANBORN, J. W. (a) *Legends, Customs and Social Life of the Seneca Indians*. Gowanda, N. Y.: Horton & Deming, 1878.

——(b) "The Mischief Maker. A Tradition of the Mythology of the Senecas," in Leland, *Algonquian Legends* ..., pp. 194–206. See above.

SCHOLEFIELD, E. O. S. *British Columbia from the Earliest Times to the Present*. 4 vols. Vancouver, Chicago: S. J. Clarke Publ. Co., [1914]. Vol. 1.

SCHOOLCRAFT, HENRY. *Algic Researches*. . . . *First Series: Indian Tales and Legends*. 2 vols. New York: Harper & Bros., 1839. Vol. 1.

SKINNER, CHAS. M. *Myths and Legends of Our Own Land*. 2 vols. Philadelphia and London: J. P. Lippincott Co., 1896. Vol. 1.

SMITH, ERMINNIE A. "Myths of the Iroquois," *BAE, Second Annual Report, 1880–81* (Washington, 1883), pp. 47–111.

SPECK, FRANK. (a) *Myths and Folklore of the Timiskaming Algonquin and Timigami Ojibway*. (Canada, Geological Survey. Memoir 71; Anthropological Series No. 9.) Ottawa, 1915.

——(b) "Malecite Tales," *JAFL*, XXX (1917), 479–85.

SPIER, LESLIE (ed.). *The Sinkaietk or Southern Okanagon of Washington*.

(General Series in Anthropology, No. 6.) Menasha, Wisconsin, Geo. Banta Publ. Co., 1938.

SQUIER, EPHRAIM. "Neshekaybenais, or the Lone Bird: An Ojibway Legend," *American Review*, VIII (1848), 255–59.

SWANTON, JOHN R. *The Indian Tribes of North America.* (BAE, Bulletin 145.) Washington, 1952.

TEIT, JAMES. (a) *Traditions of the Thompson River Indians of British Columbia,* MAFS, 1898.
——(b) "Thompson Tales," in Boas, *Folk-Tales . . .,* pp.1–64. See above.
——(c) "The Salishan Tribes of the Western Plateau," BAE, *Forty-fifth Annual Report,* 1927–28, pp. 23–396.

"Traditional History of the Confederacy of the Six Nations," in Royal Society of Canada, *Proceedings and Transactions . . .,* Vol. V, Sec. II (Ottawa, 1911), pp. 195–246.

TYRRELL, J. B. (ed.) *David Thompson's Narrative of His Explorations in Western North America, 1784–1812.* (Champlain Society, Publ. XII.) Toronto, The Champlain Society, 1916.

"Water Lily—Ojibway Legend," *The Red Man,* V (1913), 340–41.

WILSON, E. F. "Report on the Blackfoot tribes," *Report of the 57th Meeting of the British Association for the Advancement of Science, 1887* (London, 1888), pp. 183–97.

WILSON, R. N. "Blackfoot Star Myths—the Pleiades," *American Antiquarian,* XV (1893), 149–50.

WOODMAN, J. J. *Indian Legends.* Boston: The Stratford Co., 1924.

MANUSCRIPT MATERIAL

BOAS, FRANZ. "How the Animals Climbed Up into the Sky." Translated from the German by A. F. Chamberlain. BAE MS 1933, Part 2.

BRENT, MARIE H. "Coyote and Shuswap Falls," in personal letter, August, 1957.

DODD, MARGARET. Details for "The Great Rock in the Fraser River," in personal letter, March, 1960.

MCKELVIE, B. A. "Simon Fraser, Chief of the Sky People," in personal letter, August 12, 1956.

ROSS, B. R. "Legend of the Formation of the Mackenzie River." BAE MS 170 (in part) (April, 1861.)

STAUNTON, E. L. "Legend of the White Horses on Big Chief Mountain." Provincial Library, Edmonton, Alberta.

ORAL SOURCES

CHIEF WALKING BUFFALO (GEORGE MCLEAN), ELIZA HUNTER, ENOCH BAPTISTE (*interpreted* by HORACE HOLLOWAY)—the Stoney or Assiniboine.

ALBERT LIGHTNING—Cree.

ONE GUN—Blackfeet.

PAT GRASSHOPPER (*interpreted* by JIM SIMEON) *and* DAISY OTTER—Sarcee.